Names For Twins

5000+ pairs of fun and distinctive baby names for boy, girl, and mixed sets of twins

Louise Nolan

Paperback and electronic versions published by:
Magnificent Milestones, Inc.

ISBN: 9781933819716

Disclaimer:

(1) This book was written as a guide; it does not claim to be the definitive word on baby names. Accordingly, the author and publisher do not accept any liability or responsibility for any loss or damage that have been caused, or allegedly caused, through the use of information in this book.

(2) To our knowledge, all of the information in this book is correct (and current) at the time of publication. However, trends can (and do) change on a daily basis, which will affect the popularity of any given name.

Table of Contents

Chapter 1: Introduction: The Challenges of Naming Twins   4

Chapter 2: The Most Popular Names for Twins (2014)   9

Chapter 3 : Names that Rhyme   24

Chapter 4. Anagrams   32

Chapter 5. Christian & Biblical Names   49

Chapter 6. Names from Literature & Mythology   63

Chapter 7. Names from Popular Culture / the Entertainment Industry   70

Chapter 8. Names from Disney   82

Chapter 9: Names from Nature   87

Chapter 10: Last Names as First Names   92

Chapter 11: Named After Famous Places   99

Chapter 12: Named after Presidents & First Ladies   105

Chapter 13: Named after Famous Couples & Twins   107

Chapter 14: One Syllable Names   111

Chapter 15: Lengthy (Four Syllable) Names   126

Chapter 16: Gender Neutral (Unisex) Names   132

Chapter 17. Popular Names for African-American Twins   138

Chapter 18. Popular Names for Hispanic Twins   142

Chapter 19. Popular Names for Asian Twins   149

Chapter 20: The Evolution of Names Since 1900   157

Chapter 21: Names with Similar Meanings   167

Appendix A: An Alphabetical List of Boys Names   172

Appendix B. An Alphabetical List of Girls Names   205

Chapter 1: Introduction: The Challenges of Naming Twins

Few things are more exciting - or complex - than choosing a child's name. The task is particularly difficult for parents of twins, who must choose *two* names that define their children's individual identities and work together as a pair.

On a practical basis, the stakes are high for these tiny babies, who must live with *your* decision for the rest of their lives. Even worse, you must make that decision before you know your babies' personality and temperament, which determines whether or not the names you have chosen truly "fit" them.

Years ago, when I perused books of baby names, I was intrigued by the authors' arbitrary "rules" for first, middle, and last names. Yet, in reality, the beauty of a name is subjective - and what one person considers an excellent choice, another person may not. Thus, I offer only one hard and fast rule in this book: the only opinions that matter are those of the *parents* who will love and raise the twins they are naming. Other people may agree or disagree with your choices, but they don't have to live with them - and their input should be considered accordingly.

That being said, there are several factors to consider when naming children (and twins in particular):

1. **The sex of each child**. For girls, do you want a feminine name or something that is gender neutral? Likewise, do you favor strong and traditional boys' names or something modern or unisex? The difference:

Felicia, Savannah, Evangelina	vs.	Hunter, Taylor, or Dale
Joshua, Daniel, Zachary	vs.	Brett, Shay, or Finn

2. **The family's last name**. Ideally, the child's first, middle, and last names should have a pleasant flow. Ironically, what is "pleasing" to one family may seem harsh and abrupt to another.

For many parents, length and alliteration are also critical. Do you want your child to have a short name that is easy to write and spell - or do you believe that the beauty and flow of a longer name are worth the trade-off?

Patricia Paulina Petrocelli	vs.	Jane Lee Petrocelli
Jonathan Lorenzo Smith	vs.	James Hugh Smith

3. **The uniqueness of the name**. Most parents follow trends, rather than start them. As a result, there are usually five or six students with the same name in every classroom, simply because it was popular the year they were born. In contrast, there will inevitably be one or two students in the same school who have unique names that no one has heard before.

Which of these scenarios do you prefer? Do you want your child to have a popular name that is easy to spell and pronounce, but not particularly creative? Or, do you favor distinctive names that will garner your child (possibly unwanted) attention? The difference:

Sophia Ella White	vs.	Moonbeam Destiny White
Joshua James Stanton	vs.	Ziggy Maximus Stanton

Thankfully, there are thousands of names that fall between these two extremes that you can choose, depending upon your personal and familial preferences. When you consider your options, bear in mind: you are making this decision on behalf of a child whose personality may be very different from your own. Are you willing to take a risk - or would you prefer to play it safe?

4. **The longevity of the name**. That cute baby in your arms will eventually become a successful adult with dreams and aspirations of his/her own. Will the name you choose last a lifetime? In making this decision, consider the following questions - and whether the answers make a difference to you:

a. If given the choice between a physician named Sonia or Buffy, which would you choose?

b. Likewise, can you imagine a district attorney - or circuit court judge - named Bliss or Genesis?

The choice you make will affect how your child is perceived for his/her *entire life*. What seems "cute" now may not be nearly as desirable on a professional resume.

5. **Consider the initials** your child will have if you choose a particular name. If possible, avoid embarrassing combinations, such as IOU, LOL, PIG, FAG, and WTF. Many times, you can avoid bad combinations by choosing an alternative middle name.

6. If you choose a long or formal name, **consider the nickname** the child is likely to inherit. Some names, such as Katherine and Elizabeth, have multiple options, while others have only one. Even worse, once your child enrolls in school, you are unlikely to control whether or not an undesirable nickname "sticks." Bottom line: if you don't want your kids called Matty and Ginny, don't name them Matthew and Virginia.

7. **Consider the spelling and pronunciation** of the name, which can be a source of confusion and frustration for many children. If you name your child Xianthippe or Xavierius, there is an excellent chance that (s)he will spend his/her entire lifetime explaining to people how to spell and pronounce it. This isn't "bad," per se, but it may be annoying for your child.

8. **Consider the meaning of the name**, if that is important to you. Unfortunately, some popular names have truly awful meanings:

Cameron means "crooked nose"
Kennedy means "ugly head"

Granted, most people do not know - or care about - the meaning of a given name. They simply take it at face value. But if the translation of a name (and the underlying connotation) bothers you, an alternative choice may be best.

9. **Pressures from relatives to choose a "family" name**. There is nothing inherently right or wrong with naming children after beloved relatives. In many cases, it is a lovely way to honor and preserve the memory of someone important to your family. Nevertheless, problems arise when:

a. the name is question is not particularly pleasing
b. the relatives pushing it will not take no for an answer

In these cases, middle names can be an excellent solution. In my experience, a child's middle name is usually chosen for one of three reasons:

a. it is a short, pleasant, and generic "placeholder" between the first and last names:

Examples: Stephanie Ann Miller

Alexander Lee Ruggerio

b. it is the "second choice" name that was vetoed at the last moment:

Examples: Millicent Marianna Miller

Alexander Augustus Ruggerio

c. it is the name of a beloved relative that the parents did not want to use as the first name:

Examples: Jennifer Mildred Miller

Jayden Harold Ruggerio

Rather than argue with your sister, mother and spouse about a particular choice, using it as a middle name can be a great solution.

10. **Special considerations for twins**. For twins, parents face an additional hurdle: choosing two names that are pleasant, distinctive, and well coordinated with the last name (and each other). Thankfully, there are many ways to choose complementary names that work:

- names that rhyme - or sound alike
- names that begin with the same initial
- names that have the same number of syllables
- names that are anagrams (the same letters arranged differently)
- names with a similar theme: nature, flowers, presidents, etc.
- names with similar meanings
- names that honor beloved family members
- or, finally, names that are completely different from each other, but perfectly suited to your family's needs

This book, which presents more than 5,000 twin names in logical pairings, is totally devoted to point 10 - choosing distinctive names for twins that will work for you and your family. Use the lists as a starting point - and see what fits. Experiment with different combinations that capture the sound and feel that you desire. Choose the names that perfectly reflect the twins you are carrying - and your hopes and dreams for their future.

How to Use this Book

By design, this book is arranged in a logical way:

1. the chapters are clearly labeled to guide your search

2. the names are presented in logical pairs, in alphabetical order, and sorted by sex (unless noted otherwise)

3. the meaning of each name is clearly presented, although some names have multiple meanings, depending upon the original language and interpretation. Due to these variations, we encourage you to conduct additional research into the history and derivation of the names that you choose, both to learn more about them and to explore alternative spellings. By doing so, you can confirm that the name truly feels right and has no negative or unusual connotations.

4. in recent years, parents have expressed a preference for unisex, or gender neutral names that they can use for their twins, regardless of their sex. To honor this request - and to showcase the dozens of names that can be used for both boys and girls, this book presents an entire chapter of unisex names for you to consider.

5. finally, for readers who prefer a direct approach - or simply get tired or overwhelmed by reading thousands of names in various pairings, the final chapter of the book presents an alphabetical list of more than 5,000 names for boys and girls.

Why 5,000, rather than the 100,000 presented in other books? Because we have streamlined the approach by focusing on the names that you are most likely to use, rather than including odd and esoteric choices from 200 years ago that no one can spell or pronounce. We have also avoided the temptation to turn Katherine into 20 different names, simply by making a few spelling changes.

How to Create a Unique Baby Name

And, that, ultimately, is the final topic of this chapter: the emerging trend of creating unique and customized names by varying the spelling of a classic name. In most cases, **that** is how most baby name books manage to present 50,000 choices - they include every possible alternative way to spell every name they present. On one hand, that is valid, because many parents like the idea of a unique name. On the other hand, it is somewhat misleading - is the name Caryn really all that different from Karen? And do you really *want* to change the spelling of a classic name - knowing that your child will have to explain, correct, and re-spell it for the dozens of teachers, employers, and business contacts who get it wrong?

If the answer is yes, here is a quick summary of how to customize a name.

1. Change a consonant:

C to K:　Catherine/Katherine, Crystal/Krystal, Christine/Kristine
C to CH: Eric/Erich, Cris/Chris, Ciara/Chiara
C to S:　Cheryl/Sheryl, Cynthia/Synthia
F to Ph: Adolf /Adolph , Finian/Phinian, Felicia/Phylicia
G to J:　Geoffrey/Jeffrey , Gillian/Jillian
X to J:　Xavier/Javier
Z to S:　Inez/Ines
H to S:　Janesha/Janessa

2. Change a vowel:

A to E:　Megan/Meagan, Aidan/Aiden
A to Y　Megan/Megyn
CE to SS: Jocelyn/Josslyn
CI to SH: Lacrecia/Lacresha, Marcia/Marsha
E to Y:　Karen/ Karyn, Hailee/Hailey
E to O:　Conner/Connor, Ellery/Ellory
E to EI:　Andre/Andrei, Keegan/Keigan
EO to E: Geoffrey/Jeffrey
I to Y:　Nanci/ Nancy, Brandi//Brandy, Katherine/Kathryn
I to E:　Austin/Austen
IE to Y: Debbie/Debby
U to EW: Drew/Dru
U to W: Laurence/Lawrence

3. Add (or subtract) a letter or phrase:

Add an O:　Alphonso/Alphonse
Add an S:　Apollo/Apollos
Add an E:　Clancy/Clancey, Emil/Emile, Axl/Axel, Aden/Aiden
Add an L:　Alan/Allen, Chancellor/Chancelor

Add a "son:" Anders/Anderson
Add a "ton:" Fuller/Fullerton, Jack/Jackson
Add a "de:" Wayne/Dewayne
Add a "mac:" Kenize/Mackenzie
Add a "lyn:" Brooke/Brooklyn, Joss/Josslyn

4. Combine two names into one:

Ashlyn: (American): a combination of Ashley and Lynn
Deandra: (American): a combination of Dee and Andrea
Deangelo: (Italian): a combination of De and Angelo
Kaylin: (American): a combination of Kay and Lynn

5. **Use non-traditional words as names**, such as places, surnames, and personal ideals (such as honor, heaven, and bliss). The chapters in this book will provide the inspiration you need to find distinctive and creative pairs of names from unusual and unlikely places. For more traditional parents, we have also included quality choices from history, literature, and the Bible. Use the lists as guidance and inspiration for your search - and choose the names for your twins that truly work best.

Chapter 2: The Most Popular Names for Twins (2014)

For many prospective parents, this chapter is a logical place to start - with the most popular names for twins in the United States. Ironically, readers like this chapter for two very different reasons: some love the idea of giving their children popular and trendy names, while others hate the concept - and immediately dismiss all top names from consideration.

Regardless of your own inclination, it's fun to explore the current trends in names on a national basis, if only to know what other parents consider trendy and desirable. This chapter also shows you the types of combinations that parents prefer, which may (or may not) influence your thinking. As you read and consider each name, you can use this information to add (or subtract) various possibilities from your list.

Finally, a word about "popular" names in a nation as large and diverse as the United States: different names are popular in different regions, depending upon the cultural, spiritual and socioeconomic backgrounds of their residents. In an area with many Asian families, for example, names such as Ling and Ming will be more popular than those in other communities. Likewise, in regions that are predominantly Christian, Biblical names will be more popular than those in communities that are spiritually diverse.

On a practical basis, this information may not affect you (or the choices that you make). But it *does* explain why the variation among children's names is so broad in different parts of the country. In some cities, there will be five Isaiahs in every classroom, but no one named Jose or Carmen. In other places, there will be several Lings, but no one named Cynthia or Kristen. Ultimately, the names in this chapter are the most popular in the US *on average*, which may (or may not) reflect the demographics in your own community.

The Most Popular Names for Twins: Boys

Daniel & David

Daniel: (Hebrew & Biblical): God is my judge; (Irish & Welsh): attractive
David: (Hebrew, Scottish & Welsh): beloved

Jacob & Joshua

Jacob: (Biblical): supplanter; (Hebrew): he grasps the heel
Joshua: (Hebrew & Biblical): Jehovah saves

Isaac & Isaiah

Isaac: (Biblical): he will laugh
Isaiah: (Hebrew): the Lord is generous; (Israel): salvation by God

Jayden & Jordan

Jayden: (American): God has heard
Jordan: (Hebrew): to flow down; (Israel): descendant

Ethan & Evan

Ethan: (Hebrew & Biblical): firm, strong
Evan: (English): God is good; (Welsh): young; (Celtic): young fighter

Elijah & Isaiah

Elijah: (Biblical): the Lord is my God; (Hebrew): Jehovah is God
Isaiah: (Hebrew): the Lord is generous; (Israel): salvation by God

Matthew & Michael

Matthew: (Hebrew & Biblical): gift of the Lord
Michael: (Biblical & Hebrew): like God

Jayden & Jaylen

Jayden: (American): God has heard
Jaylen: (English): to rejoice

Ethan & Nathan

Ethan: (Hebrew & Biblical): firm, strong
Nathan: (Hebrew): he gives; (Israel): gift of God

Jayden & Kayden

Jayden: (American): God has heard
Kayden: (French, English & Arabic): round, gentle; companion

Landon & Logan

Landon: (English): grassy plain; from the long hill
Logan: (Irish): small cove; (Scottish): Finnian's servant; (Gaelic): from the hollow

Logan & Lucas

Logan: (Irish): small cove; (Scottish): Finnian's servant; (Gaelic): from the hollow
Lucas: (Gaelic, English & Latin America): light

Caleb & Joshua

Caleb: (Israel): faithful; (Hebrew): dog or bold
Joshua: (Hebrew & Biblical): Jehovah saves

James & John

James: (English); supplant, replace; (Israel): supplanter
John: (Israel): God is gracious; Jehovah has been gracious

Jeremiah & Josiah

Jeremiah: (Hebrew): may Jehovah exalt; (Israel): sent by God
Josiah: (Hebrew): Jehovah has healed; (Israel): God has healed

Logan & Luke

Logan: (Irish): small cove; (Scottish): Finnian's servant; (Gaelic): from the hollow
Luke: (Greek & Latin America): light

Alexander & Benjamin

Alexander: (Greek): protector of mankind
Benjamin: (English, Hebrew & Biblical): son of my right hand

Andrew & Matthew

Andrew: (English, Scottish & Biblical): manly; brave
Matthew: (Hebrew & Biblical): gift of the Lord

Chance & Chase

Chance: (English & French): good luck, keeper of records
Chase: (English): hunter

Hayden & Hunter

Hayden: (English & Welsh): in the meadow or valley
Hunter: (English): one who hunts

Alexander & Nicholas

Alexander: (Greek): protector of mankind
Nicholas: (Greek): victorious people

Gabriel & Michael

Gabriel: (Israel): hero of God; (Hebrew): man of God; (Spanish): God is my strength
Michael: (Biblical & Hebrew): like God

Jacob & Joseph

Jacob: (Biblical): supplanter; (Hebrew): he grasps the heel
Joseph: (Biblical): God will increase; (Hebrew): may Jehovah increase

Andrew & Benjamin

Andrew: (English, Scottish & Biblical): manly; brave
Benjamin: (English, Hebrew & Biblical): son of my right hand

Andrew & Anthony

Andrew: (English, Scottish & Biblical): manly; brave
Anthony: (English & Biblical): worthy of praise

Benjamin & Samuel

Benjamin: (English, Hebrew & Biblical): son of my right hand
Samuel: (Israel): God hears; (Hebrew): name of God

Aiden & Jayden

Aiden: (Irish, Celtic & Gaelic): fire, fiery
Jayden: (American): God has heard

Christian & Christopher

Christian: (English & Irish): follower of Christ
Christopher: (Biblical): Christ-bearer; (English): he who holds Christ in his heart

Brandon & Bryan (or Brian)

Brandon: (Irish): little raven
Bryan: (Irish): strong one; (Celtic): brave

Jacob & Lucas

Jacob: (Biblical): supplanter; (Hebrew): he grasps the heel
Lucas: (Gaelic, English & Latin America): light

Liam & Logan

Liam: (Irish): determined guardian; (Gaelic): helmeted
Logan: (Irish): small cove; (Scottish): Finnian's servant; (Gaelic): from the hollow

Nathan & Noah

Nathan: (Hebrew): he gives; (Israel): gift of God
Noah: (Biblical): rest, peace; (Hebrew): comfort, long-lived

Alexander & Andrew

Alexander: (Greek): protector of mankind
Andrew: (English, Scottish & Biblical): manly; brave

Alexander & Anthony

Alexander: (Greek): protector of mankind
Anthony: (English & Biblical): worthy of praise

Elijah & Ethan

Elijah: (Biblical): the Lord is my God; (Hebrew): Jehovah is God
Ethan: (Hebrew & Biblical): firm, strong

Nathan & Nicholas

Nathan: (Hebrew): he gives; (Israel): gift of God
Nicholas: (Greek): victorious people

Aiden & Ethan

Aiden: (Irish, Celtic & Gaelic): fire, fiery
Ethan: (Hebrew & Biblical): firm, strong

Aiden & Noah

Aiden: (Irish, Celtic & Gaelic): fire, fiery
Noah: (Biblical): rest, peace; (Hebrew): comfort, long-lived

Jason & Justin

Jason: (Greek): to heal
Justin: (English & French): just, true; (Irish): judicious

Logan & Mason

Logan: (Irish): small cove; (Scottish): Finnian's servant; (Gaelic): from the hollow
Mason: (French & English): stone worker

Maddox & Mason

Maddox: (English): son of the Lord; (Celtic): beneficent
Mason: (French & English): stone worker

Nicholas & Noah

Nicholas: (Greek): victorious people
Noah: (Biblical): rest, peace; (Hebrew): comfort, long-lived

Benjamin & William

Benjamin: (English, Hebrew & Biblical): son of my right hand
William: (English, German & French): protector

Garrett & Gavin

Garrett: (Irish): to watch
Gavin: (English): little hawk; (Welsh): hawk of the battle

Henry & William

Henry: (English, German & French): rules his household
William: (English, German & French): protector

Jayden & Joshua

Jayden: (American): God has heard
Joshua: (Hebrew & Biblical): Jehovah saves

Jeremiah & Jeremy

Jeremy: (Israel): God will uplift
Jeremiah: (Hebrew): may Jehovah exalt; (Israel): sent by God

Jonah & Noah

Jonah: (Hebrew & Israel): a dove
Noah: (Biblical): rest, peace; (Hebrew): comfort, long-lived

Jordan & Justin

Jordan: (Hebrew): to flow down; (Israel): descendant
Justin: (English & French): just, true; (Irish): judicious

Matthew & Nathan

Matthew: (Hebrew & Biblical): gift of the Lord
Nathan: (Hebrew): he gives; (Israel): gift of God

The Most Popular Names for Twins: Girls

Olivia & Sophia

Olivia: (Spanish & Italian): olive; (Biblical): peace of the olive tree
Sophia/Sofia/Sophie: (Greek & Biblical): wisdom

Gabriella & Isabella

Gabriella: (Israel & Hebrew): God gives strength; (Italian): woman of God
Isabella: (Hebrew): devoted to God; (Spanish): God is bountiful; (Biblical): consecrated to God

Ella & Emma

Ella: (English); beautiful fairy; (Spanish): she
Emma: (English, Danish & German): whole, complete, universal

Faith & Hope

Faith: (English): faithful; (Latin America): to trust
Hope: (English): trust, faith

Makayla & Mackenzie

Makayla: (English & Irish): like God
Mackenzie/Mackinsey: (Irish & Scottish): fair, favored one

Heaven & Nevaeh

Heaven: (American): from the heavens
Nevaeh: (American): gift from God, heaven spelled backwards

Isabella & Sophia

Isabella: (Hebrew): devoted to God; (Spanish): God is bountiful; (Biblical): consecrated to God
Sophia/Sofia/Sophie: (Greek & Biblical): wisdom

Mackenzie & Madison

Mackenzie/Mackinsey: (Irish & Scottish): fair, favored one
Madison: (English): son of Matthew

Hailey & Hannah

Hailey/Hailee/Haley/Haylee: (English): hero, field of hay
Hannah: (English & Hebrew): favor, grace; (Biblical): grace of God

Abigail & Olivia

Abigail: (Hebrew): father rejoiced; (Biblical): source of joy
Olivia: (Spanish & Italian): olive; (Biblical): peace of the olive tree

Ava & Emma

Ava: (Latin America): like a bird
Emma: (English, Danish & German): whole, complete, universal

Ava & Olivia

Ava: (Latin America): like a bird
Olivia: (Spanish & Italian): olive; (Biblical): peace of the olive tree

Ava & Mia

Ava: (Latin America): like a bird
Mia: (Italian): my; (Biblical): mine

Emma & Olivia

Emma: (English, Danish & German): whole, complete, universal
Olivia: (Spanish & Italian): olive; (Biblical): peace of the olive tree

Addison & Avery

Addison: (English): son of Adam
Avery: (English): counselor, sage, wise

Ava & Ella

Ava: (Latin America): like a bird
Ella: (English); beautiful fairy; (Spanish): she

Arianna & Brianna

Arianna: (Greek & Italian): holy
Brianna/Breanna: (Irish): strong; (Celtic & English): she ascends

Isabella & Olivia

Isabella: (Hebrew): devoted to God; (Spanish): God is bountiful; (Biblical): consecrated to God
Olivia: (Spanish & Italian): olive; (Biblical): peace of the olive tree

London & Paris

London/Londyn: (English): capital of England; fortress of the moon
Paris: (Persian): angelic face; (Greek): downfall; (French): the capital city of France

Faith & Grace

Faith: (English): faithful; (Latin America): to trust
Grace/Gracie: (Latin America): grace of God; (American): land of grace

Haylee & Kaylee

Haylee: (English): hero, field of hay
Kaylee: (American): pure

Samantha & Sophia

Samantha: (Hebrew & Biblical): listener of God
Sophia/Sofia/Sophie: (Greek & Biblical): wisdom

Abigail & Emily

Abigail: (Hebrew): father rejoiced; (Biblical): source of joy
Emily: (Latin America): admiring

Anna & Emma

Anna/Ana: (Hebrew): favor or grace; (Native American): mother; (Israel): gracious
Emma: (English, Danish & German): whole, complete, universal

Chloe & Zoe (or Zoey)

Chloe: (Greek): verdant, blooming
Zoe (or Zoey): (Greek): life, alive

Elizabeth & Emma

Elizabeth: (English): my God is bountiful; (Hebrew & Biblical): consecrated to God
Emma: (English, Danish & German): whole, complete, universal

Emily & Evelyn

Emily: (Latin America): admiring
Evelyn: (Celtic): light; (English & Hebrew); life, hazelnut

Reagan & Riley

Reagan: (Celtic): regal; (Irish): son of the small ruler
Riley/Rylee: (Irish): a small stream

Abigail & Emma

Abigail: (Hebrew): father rejoiced; (Biblical): source of joy
Emma: (English, Danish & German): whole, complete, universal

Abigail & Sophia

Abigail: (Hebrew): father rejoiced; (Biblical): source of joy
Sophia/Sofia/Sophie: (Greek & Biblical): wisdom

Sara(h) & Sophia

Sara(h): (Hebrew, Spanish & Biblical): princess
Sophia/Sofia/Sophie: (Greek & Biblical): wisdom

Elizabeth & Katherine

Elizabeth: (English): my God is bountiful; (Hebrew & Biblical): consecrated to God
Katherine/Kathryn: (Irish): clear; (English): pure; (Greek): pure, virginal

Emily & Olivia

Emily: (Latin America): admiring
Olivia: (Spanish & Italian): olive; (Biblical): peace of the olive tree

Emma & Sophia

Emma: (English, Danish & German): whole, complete, universal
Sophia/Sofia/Sophie: (Greek & Biblical): wisdom

Jayla & Kayla

Jayla: (Arabia): charity; (African American): one who is special
Kayla: (Irish): pure and beloved

Madison & Morgan

Madison: (English): son of Matthew
Morgan: (Celtic): lives by the sea; (Welsh): bright sea

Mia & Mya

Mia: (Italian): my; (Biblical): mine
Mya: (American): emerald

Natalie & Nicole

Natalia/Natalie: (French): to be born at Christmas; (Slovakian): to be born
Nicole: (French): victory of the people

Serenity & Trinity

Serenity: (Latin & English): peaceful
Trinity: (Latin): the holy three

Abigail & Isabella

Abigail: (Hebrew): father rejoiced; (Biblical): source of joy
Isabella: (Hebrew): devoted to God; (Spanish): God is bountiful; (Biblical): consecrated to God

Addison & Olivia

Addison: (English): son of Adam
Olivia: (Spanish & Italian): olive; (Biblical): peace of the olive tree

Autumn & Summer

Autumn: (English & Latin America): the fall season
Summer: (English): the summer season

Ella & Olivia

Ella: (English); beautiful fairy; (Spanish): she
Olivia: (Spanish & Italian): olive; (Biblical): peace of the olive tree

Emma & Sophie

Emma: (English, Danish & German): whole, complete, universal
Sophie: (Greek & Biblical): wisdom

Gabriella & Sophia

Gabriella: (Israel & Hebrew): God gives strength; (Italian): woman of God
Sophia/Sofia/Sophie: (Greek & Biblical): wisdom

Valentina & Valeria

Valencia/Valentina/Valene: (Spanish & Italian): brave; (Latin America): health or love
Valeria/Valerie: (French): brave, fierce one; (English): strong, valiant

The Most Popular Names for Twins: One of Each Sex

Madison & Mason

Madison: (English): son of Matthew
Mason: (French & English): stone worker

Olivia & Owen

Olivia: (Spanish & Italian): olive; (Biblical): peace of the olive tree
Owen: (English, Welsh & Celtic); young warrior; (Irish): born to nobility

Jayla & Jayden

Jayla: (Arabia): charity; (African American): one who is special
Jayden: (American): God has heard

Emma & Ethan

Emma: (English, Danish & German): whole, complete, universal
Ethan: (Hebrew & Biblical): firm, strong

Isabella & Isaiah

Isabella: (Hebrew): devoted to God; (Spanish): God is bountiful; (Biblical): consecrated to God
Isaiah: (Hebrew): the Lord is generous; (Israel): salvation by God

Addison & Aiden

Addison: (English): son of Adam
Aiden: (Irish, Celtic & Gaelic): fire, fiery

Emily & Ethan

Emily: (Latin America): admiring
Ethan: (Hebrew & Biblical): firm, strong

Aiden & Ava

Aiden: (Irish, Celtic & Gaelic): fire, fiery
Ava: (Latin America): like a bird

Ella & Ethan

Ella: (English); beautiful fairy; (Spanish): she
Ethan: (Hebrew & Biblical): firm, strong

Jada & Jaden

Jada: (Israel): wise
Jaden: (American): God has heard

Taylor & Tyler

Taylor: (English & French): a tailor
Tyler: (English): maker of tiles

Abigail & Andrew

Abigail: (Hebrew): father rejoiced; (Biblical): source of joy
Andrew: (English, Scottish & Biblical): manly; brave

Landon & London

Landon: (English): grassy plain; from the long hill
London/Londyn: (English): capital of England; fortress of the moon

Mason & Morgan

Mason: (French & English): stone worker
Morgan: (Celtic): lives by the sea; (Welsh): bright sea

Oliver & Olivia

Oliver: (French, English, Danish & Latin America): the olive tree; (German): elf army
Olivia: (Spanish & Italian): olive; (Biblical): peace of the olive tree

Zachary & Zoe

Zachary: (Israel & Hebrew): remembered by God
Zoe (or Zoey): (Greek): life, alive

Alexander & Isabella

Alexander: (Greek): protector of mankind
Isabella: (Hebrew): devoted to God; (Spanish): God is bountiful; (Biblical): consecrated to God

Ethan & Olivia

Ethan: (Hebrew & Biblical): firm, strong
Olivia: (Spanish & Italian): olive; (Biblical): peace of the olive tree

Madison & Michael

Madison: (English): son of Matthew
Michael: (Biblical & Hebrew): like God

Abigail & Benjamin

Abigail: (Hebrew): father rejoiced; (Biblical): source of joy
Benjamin: (English, Hebrew & Biblical): son of my right hand

Alexander & Sophia

Alexander: (Greek): protector of mankind
Sophia/Sofia/Sophie: (Greek & Biblical): wisdom

Emily & Matthew

Emily: (Latin America): admiring
Matthew: (Hebrew & Biblical): gift of the Lord

Emma & John

Emma: (English, Danish & German): whole, complete, universal
John: (Israel): God is gracious; Jehovah has been gracious

Mackenzie & Mason

Mackenzie/Mackinsey: (Irish & Scottish): fair, favored one
Mason: (French & English): stone worker

Michael & Michelle

Michael: (Biblical & Hebrew): like God
Michelle: (French & Hebrew): like God, close to God

Adrian & Adriana

Adrian: (German, Spanish & Italian): dark
Adriana: (Spanish & Italian): dark, rich

Charlotte & Henry

Charlotte: (French): feminine
Henry: (English, German & French): rules his household

Elizabeth & William

Elizabeth: (English): my God is bountiful; (Hebrew & Biblical): consecrated to God
William: (English, German & French): protector

Isaac & Isabella

Isaac: (Biblical): he will laugh
Isabella: (Hebrew): devoted to God; (Spanish): God is bountiful; (Biblical): consecrated to God

Samuel & Sophia

Samuel: (Israel): God hears; (Hebrew): name of God
Sophia/Sofia/Sophie: (Greek & Biblical): wisdom

Addison & Jackson

Addison: (English): son of Adam
Jackson: (English): son of Jack; (Scottish): God has been gracious

Andrew & Emma

Andrew: (English, Scottish & Biblical): manly; brave
Emma: (English, Danish & German): whole, complete, universal

Ava & Jackson

Ava: (Latin America): like a bird
Jackson: (English): son of Jack; (Scottish): God has been gracious

Blake & Brooklyn

Blake: (English): pale blond or dark; (Scottish): dark-haired
Brooklyn: (English): water, stream

Caleb & Chloe

Caleb: (Israel): faithful; (Hebrew): dog or bold
Chloe: (Greek): verdant, blooming

Chloe & Colton

Chloe: (Greek): verdant, blooming
Colton: (English): coal town, from the dark town

Chloe & Connor

Chloe: (Greek): verdant, blooming
Connor: (Irish): strong willed, much wanted

Emma & Jack

Emma: (English, Danish & German): whole, complete, universal
Jack: (English): God is gracious; (Hebrew): supplanter

Emma & Jacob

Emma: (English, Danish & German): whole, complete, universal
Jacob: (Biblical): supplanter; (Hebrew): he grasps the heel

Isabella & Jacob

Isabella: (Hebrew): devoted to God; (Spanish): God is bountiful; (Biblical): consecrated to God
Jacob: (Biblical): supplanter; (Hebrew): he grasps the heel

Jada & Jordan

Jada: (Israel): wise
Jordan: (Hebrew): to flow down; (Israel): descendant

Natalie & Nathan

Natalia/Natalie: (French): to be born at Christmas; (Slovakian): to be born
Nathan: (Israel): gift of God; (Hebrew): he gives

Robert & Sophia

Robert: (English, French, German & Scottish): famed, bright, shining
Sophia/Sofia/Sophie: (Greek & Biblical): wisdom

Trinity & Tristan

Trinity: (Latin): the holy three
Tristan: (English, Celtic & French): outcry, tumult; (Welsh): noisy; (Irish): bold

Zane & Zoey

Zane: (Hebrew): gift from God; (Arabian): beloved
Zoe (or Zoey): (Greek): life, alive

Abigail & Alexander

Abigail: (Hebrew): father rejoiced; (Biblical): source of joy
Alexander: (Greek): protector of mankind

Abigail & Jacob

Abigail: (Hebrew): father rejoiced; (Biblical): source of joy
Jacob: (Biblical): supplanter; (Hebrew): he grasps the heel

Abigail & Zachary

Abigail: (Hebrew): father rejoiced; (Biblical): source of joy
Zachary: (Israel & Hebrew): remembered by God

Addison & Austin

Addison: (English): son of Adam
Austin: (English): from the name Augustin, which means revered

Chapter 3: Twin Names That Rhyme

There are few cuter, more memorable, or distinctive ways to name twins than giving them names that rhyme. Nevertheless, this is definitely a controversial practice; in fact, for every person who likes rhyming names, there is another who thinks that the trend is juvenile and gimmicky.

In this chapter, we offer several hundred combinations of names that rhyme for girls, boys, and mixed sets of twins. Some are obvious choices because the names are so popular. However, other combinations include older and more traditional names that give the pairings an added level of cachet. As you browse the lists, consider whether (or not) each name works on its own - and whether the pairing is a good match with your family's surname. Add the best choices to your list of possibilities for your own new additions.

Twin Names That Rhyme: Boys

Aaron & Darren

Aaron: (Jewish & Hebrew): enlightened
Darren: (English, Irish & Gaelic): great

Alvin & Calvin

Alvin: (Germany): light skin, noble friend; (English): wise friend
Calvin: (English & Latin America): bald

Barrett & Garrett

Barrett: (English & German): strength of a bear
Garrett: (Irish): to watch

Bryan & Ryan

Bryan: (Irish): strong one; (Celtic): brave
Ryan: (Gaelic): little king; (Irish): kindly, young royalty

Chance & Lance

Chance: (English & French): good luck, keeper of records
Lance: (Germany): spear; (French): land

Cody & Brody

Cody: (Irish): helpful; (English): a cushion, helpful
Brody: (Irish): brother, from the muddy place; (Scottish): second son

Dustin & Justin

Dustin: (English): fighter, warrior
Justin: (English & French): just, true; (Irish): judicious

Devon, Kevin & Evan

Devon: (English & Irish): a poet, a county in England
Kevin: (Irish & Gaelic): handsome, beautiful; (Celtic): gentle
Evan: (English): God is good; (Welsh): young; (Celtic): young fighter

Donald, Arnold & Ronald

Donald: (Celtic & Gaelic): dark stranger; (Irish, English & Scottish): great leader
Arnold: (German): strong as an eagle
Ronald: (English, Gaelic & Scottish): rules with counsel

Eric & Derek

Eric: (Scandinavian): honorable ruler
Derek: (German & English): gifted ruler

Frank & Hank

Frank: (Latin America): free
Hank: (Dutch & German): rules his household

Hogan & Logan

Hogan: (Irish & Gaelic): young, young at heart
Logan: (Irish): small cove; (Scottish): Finnian's servant; (Gaelic): from the hollow

Kyle & Lyle

Kyle: (Gaelic): young; (Irish): young at heart
Lyle: (French & English): from the island

Jason & Mason

Jason: (Greek): to heal
Mason: (French & English): stone worker

Sean/Shawn & John

Sean/Shawn: (Irish): God is gracious
John: (Israel): God is gracious; Jehovah has been gracious

Taylor & Tyler

Taylor: (English & French): a tailor
Tyler: (English): tile maker

Barry, Harry & Larry

Barry: (English & Irish): fair-haired; (Celtic); marksman; (Gaelic): spear
Harry: (German): home or house ruler
Larry: (Dutch & Latin America): laurels

Jordan, Aiden, Hayden, Cayden & Jayden

Jordan: (Hebrew): to flow down; (Israel): descendant
Aiden: (Irish, Celtic & Gaelic): fire, fiery
Hayden: (English): the rosy meadow
Cayden: (Scottish): fighter
Jayden: (American): God has heard

Twin Names That Rhyme: Girls

Anna & Hannah

Anna/Ana: (Hebrew): favor or grace; (Native American): mother; (Israel): gracious
Hannah: (English & Hebrew): favor, grace; (Biblical): grace of God

Bella, Ella, & Stella

Bella: (Hebrew): devoted to God; (Spanish & Latin America): beautiful
Ella: (English); beautiful fairy; (Spanish): she
Stella: (French, Italian & Greek): star

Darcy & Marcy

Darcy: (Irish & Celtic): dark one
Marcy: (Latin America): marital

Kayla, Jayla, Layla & Shayla

Kayla: (Irish): pure and beloved
Jayla: (Arabia): charity; (African American): one who is special
Layla: (Indian): born at night; (Arabian): dark beauty
Shayla: (Irish): her gift

Cara, Mara, Sara & Tara

Cara: (Celtic): friend; (Italian & Dominican Republic): dear, beloved
Mara: (English, Italian, Hebrew & Israel): bitter
Sara(h): (Hebrew, Spanish & Biblical): princess
Tara: (Irish & Scottish): a hill where the kings meet; (Irish): tower, hillside

Carla & Marla

Carla: (Portuguese & Latin America): strong one
Marla: (Greek): high tower

Candy & Mandy

Candy: (American): bright, sweet; (Hebrew): famous bearer
Mandy: (Latin America): worthy of love

Chloe & Zoe

Chloe: (Greek): verdant, blooming
Zoe (or Zoey): (Greek): life, alive

Ellen & Helen

Ellen: (Greek): light
Helen: (Greek): light

Kiley & Riley

Kiley: (Irish): narrow land
Riley/Rylee: (Irish): a small stream

Flynn, Lynn(e) & Quinn

Flynn: (Irish): heir to the red-headed
Lynn(e): (English): waterfall
Quinn: (Celtic): wise; (Irish): fifth, counsel, intelligent

Jayne, Rain(e) & Blaine

Jayne: (Indian): victorious; (Hebrew): gift from God; (English): Jehovah has been gracious
Rain/Raine: (American): blessings from above; (French & Latin): ruler; (English): lord, wise
Blaine: (Gaelic, Irish & Celtic): thin

Callie & Tally

Callie: (Greek): beautiful; (English); lark
Tally: (Irish): surname

Addison & Madison

Addison: (English): son of Adam
Madison: (English): son of Matthew

Minnie & Winnie

Minnie: (Irish): bitter; (Hebrew): wished for a child
Winnie: (Irish & Celtic): white, fair

Clarissa, Alyssa, Melissa & Marissa

Clarissa: (Spanish & Italian): clear; (Latin America): brilliant
Alyssa: (Greek): logical
Melissa: (Greek): honey bee
Marissa: (Latin America): of the sea; (Hebrew): rebellion, bitter

Marilyn & Carolyn

Marilyn: (Israel): descendants of Mary
Carolyn: (English): joy, song of happiness

Valerie & Mallory

Valerie: (French): brave, fierce one; (English): strong, valiant
Mallory: (French): unfortunate; ill-fated; (German): war counselor

Hailey, Kaylee, & Bailey

Hailey/Hailee/Haley: (English): hero, field of hay
Kaylee: (American): pure
Bailey: (English): bailiff, steward, public official

Jess, Tess & Bess

Jess: (Israel): wealthy
Tess: (English): harvester
Bess: (Hebrew, English & Israel): oath of God, God is satisfaction

Molly, Holly, Polly & Dolly

Molly: (Israel & English): bitter
Holly: (French, English & Germany): shrub
Polly: (Latin America): bitter
Dolly: (America): cute child

Sherry and Merry

Sherry: (Israel): beloved; (French): dear one
Merry: (English): merry, joyous

Laura, Maura, Melora & Dora

Laura: (English, Spanish & Latin America): crowned with laurel, from the laurel tree
Maura: (Italian, Irish & French): dark
Melora: (Greek): golden apple
Dora: (Greek): gift

Tia, Lia, Mia, Nia & Gia

Tia: (Greek); princess; (Spanish): princess, aunt; (African American): aunt
Lia: (Greek): bearer of good news
Mia: (Italian): my; (Biblical): mine
Nia: (Irish): champion
Gia: (Italian): God is gracious

Nina, Tina, Gina & Dina

Nina: (Hebrew); grace; (Spanish): girl; (Native American): strong
Tina: (English): river
Gina: (Italian): garden; (African American): powerful mother of black people
Dina: (Hebrew & Israel): avenged, judged; (English): from the valley

Gay, Rae, Fay, Kay & May

Gay: (English): merry, happy
Rae: (Scottish): grace; (Germany): wise protection
Fay: (French): fairy; (Irish): raven; (English): faith, confidence
Kay: (Greek): rejoice; (Scottish & Welsh): fiery
May: (English): name of month; (Hebrew & Latin America): from Mary

Stacey, Casey, Tracy, Macy, Lacy & Gracie

Stacy: (English): productive, resurrection
Tracy: (English): brave
Casey: (Celtic & Gaelic): brave; (Irish): observant, alert, brave; (Spanish): honorable
Macy: (English): enduring; (American): stone worker
Lacy: (Irish): surname; (English): derived from lace
Gracie: (English & Latin America): grace

Irene, Eileen, Colleen, Darlene, Marlene & Sharlene

Irene: (Greek & Spanish): peaceful
Eileen: (Irish & French): light
Colleen: (Irish & Gaelic): girl
Darlene: (English & French): little darling
Marlene: (Germany): bitter; (Hebrew): from the tower
Sharlene: (English & French): manly, from the name Charles

Twin Names That Rhyme: One of Each Sex

Adonis & Beatrice

Adonis: (Greek): beautiful
Beatrice: (Italian): blesses; (French): bringer of joy

Beth & Seth

Beth: (Scottish): lively
Seth: (Hebrew): anointed; (Israel): appointed

Cleo & Leo

Cleo: (Greek): to praise, acclaim
Leo: (Italian & English): a lion

Dale & Gayle

Dale: (Germany): valley; (English): lives in the valley
Gayle: (English): lively

Doris & Morris

Doris: (Greek): sea
Morris: (Latin America): dark skinned; (English): son of More

Gwen & Ken

Gwen: (Celtic): mythical son of Gwastad
Ken: (Welsh): clear water; (English): royal obligation; (Irish): handsome; (Japanese): strong

Jade & Wade

Jade: (Spanish): jewel, green gemstone
Wade: (English): ford, cross the river

Jody & Cody

Jody: (Hebrew): praised
Cody: (Irish): helpful; (English): a cushion, helpful

Tristan & Kristen

Tristan: (English, Celtic & French): outcry, tumult; (Welsh): noisy; (Irish): bold
Kristen: (Irish): Christ-bearer

Jake, Lake & Blake

Jake: (Hebrew): he grasps the heel
Lake: (American): body of water, from the lake
Blake: (English): pale blond or dark; (Scottish): dark-haired

Troy, Roy & Joy

Troy: (French): curly haired; (Irish): foot soldier
Roy: (Irish & French): king; (Scottish & Celtic): red
Joy: (French, English & Latin America): rejoicing

Lori, Cory & Tori

Lori: (English): the laurel tree; (Latin America): crowned with laurel
Cory: (English & Irish): hill, hollow
Tori: (English): triumphant

Gage, Paige & Saige/Sage

Gage: (French): a pledge or pawn
Paige: (French): assistant, attendant
Saige/Sage: (English & French): wise one; (English): from the spice

John, Dawn, Fawn & Sean/Shawn

John: (Israel): God is gracious; Jehovah has been gracious
Dawn: (Greek): sunrise; (English): aurora
Fawn: (French & English): young deer
Sean/Shawn: (English & Irish): from the shady grove; (Irish): God is gracious

Jane, Shane, Cain, Layne & Zane

Jane: (Hebrew): gift from God; (English): gracious, merciful
Shane: (Hebrew): gift from God; (Irish): God is gracious
Cain/Kane: (Israel): craftsman; (Hebrew): spear; (Welsh): clear water; (Irish): archaic
Layne: (English): path, roadway
Zane: (Hebrew): gift from God; (Arabian): beloved

Darian, Giddeon & Jillian

Darian: (Irish): from the name Darrin, which means great
Giddeon: (Hebrew & Israel): great warrior
Jillian: (English): child of the gods; (Latin America): youthful, young at heart

Andy, Sandy, Brandy & Randy

Andy: (French, English & Scottish): manly, brave
Sandy: (Greek): from the name Alexander, which means defender
Brandy: (American): warm; (English): the beverage brandy
Randy: (English): son of Rand

Erin, Karen, Sharon & Darren

Erin: (Gaelic): peace; (Irish): Ireland
Karen: (Greek): pure
Sharon: (Hebrew & Israel): a flat clearing
Darren: (English, Irish & Gaelic): great

Amber, Elmer, Oliver & Parker

Amber: (Gaelic): fierce; (American): precious jewel
Elmer: (English): noble, famous
Oliver: (English): the olive tree; (German): elf army; (Latin America): peace, olive tree
Parker: (English): keeper of the park or forest

Eugene, Irene, Eileen, Colleen, Darlene, Marlene & Sharlene

Eugene: (Greek): born with good fortune
Irene: (Greek & Spanish): peaceful
Eileen: (Irish & French): light
Colleen: (Irish & Gaelic): girl
Darlene: (English & French): little darling
Marlene: (Germany): bitter; (Hebrew): from the tower
Sharlene: (English & French): manly, from the name Charles

Eleanor, Isadore & Theodore

Eleanor: (Greek & English): light
Isadore: (Greek): strong gift, gift of isis
Theodore: (Greek): divine gift

Chapter 4. Twin Names that are Anagrams

For parents who seek similar - and symmetrical - names for their twins that are not cutesy or rhyming, anagrams are an intriguing choice. By definition, anagrams are words that have exactly the same letters, but in a different order. Consequently, they are always the same length - and often have a similar feel. As an added bonus, names that are anagrams are rarely trendy or popular, which gives them a certain cachet. If nothing else, the pairings in this chapter will open your mind to new ways of thinking about names - and to possibilities you might not have considered.

Twin Names that are Anagrams - Boys

Adrian & Darian

Adrian: (German, Spanish & Italian): dark
Darian: (Irish): from the name Darren, which means great

Adrien & Andrei

Adrien: (German, Spanish & Italian): dark
Andrei: (Italian): manlike

Arnold & Orland & Roland & Ronald

Arnold: (German): strong as an eagle
Orland: (English): from the pointed hill; (Spanish & German): renowned in the land
Roland: (French, German & English): renowned in the land
Ronald: (English, Gaelic & Scottish): rules with counsel

Ary & Ray

Ary: (Hebrew): lion of God
Ray: (French): regal: (Scottish): grace; (English): wise protector

Brendan & Branden

Brendan: (Irish): prince; (Gaelic): brave; (Celtic & Irish): raven; (German): flame
Brandon: (Irish): little raven

Benito & Benoit

Benito: (Italian): blessed
Benoit: (French): bland

Bret & Bert

Bret: (French, English & Celtic): a native of Brittany
Bert: (German & English): bright light

Claus & Lucas

Claus: (Greek): people's victory
Lucas: (Gaelic, English & Latin America): light

Dane & Dean & Aden

Dane: (Hebrew & Scandinavian): God will judge; (English): brook
Dean: (English): head, leader
Aden: (Irish, Celtic & Gaelic): fire, fiery

Darnel & Lenard

Darnel: (English): hidden
Lenard: (French & German): lion, bold

Earl & Lear

Earl: (Irish): pledge; (English): nobleman
Lear: (English): Shakespearean king

Elgin & Nigel

Elgin: (English & Celtic): noble, white
Nigel: (English, Gaelic & Irish): champion; (American): ahead

Elroy & Leroy

Elroy: (French, English & African American): king; (Irish): red-haired youth
Leroy: (French): king

Elmer & Merle

Elmer: (English): famous, noble
Merle: (French): blackbird; (English): falcon

Ewan & Wane

Ewan: (Celtic, Scotch & Irish): young
Wane: (English): craftsman, wagon maker

Forrest & Forster

Forrest: (English & French): from the woods
Forster: (American & French): from the woods

Gray & Gary

Gray: (English): gray-haired
Gary: (German & English): spear

Hans & Nash

Hans: (German & Hebrew): gift from God; (Scandinavian): God is gracious
Nash: (American): adventurer

Jason & Jonas

Jason: (Greek): to heal
Jonas: (Hebrew): gift from God; (Spanish): dove; (Israel): accomplishing

Kaleb & Blake

Kaleb: (Israel): faithful; (Hebrew): dog or bold
Blake: (English): pale blond or dark; (Scottish): dark-haired

Leon & Noel

Leon: (Spanish, German, French & Lain America): lion
Noel: (French): Christmas

Marcelo & Carmelo

Marcelo: (Italian & Latin): hammer
Carmelo: (Hebrew & Israel): fruit orchard

Nicol & Colin

Nicol: (Scottish & English): victorious
Colin: (Irish & Gaelic): young; (Scottish): young dog; (English): of a triumphant people

Romeo & Moore

Romeo: (Italian, Spanish, Latin America & African American): from Rome
Moore: (French): dark-skinned; (Irish & French): surname

Ryder & Derry

Ryder: (English): knight
Derry: (English, Irish, German & Gaelic): red-haired, from the oak grove

Seaton & Easton

Seaton: (English): from the farm by the sea
Easton: (English): from east town

Seton & Stone

Seton: (English): from the farm by the sea
Stone: (English): stone

Tyson & Stony

Tyson: (French): explosive; (English): son of Tye
Stony: (English): stone

Warden & Andrew

Andrew: (English, Scottish & Biblical): manly; brave
Warden: (English): guard

Warner & Warren

Warner: (German & English): defender
Warren: (English): to preserve; (German): protector, loyal

Twin Names that Are Anagrams - Girls

Amy & May & Mya

Amy: (English, French & Latin America): beloved
May: (English): name of month; (Hebrew & Latin America): from Mary
Mya: (American): emerald

Adelina & Daniela

Adelina: (French & Spanish): of the nobility
Daniela: (Hebrew & Spanish): God is my judge

Alexi & Lexia

Alexi: (English): helper, defender
Lexa: (Czech): defender of mankind

Ali & Lia

Ali: (Arabia): noble, sublime
Lia: (Greek): bearer of good news

Alice & Celia & Lacie

Alice: (Spanish): of the nobility
Celia: (Italian): heavenly
Lacie: (Irish): surname; (English): derived from lace

Alli & Lila

Alli: (Arabia): noble, sublime
Lila: (Arabia): night

Alyce & Lacey

Alyce: (Spanish): of the nobility
Lacey: (Irish): surname; (English): derived from lace

Alysha & Shayla

Alysha: (English): of noble birth; (Spanish & German): sweet
Shayla: (Irish): her gift

Ashlie & Elisha & Sheila

Ashlie: (English & Biblical): lives in the ash tree
Elisha: (Hebrew): God is salvation; (Israel): God is gracious
Sheila: (English & Irish): blind; (Italian): music

Aileen & Elaine & Ileana

Aileen: (Dutch): alone; (Celtic & Irish): fair, good looking
Elaine: (French): light
Ileana: (Roman): torch; (Greek): from the city of lion

Anita & Tania & Tiana

Anita: (Italian, Hebrew & Latin America): gracious
Tania: (Slovakian): a fairy queen
Tiana: (Greek): princess

Anja & Jana

Anja: (Russian): grace of God
Jana: (Slovakian): God is gracious

Ann & Nan

Ann: (Hebrew & Israel): favor or grace
Nan: (English): gracious

Anne & Nena

Anne: (Hebrew & Israel): favor or grace
Nena: (English): girl

Annette & Nanette

Annette: (French & Hebrew): gracious
Nanette: (English): favor; (French & Hebrew): gracious

April & Pilar

April: (English): opening buds of spring; (Latin America): opening, fourth month
Pilar: (Spanish): pillar of strength

Ashlee & Sheela

Ashlee: (English & Biblical): lives in the ash tree
Sheela: (English & Irish): blind; (Italian): music

Ashley & Halsey

Ashley: (English & Biblical): lives in the ash tree
Halsey: (English); from the Hals island, residence name

Carlie & Claire

Carlie: (American): strong one; (Latin America): little, womanly
Claire: (English): clear; (French): bright

Carmela & Marcela

Carmela/Carmella: (Hebrew & Israel): golden; (Spanish): garden
Marcela: (Spanish): warring

Carrie & Cierra

Carrie: (American): melody, song
Cierra: (Spanish): dark-skinned

Cilla & Lilac

Cilla: (Latin): sturdy, vision
Lilac: (Latin America): bluish purple; (American): a flowering bluish purple shrub

Cornelia & Caroline

Cornelia: (Latin): horn
Caroline: (Mexico): beautiful woman; (French & English): song of happiness

Della & Adell

Adell: (German & French): noble, kind
Della: (German, Greek & English): noble

Delora & Eldora

Delora: (Latin America): of the seashore; (English): sorrow
Eldora: (Spanish): golden, blond, gift of the sun

Dianne & Nadine

Dianne: (Latin America): hunter
Nadine: (French): hopeful; (German): the courage of a bear

Deanna & Nadene

Deanna: (English & Latin America): from the valley
Nadene: (French): hopeful; (German): the courage of a bear

Dena & Edna

Dena: (Hebrew & Israel): vindicated; (Native American): valley
Edna: (Celtic): fire; (Hebrew): rejuvenation; (Israel): spirit renewed

Erika & Kiera

Erika: (Denmark): honorable ruler
Kiera: (Irish): dusky

Elisha & Ashlie & Sheila

Elisha: (English): of noble birth; (Spanish & German): sweet
Ashlie: (English & Biblical): lives in the ash tree
Sheila: (English & Irish): blind; (Italian): music

Ellen & Nelle

Ellen: (Greek): light
Nelle: (English): torch

Ellyn & Nelly

Ellyn: (Greek): light
Nelly: (English): torch

Erica & Ciera

Ciera: (Spanish): dark-skinned
Erica: (Denmark): honorable ruler

Esther & Hester

Esther: (Hebrew & Africa): star
Hester: (Greek): star

Gina & Inga

Gina: (Italian): garden; (African American): powerful mother of black people
Inga: (Danish & Swedish): beautiful daughter

Hera & Rhea

Hera: (Greek): goddess of marriage
Rhea: (Greek): rivers

Lina & Nila

Lina: (Arabic): tender
Nila: (Indian): blue

Ilene & Eleni

Ilene: (English & Irish): light
Eleni: (Greek): light

Ilsa & Isla & Lisa

Ilsa: (German): abbreviation of Elizabeth, which means God is bountiful
Isla: (Irish): island
Lisa: (German): devoted to God; (Israel): consecrated to God

Iris & Siri

Iris: (Greek): colorful, rainbow; (Hebrew & English): the flower
Siri: (Scandinavian): beautiful victory

Irena & Reina

Irena: (Greek): peace
Reina: (French & Spanish): queen; (English): wise ruler

Joann & Jonna

Joann: (English & Hebrew): God is gracious
Jonna: (Danish): God is gracious

Kamala & Makala

Kamala: (Hindu): lotus
Makala: (English): princess

Kami & Mika

Kami: (Hindu): loving
Mika: (Finnish): like God

Kari & Kira

Kari: (Norwegian): blessed, pure, holy
Kira: (Russian): sun

Keely & Kylee

Keely: (Irish): beautiful
Kylee: (Celtic): a straight and narrow channel

Laryn & Rylan

Laryn: (French): crowned with laurel
Rylan: (English): dweller in the rye field

Leila & Allie

Leila: (Indian): born at night; (Arabian): dark beauty
Allie: (Arabia): noble, sublime

Leilah & Hallie

Leilah: (Indian): born at night; (Arabian): dark beauty
Hallie: (English): hay meadow

Liza & Zila

Liza: (Hebrew): consecrated to God
Zila: (Hebrew): shadow, shade

Lona & Nola

Lona: (English): ready for battle
Nola: (Irish): champion

Lorita & Tailor

Lorita: (Latin America): laurel
Tailor: (English & French): a tailor

Luna & Nula

Luna: (Latin): moon
Nula: (Irish): white: shouldered

Marian & Marina

Marian: (French): bitter
Marina: (Italian): of the sea

Mabel & Melba

Mabel: (English): lovable, beautiful
Melba: (Greek): slender, thin-skinned

Mariel & Elmira & Marlie

Mariel: (Hebrew): bitter
Elmira: (English): noble
Marlie: (American): bitter

Maci & Cami & Mica

Maci: (English): enduring; (American): stone worker
Kami: (Hindu): loving
Mika: (Finnish): like God

Malika & Kamila & Mikala

Malika: (African): queen, princess
Kamila: (Czech): young ceremonial attendant
Mikala: (Hawaiian): who is like God

Mary & Myra

Mary: (Biblical, English & Slovakian): bitter
Myra: (Greek): fragrant

Marisa & Samira

Marisa: (Latin America): of the sea; (Hebrew): rebellion, bitter
Samira: (Arabic): entertaining

Maria & Amira

Maria: (Latin): bitter
Amira: (Arabic): prince

Nevada & Davena

Nevada: (English): covered in snow
Davena: (Scottish): feminine form of David, which means beloved one

Nuala & Luana

Nuala: (Irish): white, fair-shouldered
Luana: (English): gracious light

Oliva & Viola

Oliva: (Latin): olive tree
Viola: (Italian): violet flower

Raven & Verna

Raven: (English): to be black, blackbird
Verna: (English): alder tree

Reba & Brea

Reba: (Hebrew): fourth
Brea: (French): champion

Rein & Erin

Rein: (German); advisor, counselor
Erin: (Irish): peace

Rhona & Norah

Rhona: (Hebrew): my joy
Norah: (Hebrew): light

Roza & Zora

Roza: (Polish): rose
Zora: (Slavic): sunrise

Rosina & Sorina

Rosina: (Celtic): little rose
Sorina: (Romanian): sun

Salina & Alanis

Salina: (French): peaceful, solemn
Alanis: (English): attractive

Tamira & Amrita & Marita

Tamira: (Hebrew): palm tree, spice
Amrita: (Hindu): nectar of eternal immortality
Marita: (Dutch): bitter

Tanisha & Ashanti

Tanisha: (English): worthy of praise
Ashanti: (African): great African woman

Theodora & Dorothea

Theodora: (English): gift of God
Dorothea: (Dutch): gift of God

Teresa & Easter

Teresa: (Finnish): summer, harvester
Easter: (American): from the holiday or Christian festival

Tia & Tai

Tia: (Greek); princess; (Spanish): princess, aunt; (African American): aunt
Tai: (Chinese): large

Trisha & Ishtar

Trisha: (English): noble
Ishtar: (Arabic): mythical goddess of love and fertility

Vera & Reva

Vera: (Russian): verity, truth
Reva: (Hebrew): rain

Liane & Aline & Laine & Lanie & Neila

Liane: (English): daughter of the sun
Aline: (Dutch): alone; (Celtic & Irish): fair, good looking
Laine: (English): narrow road, from the long meadow
Lanie: (English): path or roadway
Neila: (Irish): champion

Twin Names that Are Anagrams - One of Each Sex

Abe & Bea

Abe: (Jewish): father of nations
Bea: (American): blessed

Abel & Bela

Abel: (Biblical & Hebrew): breath
Bela: (Slovakian): she of fair skin; (Indian): seas shore; (Hebrew): destruction

Abram & Ambra

Abram: (Hebrew): high father; (Israel): father of nations
Ambra: (French): jewel; (Italian): amber color

Adan & Dana

Adan: (Irish, Celtic & Gaelic): fire, fiery
Dana: (English, Danish, Irish & Hebrew): a person from Denmark

Alan & Nala

Alan: (English & Irish): handsome; (Celtic): harmony, stone or noble
Nala: (African): successful

Alek & Lake

Alek: (Russian): defender of mankind
Lake: (American): body of water, from the lake

Nora & Roan & Rona

Nora: (Hebrew): light
Roan: (English): from the Rowan tree
Rona: (Hebrew): my joy

Axel & Alex & Lexa

Axel: (German & Hebrew): father of peace; (German): source of all life
Alex: (Greek): protector of mankind
Lexa: (Czech): defender of mankind

Aden & Dane & Dean & Dena & Edna & Neda

Aden: (Irish, Celtic & Gaelic): fire, fiery
Dane: (Hebrew & Scandinavian): God will judge; (English): brook
Dean: (English): head, leader
Dena: (Hebrew & Israel): avenged, judged; (English): from the valley
Edna: (Celtic): fire; (Hebrew): rejuvenation; (Israel): spirit renewed
Neda: (Slovakian): Sunday's child; (English): wealthy guardian

Ashley & Halsey

Ashley: (English & Biblical): lives in the ash tree
Halsey: (English): from Hals island

Adrien & Andrei & Darien & Randie

Adrien: (German, Spanish & Italian): dark
Andrei: (Italian): manlike
Darien: (Irish): from the name Darren, great
Randie: (English): shield-wolf

Bryon & Byron & Robyn

Bryan: (Irish): strong one; (Celtic): brave
Byron: (French & English): barn or cottage
Robyn: (English): a small bird

Booker & Brooke

Booker: (English): bible, book maker
Brooke: (English): lives by the stream

Braden & Brande & Brenda

Braden: (Irish & English): broad hillside; (Scottish): salmon
Brande: (English): firebrand
Brenda: (Gaelic): little raven; (Scandinavian): sword

Brady & Darby

Brady: (Gaelic & Irish): spirit; (Irish): broad-shouldered
Darby: (Irish & Gaelic): free man; (English): deer park

Cari & Rico

Cari: (Latin America): beloved
Rico: (German): glory; (Spanish & Cuban): strong ruler

Carle & Clare

Carle: (English): man; (German): strong one
Clare: (English): clear; (French): bright

Carlo & Carol & Coral

Carlo: (French): strong; Italian: manly
Carol: (French): melody, song
Coral: (English): a reef formation

Casia & Isaac

Casia: (English): alert, vigorous
Isaac: (Biblical): he will laugh

Clay & Lacy

Clay: (English): clay maker, immortal
Lacy: (Irish): surname; (English): derived from lace

Cleo & Cole

Cleo: (Greek): to praise, acclaim
Cole: (Irish): warrior

Cyril & Lyric

Cyril: (English & Greek): master, lord
Lyric: (Greek): melodic word; (French): of the lyre

Dania & Adina & Aidan & Diana & Nadia

Dania: (English, Hebrew & Denmark): God is my judge
Adina: (Israel): beautiful; (Hebrew): slender
Aidan: (Irish, Celtic & Gaelic): fire, fiery
Diana: (Greek): divine, goddess of the moon and the hunt
Nadia: (Slovakian): hopeful

Dolly & Lloyd

Dolly: (American): cute child
Lloyd: (Celtic, Welsh & English): gray

Dale & Dela

Dale: (German): valley; (English): lives in the valley
Dela: (German, Greek & English): noble

Daisy & Sayid

Daisy: (American): flower
Sayid: (African): lord and master

Dilan & Linda

Dilan: (English & Welsh): born from the ocean, son of the wave
Linda: (Spanish): pretty; (English): lime tree; (German): snake, lime tree

Elvin & Levin

Elvin: (Irish): friend of elves
Levin: (Hebrew): heart; (English): dear friend

Erik & Keri

Erik: (Scandinavian): honorable ruler
Keri: (Irish): dusky, dark

Galen & Angel

Galen: (Gaelic): tranquil; (English): festive party: (Greek): healer, calm
Angel: (Spanish & Greek): angelic

Isabel & Blaise

Isabel: (Hebrew): devoted to God; (Spanish & Biblical): consecrated to God
Blaise: (French & English): stutter, stammer

Jason & Jonas & Sonja

Jason: (Greek): to heal
Jonas: (Hebrew): gift from God; (Spanish): dove; (Israel): accomplishing
Sonja: (Scandinavian): wisdom

Karl & Lark

Karl: (English & Icelandic): man; (French): strong, masculine; (Danish): one who is free
Lark: (English): a lark; (American): songbird

Lane & Lena & Neal

Lane: (English): narrow road, from the long meadow
Lena: (Israel): illustrious
Neal: (Irish, English & Celtic): a champion

Liam & Mila

Liam: (Irish): determined guardian; (Gaelic): helmeted
Mila: (Serbia): favor, glory

Lamar & Marla

Lamar: (German): famous land; (French): of the sea
Marla: (Greek): high tower

Marsha & Shamar

Marsha: (Latin America): brave
Shamar: (Arabian): ready for battle

Moira & Mario

Moira: (Irish): bitter
Mario: (Hebrew): bitter, king-ruler

Mari & Amir & Irma & Mira

Mari: (Finnish): bitter
Amir: (Arabic): prince
Irma: (German): whole, universal
Mira: (Hindu): prosperous

Nia & Ian

Nia: (Irish): champion; (African): purpose
Ian: (Scottish): gift from God

Norma & Ramon & Roman

Norma: (Latin America): from the north
Ramon: (Spanish): a wise or mighty protector
Roman: (Spanish & Latin America): from Rome

Adrian & Andria & Darian

Adrian: (German, Spanish & Italian): dark
Andrei: (Italian): manlike
Darian: (Irish): from the name Darren, which means great

Royce & Corey

Royce: (English): royal, son of the king: (German): famous
Corey: (English & Irish): hill, hollow

Sean & Sena

Sean: (Irish): God is gracious
Sena: (Persian): blessed

Salem & Selma

Salem: (Hebrew): peace
Selma: (Scandinavian): divinely protected

Anders & Andres

Anders: (Scandinavian): a courageous, valiant man
Andres: (Spanish): manly, courageous

Shawnda & Dashawn

Shawnda: (English): God is gracious
Dashawn: (English): God is willing

Thelma & Hamlet

Thelma: (English): ambitious, nurturing
Hamlet: (English): home

Thema & Ahmet

Thema: (African): queen
Ahmet: (Turkish): worthy of praise

Tory & Troy

Tory: (English): triumphant
Troy: (French): curly haired; (Irish): foot soldier

Vonda & Davon

Vonda: (Latin): true image
Davon: (English): river

Evan & Neva

Evan: (English): God is good; (Welsh): young; (Celtic): young fighter
Neva: (Spanish): covered with snow

York & Kory

York: (Celtic, English & Latin America): from the yew tree
Kory: (English & Irish): hill, hollow

Zane & Zena

Zane: (Hebrew): gift from God; (Arabian): beloved
Zena: (African): famous; (Greek): hospitable

Liane & Aline & Elian & Laine & Lanie & Neila

Liane: (English): daughter of the sun
Aline: (Dutch): alone; (Celtic & Irish): fair, good looking
Elian: (Spanish): consecrated to the gracious God
Laine: (English): narrow road, from the long meadow
Lanie: (English): path or roadway
Neila: (Irish): champion

Chapter 5. Christian & Biblical Names for Twins

Across the U.S., Christian and Biblical names continue to be perennial favorites for twins. Depending upon your preference, you can follow this trend in a traditional or nonconventional way. Some names, such as Daniel and David, are extremely popular, while others, such as Demetrius and Zebulun, are relatively rare. Nevertheless, their place in history and religion gives them a strong global appeal.

In this chapter, we present several hundred Christian and Biblical names in potential pairings for girl, boy, and mixed sets of twins. Find the ones that suit your preference - and add them to your list.

Christian & Biblical Names for Twins - Boys

Aaron & Abel

Aaron: (Jewish): enlightened; (Hebrew): lofty, exalted
Abel: (Hebrew & Biblical): breathe, son

Abner & Abraham

Abner: (Israel & Hebrew): father is light, father of light
Abraham: (Hebrew & Biblical): exalted father

Adam & Abram

Adam: (Hebrew): red; (Israel): man of the earth; (English): of the red earth
Abram: (Hebrew): high father; (Israel): father of nations

Asa & Asher

Asa: (Hebrew): physician; (Japanese): born at dawn
Asher: (Hebrew & Israel): happy, blessed

Andrew & Anthony

Andrew: (English, Scottish & Biblical): manly; brave
Anthony: (English & Biblical): worthy of praise

Amos & Azariah

Amos: (Hebrew): strong, carried, brave: (Israel): troubled
Azariah: (Hebrew & Israel): God helps

Alexander & Apollos

Alexander: (Greek): protector of mankind
Apollos: (Israel): one who destroys

Barak & Benjamin

Barak: (Hebrew & Israel): flash of lightening
Benjamin: (English, Hebrew & Biblical): son of my right hand

Barnabus & Bartholomew

Barnabus: (Hebrew & Israel): comfort
Bartholomew: (English, Hebrew & Biblical): son of a farmer

Cain & Caleb

Cain: (Israel): craftsman; (Hebrew): spear; (Welsh): clear water; (Irish): archaic
Caleb: (Israel): faithful; (Hebrew): dog or bold

Christian & Claudius

Christian: (English & Irish): follower of Christ
Claudius: (English): lame

Cornelius & Christopher

Cornelius: (Irish): strong willed, wise; (Latin America): horn-colored
Christopher: (Biblical): Christ-bearer; (English): he who holds Christ in his heart

Daniel & David

Daniel: (Hebrew & Biblical): God is my judge; (Irish & Welsh): attractive
David: (Hebrew, Scottish & Welsh): beloved

Demetrius & Ebenezer

Demetrius: (Greek): goddess of fertility, one who loves the earth
Ebenezer: (Hebrew & Israel): rock of help

Eli & Elijah

Eli: (Hebrew): ascended, uplifted, high; (Greek): defender of man
Elijah: (Biblical): the Lord is my God; (Hebrew): Jehovah is God

Ephraim & Emmanuel

Ephraim: (Hebrew & Israel): fruitful
Emmanuel: (Hebrew): God with us

Ethan & Esau

Ethan: (Hebrew & Biblical): firm, strong
Esau: (Hebrew): hairy, famous bearer; (Israel): he that acts or finishes

Ezekiel & Ezra

Ezekiel: (Hebrew & Israel): strength of God
Ezra: (Hebrew & Israel): helper

Evan & Ethan

Evan: (English): God is good; (Welsh): young; (Celtic): young fighter
Ethan: (Hebrew & Biblical): firm, strong

Gabriel & Gideon

Gabriel: (Israel): hero of God; (Hebrew): man of God; (Spanish): God is my strength
Gideon: (Hebrew & Israel): great warrior

Ira & Isaac

Ira: (Hebrew & Israel): watchful
Isaac: (Biblical): he will laugh

Isaiah & Ishmael

Isaiah: (Hebrew): the Lord is generous; (Israel): salvation by God
Ishmael: (Hebrew, Israel & Spanish): God listens, God will hear

Jacob & James

Jacob: (Biblical): supplanter; (Hebrew): he grasps the heel
James: (English); supplant, replace; (Israel): supplanter

Jeremy & Jeremiah

Jeremy: (Israel): God will uplift
Jeremiah: (Hebrew): may Jehovah exalt; (Israel): sent by God

Jesse & Jethro

Jesse: (Hebrew): wealthy; (Israel): God exists; (English): Jehovah exists
Jethro: (Hebrew & Israel): excellence

Joel & Joab

Joel: (Hebrew): Jehovah is God; (Israel): God is willing
Joab: (Israel): paternity, voluntary

John & Jonah

John: (Israel): God is gracious; Jehovah has been gracious
Jonah: (Hebrew & Israel): a dove

Jordan & Jonathan

Jordan: (Hebrew): to flow down; (Israel): descendant
Jonathan: (Hebrew): Jehovah has given: (Israel): gift of God

Joshua & Josiah

Joshua: (Hebrew & Biblical): Jehovah saves
Josiah: (Hebrew): Jehovah has healed; (Israel): God has healed

Judas & Justus

Judas: (Hebrew & Israel): praised
Justus: (Israel): fairness, justice

Jaden & Justin

Jaden: (American): God has heard
Justin: (English & French): just, true; (Irish): judicious

Jude & Jesse

Jude: (Israel): one who is praised
Jesse: (Hebrew): wealthy; (Israel): God exists; (English): Jehovah exists

Lucas & Lazarus

Lucas: (Gaelic, English & Latin America): light
Lazarus: (Hebrew & Israel): God will help

Luke & Levi

Luke: (Greek & Latin America): light
Levi: (Hebrew & Israel): attached, united as one

Marcus & Matthew

Marcus: (Gaelic): hammer; (Latin America): warlike
Matthew: (Hebrew & Biblical): gift of the Lord

Mark & Micah

Mark: (Latin America): warlike
Micah: (Israel): like God

Michael & Moses

Michael: (Biblical & Hebrew): like God
Moses: (Hebrew & Biblical): saved from the water

Nathan & Nicholas

Nathan: (Hebrew): he gives; (Israel): gift of God
Nicholas: (Greek): victorious people

Noah & Nathaniel

Noah: (Biblical): rest, peace; (Hebrew): comfort, long-lived
Nathaniel: (Hebrew & Israel): gift of God

Paul & Peter

Paul: (English & French): small, apostle in the bible
Peter: (Greek & English): a small stone or rock, apostle in the bible

Philip & Phineas

Philip: (French, Greek & English): lover of horses
Phineas: (Hebrew): oracle; (Israel): loudmouth

Reuben & Rufus

Reuben: (Hebrew & Israel): behold - a son
Rufus: (Latin America): redhead

Samson & Omar

Samson: (Hebrew & Israel): bright as the sun
Omar: (Arabian): ultimate devotee; (Hebrew): eloquent speaker

Saul & Samuel

Saul: (Israel): borrowed; (Hebrew & Spanish): asked for
Samuel: (Israel): God hears; (Hebrew): name of God

Seth & Sean

Seth: (Hebrew): anointed; (Israel): appointed
Sean: (Irish): God is gracious

Silas & Simon

Silas: (Latin America): man of the forest
Simon: (Israel): it is heard

Solomon & Stephen

Solomon: (Hebrew & Israel): peaceful
Stephen: (English & Greek): crowned one

Thaddeus & Tobias

Thaddeus: (Hebrew): valiant, wise: (Greek): praise, one who has courage
Tobias: (Hebrew & Israel): God is good

Thomas & Timothy

Thomas: (Hebrew, Greek & Dutch): twin
Timothy: (Greek & English): to honor God

Victor & Vincent

Victor: (Spanish & Latin America): winner
Vincent: (English & Latin America): conquering, victorious

Zachariah & Zebulun

Zachariah: (Hebrew): Jehovah has remembered; (Israel): remembered by the Lord
Zebulun: (Hebrew & Israel): habitation

Christian & Biblical Names for Twins - Girls

Abigail & Ada

Abigail: (Hebrew): father rejoiced; (Biblical): source of joy
Ada: (English): wealthy; (Hebrew): ornament; (German): noble; (African): first daughter

Anna & Angela

Anna/Ana: (Hebrew): favor or grace; (Native American): mother; (Israel): gracious
Angela: (Spanish, French, Italian & Latin America): angel

Bernice & Bethany

Bernice: (French & Greek): one who brings victory
Bethany: (Hebrew & Israel): a life-town near Jerusalem

Bathsheba & Beulah

Bathsheba: (Hebrew): oath, voluptuous, famous bearer; (Biblical): seventh daughter
Beulah: (Hebrew & Israel): married

Candace & Carmel

Candace: (English): pure, glittering white
Carmel: (Hebrew): garden; (Israel): woodland; (Celtic): from the vineyard

Charity & Chloe

Charity: (English): kindness, generous, goodwill
Chloe: (Greek): verdant, blooming

Deborah & Dinah

Deborah: (Hebrew & Israel): honey bee
Dinah: (Hebrew & Israel): judgment

Drusilla & Diana

Drucilla/Drusilla: (Bible): fruitful, dewy-eyed; (Latin America): mighty
Diana: (Greek): divine, goddess of the moon and the hunt

Eden & Edna

Eden: (Hebrew): delight; (Israel): paradise
Edna: (Celtic): fire; (Hebrew): rejuvenation; (Israel): spirit renewed

Elisha & Elizabeth

Elisha: (Hebrew): God is salvation; (Israel): God is gracious
Elizabeth: (English): my God is bountiful; (Hebrew & Biblical): consecrated to God

Esther & Eunice

Esther: (Hebrew & African): star
Eunice: (Greek): happy, victorious

Eva & Eve

Eva: (Hebrew, Israel, Indian & Spanish): one who gives life
Eve: (Hebrew): to breathe

Faith & Hope

Faith: (English): faithful; (Latin America): to trust
Hope: (English): trust, faith

Hannah & Grace

Hannah: (English & Hebrew): favor, grace; (Biblical): grace of God
Grace/Gracie: (Latin America): grace of God; (America): land of grace

Joanna & Judith

Joanna: (Hebrew & French): gift from God
Judith: (Hebrew): praised; (Israel): from Judah

Jewel & Joy

Jewel: (English & French): precious gem
Joy: (French, English & Latin America): rejoicing

Hagar & Honey

Hagar: (Hebrew): forsaken, flight, famous bearer; (Israel): flight
Honey: (English): sweet

Julia & Lia

Julia: (French): youthful; (Latin America): soft-haired, youthful
Lia: (Greek): bearer of good news

Leah & Lily

Leah: (Hebrew): weary
Lily: (Hebrew, English & Latin America): lily, blossoming flower

Lydia & Lois

Lydia: (Greek): maiden
Lois: (Israel): good

Magdalena & Mara

Magdalena: (Hebrew): from the tower; (Spanish): bitter
Mara: (English, Italian, Hebrew & Israel): bitter

Martha & Miriam

Martha: (Israel): lady
Miriam: (Hebrew): rebellious; (Israel): strong-willed

Mary & Merry

Mary: (Biblical, English & Slovakian): bitter
Merry: (English): joyful, mirthful

Myra & Mara

Myra: (Greek): fragrant
Mara: (English, Italian, Hebrew & Israel): bitter

Naomi & Neriah

Naomi: (Hebrew & Israel): pleasant
Neriah: (Israel): light lamp of the Lord

Olive & Orpah

Olive: (Irish): olive; (Latin America): olive branch, peace
Orpah: (Israel): fawn

Priscilla & Phoebe

Priscilla: (Latin America): ancient
Phoebe: (Greek): bright, shining one

Rachel & Rebecca

Rachel: (Hebrew): ewe; (Israel): innocent lamb
Rebecca: (Biblical): servant of God

Rhoda & Rose

Rhoda: (Greek): roses
Rose: (English, French & Scottish): flower, a rose; (German): horse, fame

Ruby & Ruth

Ruby: (English & French): a precious jewel, a ruby
Ruth: (Hebrew & Israel): companion, friend

Sharon & Sela(h)

Sharon: (Hebrew & Israel): a flat clearing
Sela(h): (Israel): pause and reflect

Sarah & Shiloh

Sara(h): (Hebrew, Spanish & Biblical): princess
Shiloh: (Hebrew): the one to whom it belongs; (Israel): peaceful

Sappira & Susannah

Sapphira: (Hebrew): sapphire; (Israel): beautiful
Susannah: (Hebrew): graceful lily; (Israel): lily

Tabitha & Tamara

Tabitha: (Hebrew): beauty, grace; (Israel): a gazelle
Tamara: (Hebrew): palm tree; (Israel): spice

Zina & Zillah

Zina: (English): welcoming
Zillah: (Hebrew): shade

Zipporah & Zemira

Zipporah: (Hebrew & Israel): bird
Zemira: (Hebrew & Israel): praised

Christian & Biblical Names for Twins - One of Each Sex

Ada & Adam

Ada: (English): wealthy; (Hebrew): ornament; (German): noble; (African): first daughter
Adam: (Hebrew): red; (Israel): man of the earth; (English): of the red earth

Abigail & Abraham

Abigail: (Hebrew): father rejoiced; (Biblical): source of joy
Abraham: (Hebrew & Biblical): exalted father

Anna & Andrew

Anna/Ana: (Hebrew): favor or grace; (Native American): mother; (Israel): gracious
Andrew: (English, Scottish & Biblical): manly; brave

Angela & Anthony

Angela: (Spanish, French, Italian & Latin America): angel
Anthony: (English & Biblical): worthy of praise

Ada & Alexander

Ada: (English): wealthy; (Hebrew): ornament; (German): noble; (African): first daughter
Alexander: (Greek): protector of mankind

Bethany & Benjamin

Bethany: (Hebrew & Israel): a life-town near Jerusalem
Benjamin: (English, Hebrew & Biblical): son of my right hand

Beulah & Barnabus

Beulah: (Hebrew & Israel): married
Barnabus: (Hebrew & Israel): comfort

Candace & Caleb

Candace: (English): pure, glittering white
Caleb: (Israel): faithful; (Hebrew): dog or bold

Carmel & Cain

Carmel: (Hebrew): garden; (Israel): woodland; (Celtic): from the vineyard
Cain: (Israel): craftsman; (Hebrew): spear; (Welsh): clear water; (Irish): archaic

Charity & Christian

Charity: (English): kindness, generous, goodwill
Christian: (English & Irish): follower of Christ

Chloe & Claudius

Chloe: (Greek): verdant, blooming
Claudius: (English): lame

Claudia & Christopher

Claudia: (Spanish & Latin America): lame
Christopher: (Biblical): Christ-bearer; (English): he who holds Christ in his heart

Caleb & Cordelia

Caleb: (Israel): faithful; (Hebrew): dog or bold
Cordelia: (English, Welsh & Celtic): of the sea

Deborah & Daniel

Deborah: (Hebrew & Israel): honey bee
Daniel: (Hebrew & Biblical): God is my judge; (Irish & Welsh): attractive

Dinah & David

Dinah: (Hebrew & Israel): judgment
David: (Hebrew, Scottish & Welsh): beloved

Drusilla & Demetrius

Drucilla/Drusilla: (Bible): fruitful, dewy-eyed; (Latin America): mighty
Demetrius: (Greek): goddess of fertility, one who loves the earth

Eden & Eli

Eden: (Hebrew): delight; (Israel): paradise
Eli: (Hebrew): ascended, uplifted, high; (Greek): defender of man

Edna & Esau

Edna: (Celtic): fire; (Hebrew): rejuvenation; (Israel): spirit renewed
Esau: (Hebrew): hairy, famous bearer; (Israel): he that acts or finishes

Elisha & Emmanuel

Elisha: (Hebrew): God is salvation; (Israel): God is gracious
Emmanuel: (Hebrew): God with us

Elizabeth & Ethan

Elizabeth: (English): my God is bountiful; (Hebrew & Biblical): consecrated to God
Ethan: (Hebrew & Biblical): firm, strong

Eva & Elijah

Eva: (Hebrew, Israel, Indian & Spanish): one who gives life
Elijah: (Biblical): the Lord is my God; (Hebrew): Jehovah is God

Eve & Evan

Eve: (Hebrew): to breathe
Evan: (English): God is good; (Welsh): young; (Celtic): young fighter

Grace & Gabriel

Grace/Gracie: (Latin America): grace of God; (American): land of grace
Gabriel: (Israel): hero of God; (Hebrew): man of God; (Spanish): God is my strength

Julia & Jacob

Julia: (French): youthful; (Latin America): soft-haired, youthful
Jacob: (Biblical): supplanter; (Hebrew): he grasps the heel

Leah & Lucas

Leah: (Hebrew): weary;
Lucas: (Gaelic, English & Latin America): light

Lily & Levi

Lily: (Hebrew, English & Latin America): lily, blossoming flower
Levi: (Hebrew & Israel): attached, united as one

Lydia & Lazarus

Lydia: (Greek): maiden
Lazarus: (Hebrew & Israel): God will help

Lois & Luke

Lois: (Israel): good
Luke: (Greek & Latin America): light

Martha & Marcus

Martha: (Israel): lady
Marcus: (Gaelic): hammer; (Latin America): warlike

Miriam & Micah

Miriam: (Hebrew): rebellious; (Israel): strong-willed
Micah: (Israel): like God

Mary & Marcus

Mary: (Biblical, English & Slovakian): bitter
Marcus: (Gaelic): hammer; (Latin America): warlike

Merry & Matthew

Merry: (English): joyful, mirthful
Matthew: (Hebrew & Biblical): gift of the Lord

Mara & Michael

Mara: (English, Italian, Hebrew & Israel): bitter
Michael: (Biblical & Hebrew): like God

Myra & Moses

Myra: (Greek): fragrant
Moses: (Hebrew & Biblical): saved from the water

Naomi & Nathan

Naomi: (Hebrew & Israel): pleasant
Nathan: (Hebrew): he gives; (Israel): gift of God

Neriah & Nicholas

Neriah: (Israel): light lamp of the Lord
Nicholas: (Greek): victorious people

Paula & Peter

Paula: (Latin America): small
Peter: (Greek & English): a small stone or rock, apostle in the Bible

Phoebe & Philip

Phoebe: (Greek): bright, shining one
Philip: (French, Greek & English): lover of horses

Priscilla & Phineas

Priscilla: (Latin America): ancient
Phineas: (Hebrew): oracle; (Israel): loudmouth

Rose & Reuben

Rose: (English, French & Scottish): flower, a rose; (German): horse, fame
Reuben: (Hebrew & Israel): behold - a son

Ruby & Rufus

Ruby: (English & French): a precious jewel, a ruby
Rufus: (Latin America): redhead

Sapphira & Solomon

Sapphira: (Hebrew): sapphire; (Israel): beautiful
Solomon: (Hebrew & Israel): peaceful

Sarah & Seth

Sara(h): (Hebrew, Spanish & Biblical): princess
Seth: (Hebrew): anointed; (Israel): appointed

Sela(h) & Stephen

Sela(h): (Israel): pause and reflect
Stephen: (English & Greek): crowned one

Shiloh & Samuel

Shiloh: (Hebrew): the one to whom it belongs; (Israel): peaceful
Samuel: (Israel): God hears; (Hebrew): name of God

Tabitha & Thomas

Tabitha: (Hebrew): beauty, grace; (Israel): a gazelle
Thomas: (Hebrew, Greek & Dutch): twin

Tamara & Timothy

Tamara: (Hebrew): palm tree; (Israel): spice
Timothy: (Greek & English): to honor God

Victoria & Vincent

Victoria: (Latin America): winner
Vincent: (English & Latin America): conquering, victorious

Zina & Zachary

Zina: (English): welcoming
Zachary: (Israel & Hebrew): remembered by God

Zemira & Zebulun

Zemira: (Hebrew & Israel): praised
Zebulun: (Hebrew & Israel): habitation

Chapter 6: Twin Names from Literature & Mythology

Many times, when you encounter a baby name that is mature, sophisticated, with a global appeal, it has its roots in literature and mythology. As expected, the popularity of these names has varied over time (and across geographical borders). Nevertheless, names from literature and mythology continue to hold a strong appeal for American parents who are passionate about history and the arts.

In this chapter, we present a comprehensive list of names from literature and mythology that are grouped in logical pairs. See if you find your own babies' names on the lists!

Names from Literature & Mythology - Boys

Andre & Aristotle

Andre: (French): manly, brave
Aristotle: (Greek): thinker with a great purpose

Beau & Burke

Beau: (French): handsome, beautiful
Burke: (German): birch tree

Balthazar & Barrington

Balthazar: (English): the comedy of errors a merchant
Barrington: (English): town of Barr

Charles & Carleton

Charles: (English): strong, manly
Carleton: (English): town of Charles

Connor & Clement

Connor: (Irish): strong willed, much wanted
Clement: (French): compassionate

Damon & Dion

Damon: (English): calm, tame
Dion: (French): mountain of Zeus

Eamon & Ellison

Eamon: (Irish): blessed guardian
Ellison: (English): son of Elias

Fraser & Faust

Fraser: (Scottish): strawberry flowers
Faust: (Latin): fortunate

Galen & Griffin

Galen: (Gaelic): tranquil; (English): festive party: (Greek): healer, calm
Griffin: (Latin): prince

Hewitt & Henderson

Hewitt: (English): little smart one
Henderson: (Scottish): son of Henry

Hans & Jules

Hans: (German & Hebrew): gift from God; (Scandinavian): God is gracious
Jules: (French): youthful, downy-haired

Homer & Hector

Homer: (Greek & English): pledge, promise
Hector: (Greek): anchor; (Spanish): tenacious

Jasper & Israel

Jasper: (Hebrew, French & English): precious stone
Israel: (Israel): prince of God; (Hebrew): may God prevail

Jonathan & Johann

Jonathan: (Hebrew): Jehovah has given: (Israel): gift of God
Johann: (German): God's gracious gift

Justin & Julian

Justin: (English & French): just, true; (Irish): judicious
Julian: (Spanish, French & Greek): youthful

Leo & Lewis

Leo: (Italian & English): a lion
Lewis: (German): famous warrior

McKenna & Malloy

McKenna: (English): handsome, fiery
Malloy: (Irish): noble chief

Otto & Oberon

Otto: (German): wealthy or prosperous
Oberon: (German): bear heart

Orion & Oliver

Orion: (Greek): a hunter in Greek mythology
Oliver: (French, English, Danish & Latin America): the olive tree; (German): elf army

Quentin & Pierre

Quentin: (French, English & Latin America): fifth
Pierre: (French): a rock

Puck & Phinneas

Puck: (English): elf
Phineas: (Hebrew): oracle; (Israel): loudmouth

Phillip & Paris

Philip: (French, Greek & English): lover of horses
Paris: (Persian): angelic face; (Greek): downfall; (French): the capital city of France

Plato & Ridley

Plato: (Greek): strong shoulders
Ridley: (English): from the red meadow

Sheridan & Stuart

Sheridan: (Irish, English & Celtic): untamed; (Gaelic): bright
Stuart: (Scottish): steward; (English): bailiff; (Irish): keeper of the estate

Santiago & Stern

Santiago: (Spanish): named for Saint James
Stern: (English): austere

Virgil & Zeus

Virgil: (English): flourishing; (Latin America): strong
Zeus: (Greek): powerful one

Names from Literature & Mythology - Girls

Aimee & Ava

Aimee: (English, French & Latin America): beloved
Ava: (Latin America): like a bird

Agatha & Aphrodite

Agatha: (Latin): virtuous, good
Aphrodite: (Greek): beauty, love goddess

Athena & Aurora

Athena: (Greek): wisdom, goddess of war
Aurora: (Latin): dawn

Alejandra & Annika

Alejandra: (Spanish): defender of mankind
Annika: (Dutch): gracious

Antoinette & Apollonia

Antoinette: (French): flower
Apollonia: (Greek): strength

Beatrice & Bronte

Beatrice: (Italian): blesses; (French): bringer of joy
Bronte: (Greek): thunder

Constance & Colette

Constance: (American): strong-willed
Colette: (English): victorious people

Chloe & Clio

Chloe: (Greek): verdant, blooming
Cleo/Clio: (English): father's glory

Calliope & Cynthia

Calliope: (Greek): beautiful voice
Cynthia: (Greek): moon

Clair & Candace

Clair: (English): clear; (French): bright
Candace: (English): pure, glittering white

Cassandra & Cecilia

Cassandra: (Greek): prophet of doom
Cecilia: (Latin): blind

Cleopatra & Cordelia

Cleopatra: (Greek): glory to the father; (African American): queen
Cordelia: (English, Welsh & Celtic): of the sea

Dalia & Echo

Dalia: (Hebrew): tree branch
Echo: (Greek): sound returned

Elinor & Eudora

Elinor: (English): torch
Eudora: (Greek): honored gift

Eunice & Electra

Eunice: (Latin): victory
Electra: (Greek): bright, the shining one

Flora & Faith

Flora: (English): flower: (Latin): flowering
Faith: (English): faithful; (Latin America): to trust

Felicia & Felicity

Felicia: (French & Latin America): happiness
Felicity: (French, English & Latin America): happiness

Geraldine & Gillian

Geraldine: (French, English & German): rules by the spear
Gillian: (English): child of the gods; (Irish): young at heart

Helen & Hera

Helen: (Greek): light
Hera: (Greek): goddess of marriage

Harriet & Hester

Harriet: (English & German): rules the home
Hester: (Greek): star

Helene & Justine

Helene: (French): in the light of the sun
Justine: (English): just, upright; (Latin America): fairness

Josephina & Juliana

Josephina: (Hebrew): God will add
Juliana: (Spanish): soft-haired

Janine & Justina

Janine: (Hebrew): gift from God
Justina: (Greek): just

Kamala & Kelly

Kamala: (Hawaiian & Indian): lotus
Kelly: (Gaelic & Irish): warrior; (Scottish): wood

Ida & Livia

Ida: (English): hardworking
Livia: (English): life

Laurie & Lucy

Laurie: (English): crowned with laurels
Lucy: (Latin America): bringer of light

Muriel & Martha

Muriel: (Arabian): myth; (Celtic): shining sea
Martha: (Israel): lady

Ming & Maia

Ming: (Chinese): brilliant light
Maia: (French): May, (Greek): mother

Mariana & Melia

Mariana: (French): bitter
Melia: (German): industrious

Melissa & Mirabel

Melissa: (Greek): honey bee
Mirabel: (Spanish): of uncommon beauty

Nyssa & Natasha

Nyssa: (Greek): the beginning
Natasha: (Greek): rebirth

Olga & Ophelia

Olga: (Slovakian): holy
Ophelia: (Greek): useful, wise

Octavia & Odessa

Octavia: (Latin America): eighth; (Italian): born eighth
Odessa: (Latin America): the odyssey

Portia & Patience

Portia: (Latin): offering
Patience: (English): patient, enduring

Patricia & Rosemary

Patricia: (Spanish & Latin America): noble
Rosemary: (English): bitter rose

Regina & Raven

Regina: (Italian, Spanish & Latin America): queen
Raven: (English): to be black, blackbird

Thea & Tess

Thea: (Greek): gift of God
Tess: (English): harvester

Ursula & Venus

Ursula: (Danish & Scandinavian): female bear
Venus: (Greek): love goddess, little bird

Winnifred & Zenia

Winifred: (Irish): friend of peace; (Welsh): reconciled, blessed
Zenia: (Greek): hospitable

Zora & Zoya

Zora: (Slavic): sunrise
Zoya: (Greek): life

Chapter 7. Names from Popular Culture & the Entertainment Industry

Every year, parents seek new inspiration for their babies' names, including the world of music, movies, sports, and television. As a result, the rise of a popular athlete, singer, or reality star can have a strong - and immediate - impact on a parent's choice of names. In some cases, such as Cyrus and Angus, the phenomenon brings new interest to classic names that had fallen out of favor. In other cases, such as Ashton and Ozzy, the phenomenon brings new names to the forefront that would otherwise not be considered.

My only caveat about names from popular culture is their shelf-life. Sixty years ago, millions of parents named their baby girls after Marilyn Monroe; however, its popularity waned within a few years. Nevertheless, some trends **do** manage to stick. After *Love Story* was released in 1970, millions of parents named their baby girls after the doomed heroine Jennifer ..... and the name continued to remain a top choice for more than 25 years.

When reviewing these names, try to be objective - and determine if you would still like the name if it was *not* associated with a famous person, character, movie, or song. Also consider the popularity of the name - and whether you want your child to be one of the seven Ashtons in his kindergarten class. In the end, there is no right or wrong answer - simply what feels right to **you**.

Names from Popular Culture - Boys

Adrian & Anderson

Adrian: (German, Spanish & Italian): dark
Anderson: (Scottish): son of Andrew

Ashton & Angus

Ashton: (Hebrew): shining light; (English): ash tree settlement
Angus: (Irish): vigorous one

Avi & Ari

Avi: (Hebrew): my God, father; (Latin America): Lord of mine
Ari: (Hebrew): lion of God

Axl & Armand

Axl: (German & Hebrew): father of peace; (German): source of all life
Armand: (French): of the army

Beckett & Boston

Beckett: (English) : brook
Boston: (English): the city Boston

Boone & Brody

Boone: (French): good
Brody: (Irish): brother, from the muddy place; (Scottish): second son

Bryce & Bowie

Bryce: (Scottish): speckled
Bowie: (Celtic): yellow-haired

Bodhi & Barrett

Bodhi: (Indian): awakens
Barrett: (English & German): strength of a bear

Chauncey & Carlton

Chauncey: (Latin): chancellor
Carlton: (English): town of Charles

Chase & Cole

Chase: (English): hunter
Cole: (Irish): warrior

Casper & Cosmo

Casper: (Persian): treasurer; (German): imperial
Cosmo: (Greek): the order of the universe

Cato & Cullen

Cato: (Latin): sagacious, wise one, good judgment
Cullen: (Irish & Gaelic): handsome; (Celtic): cub; (English): city in Germany

Chandler & Creed

Chandler: (French): candle maker
Creed: (English): belief, guiding principle

Cyrus & Carlisle

Cyrus: (English): far-sighted
Carlisle: (English): from the walled city

Crosby & Cooper

Crosby: (English): town crossing
Cooper: (English): barrel maker

Cameron & Dylan

Cameron: (Irish & Gaelic): crooked nose
Dylan: (English & Welsh): born from the ocean, son of the wave

Dane & Drew

Dane: (Hebrew & Scandinavian): God will judge; (English): brook
Drew: (English): courageous, valiant

Dax & Dixon

Dax: (English & French): water
Dixon: (English): power, brave ruler

Dawayne & Denzel

Dawayne: (Irish): dark
Denzel: (English): fort; African: wild

Dierks & Drake

Dierks: (Danish): ruler of the people
Drake: (English): male duck, dragon

Duncan & Dexter

Duncan: (Scottish): brown warrior
Dexter: (Latin): right-handed, skillful; (Latin America): flexible

Eli & Emmett

Eli: (Hebrew): ascended, uplifted, high; (Greek): defender of man
Emmett: (English): whole, universal

Ewen & Edward

Ewan: (Celtic, Scotch & Irish): young
Edward: (English): blesses guardian

Elton & Elvis

Elton: (English): old town
Elvis: (Scandinavian): wise

Fox & Finn

Fox: (English): fox
Finn: (English): blond

Frasier & Franco

Frasier: (French): strawberry, curly-haired
Franco: (Italian): of France

Gray & Grayson

Gray: (English): gray-haired
Grayson: (English): son of the bailiff

Godric & Graham

Godric: (English): power of God
Graham: (Scottish): from the gray home

Jagger & Jasper

Jagger: (English): a carter, to carry
Jasper: (Persian): treasurer

Luka & Levon

Luka: (Latin America): light; (Russian): of Luciana
Levon: (Armenian): lion

Laird & Maddox

Laird: (Scottish): lord; (Irish): head of household
Maddox: (English): son of the Lord; (Celtic): beneficent

Magnus & Marston

Magnus: (Latin): great
Marston: (English): from the town near the marsh

Maximus & Milo

Maximus: (Greek): greatest
Milo: (English): soldier

Miller & Montel

Miller: (English): one who works at the mill
Montel: (Italian): mountain

Nash & Niles

Nash: (American): adventurer
Niles: (English): champion

Ozzy & Neo

Ozzy: (English): divine ruler
Neo: (Greek & American): new

Quinn & Quincy

Quinn: (Celtic): wise; (Irish): fifth, counsel, intelligent
Quincy: (English): fifth; (French): estate belonging to Quintus

Pax & Rio

Pax: (English): peaceful
Rio: (Portuguese): river

Percy & Peeta

Peeta: (Indian): yellow silk cloth
Percy: (English): piercing the valley

Phineas & Presley

Phineas: (Hebrew): oracle; (Israel): loudmouth
Presley: (English): priest's land

Regis & Radcliff

Regis: (Latin): regal; (Latin America): rules
Radcliff: (English): red cliff

Rupert & Roman

Rupert: (German): bright fame
Roman: (Spanish & Latin America): from Rome

River & Rain

River: (English): from the river
Rain/Raine: (American): blessings from above; (French & Latin): ruler; (English): lord, wise

Ripley & Rocco

Ripley: (English): from the noisy meadow
Rocco: (Italian & German): rest

Rocket & Ryder

Rocket: (English): fast
Ryder: (English): knight

Sanjay & Shepherd

Sanjay: (American): a combination of Sanford and Jay
Shepherd: (English): one who herds sheep

Satchel & Sawyer

Satchel: (French): Saturn
Sawyer: (English): one who works with wood

Seven & Speck

Seven: (American): the number seven
Speck: (German): bacon

Shane & Silas

Shane: (Hebrew): gift from God; (Irish): God is gracious
Silas: (Latin America): man of the forest

Stanford & Spencer

Stanford: (English): from the stony ford
Spencer: (English): provider

Tucker & Terence

Tucker: (English): tucker of cloth
Terence: (Latin America): tender, gracious

Tex & Troy

Tex: (English): of Texas
Troy: (French): curly haired; (Irish): foot soldier

Trigg & Tripp

Trigg: (Norse): truthful
Tripp: (English): traveler

Tiger & Vaughn

Tiger: (English): powerful cat
Vaughn: (Celtic): small

Trey & True

Trey: (English & Latin): third-born child
True: (English): loyal

Wentworth & Weston

Wentworth: (English): village, from the white one's estate
Weston: (English): west town

Wesley & West

Wesley: (English): from the west meadow
West: (English): from the west

Names from Popular Culture - Girls

Alexis & Amber

Alexis: (English): helper, defender; (Biblical): protector of mankind
Amber: (Arabic): precious jewel, yellow-brown color

75

Avril & Audrey

Avril: (English): born in April
Audrey: (English): noble strength

Ashley & Arial

Ashley: (English & Biblical): lives in the ash tree
Arial: (Hebrew): lioness of God

Aria & Addison

Aria: (Italian): melody
Addison: (English): son of Adam

Alanis & America

Alanis: (English): attractive
America: (English): ruler of the home

Angelina & Ashanti

Angelina: (Italian): little angel
Ashanti: (African): great African woman

Audrina & Adele

Audrina: (English): nobility, strength
Adele: (German & French): noble, kind

Bailey & Bettina

Bailey: (English): bailiff, steward, public official
Bettina: (English): consecrated to God

Blythe & Brandy

Blythe: (English): happy
Brandy: (English): firebrand

Bree & Blair

Bree: (Celtic): broth; (Irish): hill, strong one
Blair: (Irish & Celtic): from the plain, (Gaelic): child of the fields; (Scottish): peat moss

Clove & Cher

Clove: (German): spice
Cher: (English): beloved

Campbell & Contessa

Campbell: (Scottish): crooked mouth
Contessa: (Italian): a countess

Carrie & Cordelia

Carrie: (American): melody, song
Cordelia: (English, Welsh & Celtic): of the sea

Charlize & Carmen

Charlize: (French): manly
Carmen: (English): garden; (Spanish & Latin America): song

Charisma & Chloe

Charisma: (Greek): grace
Chloe: (Greek): verdant, blooming

Crimson & Clover

Crimson: (English): deep red color
Clover: (English): meadow flower

Dana & Dominique

Dana: (English, Danish, Irish & Hebrew): a person from Denmark
Dominique: (French): belonging to God

Danica & Destiny

Danica: (Slavic): the morning star
Destiny: (English): fate

Effie & Rue

Effie: (Greek): melodious talk
Rue: (English): bitter, medicinal plant

Edie & Elle

Edie: (English): blessed
Elle: (English): torch

Elliott & Evangeline

Elliott: (Israel): close to God; (English): the Lord is my God
Evangeline: (Greek): like an angel

Felicity & Fantasia

Felicity: (French, English & Latin America): happiness
Fantasia: (Latin): from a fantasy land

Gabrielle & Giselle

Gabrielle: (French): strength of God
Giselle: (French): pledge

Gwyneth & Goldie

Gwyneth: (Welsh): blessed with happiness
Golda/Goldie: (English): resembling the precious metal

Hoda & Hermoine

Hoda: (Indian): child of God
Hermione: (Greek): earthly

Hannah & Hayden

Hannah: (English & Hebrew): favor, grace; (Biblical): grace of God
Hayden: (English & Welsh): in the meadow or valley

Haven & Honor

Haven: (English): safe place
Honor: (Spanish & Irish): honor; (Latin America): integrity

Isla & Ivy

Ilsa: (German): abbreviation of Elizabeth, which means God is bountiful
Ivy: (English): vine

Ivanka & Jorja

Ivanka: (Slavic): God is gracious
Jorja: (English): farmer

Jamie & Juno

Jamie: (English): supplanter, representative
Juno: (Roman): mythical queen of the heavens

Jada & January

Jada: (Israel): wise
January: (American): born in January

Katniss & Clove

Katniss: (American): female warrior
Clove: (German): spice

Keisha & Keira

Keisha: (African): favorite
Keira: (Celtic): black-haired

Kristi & Kerri

Kristi: (Greek): anointed, follower of Christ
Kerri: (Irish): dusky, dark

Leighton & Layla

Leighton: (English): herb garden, town by the meadow
Layla: (Indian): born at night; (Arabian): dark beauty

Martina & Miranda

Martina: (Latin America): warlike
Miranda: (Latin): worthy of admiration

Murphy & Nona

Murphy: (Irish): sea warrior
Nona: (English): ninth

Nadia & Mariah

Nadia: (Slovakian): hopeful
Mariah: (English): biter

Mischa & Neve

Mischa: (Russian): like God
Neve: (Irish): radiant

Mya & Ophelia

Mya: (American): emerald
Ophelia: (Greek): useful, wise

Remy & Peyton

Remy: (French): oarsman or rower, from Rheims
Peyton: (English): village

Pippa & Piper

Pippa: (English): friend of horses
Piper: (English): plays the flute

Prudence & Primrose

Prudence: (English): prudent or cautious
Primrose: (English): the first rose, primrose flower

Posy & Quinn

Posy: (English): God will increase
Quinn: (Celtic): wise; (Irish): fifth, counsel, intelligent

Rhoda & Roseanne

Rhoda: (Greek): roses
Roseanne: (Greek): graceful rose

Riley & Rumer

Riley: (Irish): a small stream
Rumer: (English): gypsy

Reese & Rory

Reese: (Welsh): enthusiastic
Rory: (Irish): famous brilliance, famous ruler; (Gaelic): red-haired

Rhianna & Rosanna

Rhianna: (English): goddess
Roseanna: (Greek): graceful rose

Summer & Scarlett

Summer: (English): the summer season
Scarlett: (English): red

Shania & Santana

Shania: (Native American): on my way
Santana: (Spanish): saintly

Sherri & Sasha

Sherri: (Israel): beloved; (French): dear one
Sasha: (English): defender of mankind

Shakira & Sienna

Shakira: (Arabic): grateful
Sienna: (Italian): reddish brown in color

Sunshine & Shiloh

Sunshine: (English): brilliant rays from the sun
Shiloh: (Israel): peaceful

Sheryl & Serena

Sheryl: (English): beloved
Serena: (English): calm, serene

Simone & Sydney

Simone: (French): one who listens well
Sydney: (French): from Saint Denis

Soledad & Signourney

Soledad: (Spanish): solitary
Signourney: (English): victorious conquerer

Tanya & Trisha

Tanya: (Slovakian): a fairy queen
Trisha: (English & Latin): noble

Temperance & Xena

Temperance: (English): temperate, moderate
Xena: (Greek): hospitable

Tyra & Tiana

Tyra: (Scandinavian): God of battle; (Scottish): land
Tiana: (Greek): princess

Willow & Whitney

Willow: (English): willow tree
Whitney: (English & African American): white island

Venus &Vivienne

Venus: (Greek): love goddess, little bird
Vivianne: (English): the lady of the lake

Zoe & Zahara

Zoe (or Zoey): (Greek): life, alive
Zahara: (Arabic): shining, luminous

Chapter 8: Names from Disney

In reality, this material could easily be included in Chapter 7, which presents baby names from popular culture and the entertainment industry. But, on a practical basis, Disney has a greater reach - and longer staying power - than most musical, athletic, and movie franchises, which is why we have given it a chapter all its own.

Within a few months of a Disney release, the names of its characters begin to ascend the list of popular baby names. As a result, they bring the same benefits and pitfalls of other trendy names: everyone knows why you chose it..... and they probably chose it, too!

In the past few years, here are the most popular baby names from Disney movies.

Names from Disney - Boys

Aladdin & Apollo

Aladdin: (Arabian): faithful
Apollo: (Latin): strength, sun god

Archimedes & Arthur

Archimedes: (Greek): to think about first
Arthur: (English): bear, stone

Ben & Clayton

Ben: (English): son of my right hand
Clayton: (English): mortal

Eli & Fagin

Eli: (Hebrew): ascended, uplifted, high; (Greek): defender of man
Fagin: (Gaelic): ardent; (Irish): eager

Fenton & Flynn

Fenton: (English): from the farm on the fens
Flynn: (Irish): heir to the red-headed

Gaetan & Gideon

Gaetan: (French & Italian): from Italy
Gideon: (Hebrew & Israel): great warrior

Hermes & Horace

Hermes: (Greek): stone pile
Horace: (French): hour, time

Iago & Ian

Iago: (Welsh): Spanish supplanter
Ian: (Scottish): gift from God

Jafar & Jasper

Jafar: (Hindu): little stream
Jasper: (Persian): treasurer

Jock & Lafayette

Jock: (Scottish): God is gracious
Lafayette: (Israel): to God to the mighty

Louis & Lyle

Louis: (French): famous warrior
Lyle: (French & English): from the island

Max & Milo

Max: (English): greatest
Milo: (English): soldier

Oliver & Orville

Oliver: (French, English, Danish & Latin America): the olive tree; (German): elf army
Orville: (French): golden city; (English): spear-strength

Otto & Pascal

Otto: (German): wealthy or prosperous
Pascal: (French): born at Easter

Percy & Preston

Percy: (English): piercing the valley
Preston: (English): from the priest's farm

Robin & Roscoe

Robin: (English): a small bird
Roscoe: (Norwegian): deer forest

Rufus & Simba

Rufus: (Latin America): redhead
Simba: (African): lion

Timon & Tito

Timon: (Hebrew): honor
Tito: (Italian): honor

Winston & Zeus

Winston: (English): joy stone
Zeus: (Greek): powerful

Names from Disney - Girls

Abigail & Amelia

Abigail: (Hebrew): father rejoiced; (Biblical): source of joy
Amelia: (English & Latin America): industrious, striving

Adelaide & Adella

Adelaide: (French & German): noble, kind
Adella: (German & French): noble, kind

Alana & Alice

Alana: (Irish): beautiful, peaceful
Alice: (Spanish): of the nobility

Anastasia & Andrina

Anastasia: (Greek): resurrection
Andrina: (English): courageous, valiant

Ariel & Arista

Ariel: (Hebrew): lioness of God
Arista: (Latin): harvest

Aurora & Audrey

Aurora: (Latin): dawn
Audrey: (English): noble strength

Belle & Bianca

Belle: (French): beautiful
Bianca: (Italian): white, fair

Cleo & Calliope

Cleo: (English); father's glory
Calliope: (Greek): beautiful voice

Carlotta & Felicia

Carlotta: (Italian): a derivative of Charlotte, which means feminine
Felicia/Felice/Phylicia: (French & Latin America): happiness

Daisy & Eudora

Daisy: (English); day's eve; (American): daisy flower
Eudora: (Greek): honored gift

Faline & Flora

Faline: (Irish): in charge
Flora: (English): flower: (Latin): flowering

Georgette & Giselle

Georgette: (French): farmer
Giselle: (French): pledge

Helga & Hera

Helga: (German): wealthy, blessed
Hera: (Greek): Goddess of marriage

Jasmine & Kala

Jasmine: (English): a fragrant flower
Kala: (Hawaiian): princess

Marian & Megara

Marian: (French): bitter
Megara: (Greek): wife of Hercules

Myrtle & Mulan

Myrtle: (Greek): the tree, victory; (English): the flowering shrub
Mulan: (Chinese): magnolia blossom

Penny & Perdita

Penny: (English): duck
Perdita: (English): lost

Thalia & Tiana

Thalia: (Greek): plentiful, blooming
Tiana: (Greek): princess

Ursula & Seraphina:

Ursula: (Danish & Scandinavian): female bear
Seraphina: (Israel): burning fire; (Hebrew): fiery-ringed

Wendy & Wilhemina

Wendy: (English): white-skinned, literary
Wilhemina: (German): resolute protector

Willow & Winifred

Willow: (English): willow tree
Winifred: (Irish): friend of peace; (Welsh): reconciled, blessed

Chapter 9: Names from Nature

People differ greatly in their temperament and ideals. Many times, our only commonality is the planet we inhabit - and the beautiful flowers, oceans, colors, and gemstones that we all enjoy. As a result, names from nature are perennial favorites for boys and girls in all cultures. In this chapter, we present an intriguing collection of names for twins that honor the incomparable beauty of nature.

Names of Flowers, Fruit, Spices & Colors

Sage & Ginger

Sage: (English & French): wise one; (English): from the spice
Ginger: (English): the spice

Apple & Peaches

Apple: (American): sweet fruit
Peaches: (English): fruit

Olive & Zinnia

Olive: (Irish): olive; (Latin America): olive branch, peace
Zinnia: (English): the flower: (Latin America): beautiful

Blossom & Cherise

Blossom: (English): fresh, flowerlike
Cherise: (French): cherry, dear one

Cherry & Cyan

Cherry: (French): dear one; (American): cherry
Cyan: (American): light blue or green

Indigo & Leighton

Indigo: (Latin America): dark blue
Leighton: (English): herb garden, town by the meadow

Laurel & Lotus

Laurel: (English & French): crowned with laurel, from the laurel tree
Lotus: (Greek): the flower

Honey & Clover

Honey: (English): sweet
Clover: (English): meadow flower

Ivy & Iris

Ivy: (English): vine
Iris: (Greek): colorful, rainbow; (Hebrew & English): the flower

Daisy & Rose

Daisy: (English); day's eve; (American): daisy flower
Rose: (English, French & Scottish): flower, a rose; (German): horse, fame

Lily & Lilac

Lilac: (Latin America): bluish purple; (American): a flowering bluish purple shrub
Lily: (Hebrew, English & Latin America): lily, blossoming flower

Jasmine & Violet

Jasmine: (Persian): a climbing plant; (English): a fragrant flower
Violet: (Italian): violet flower

Poppy & Amaranth

Poppy: (English & Latin America): the poppy flower
Amaranth: (Greek): an unfading flower

Silver & Scarlett

Silver: (English): the color silver
Scarlett: (English): red

Names of Gemstones

Ruby & Jade

Ruby: (English & French): a precious jewel, a ruby
Jade: (Spanish): jewel, green gemstone

Azure & Amethyst

Azura/Azure: (Persian): a blue, semi-precious stone
Amethyst: (Greek): a semi-precious stone

Pearl & Topaz

Pearl: (English): gemstone
Topaz/Topaza: (Mexican): golden gem

Emerald & Garnet

Emerald: (English, Spanish & French): a bright green gem
Garnet: (English): gem, armed with a spear; (French): keeper of grain

Opal & Sapphire

Opal: (English & Indian): precious gem
Sapphire: (Greek): the sapphire gem; (Hebrew): sapphire gem, beautiful

Crystal & Cameo

Crystal: (English): jewel; (Latin America): a clear brilliant glass
Cameo: (Italian): sculptured jewel; (English & Latin America): a shadow or carved gem portrait

Amber & Beryl

Amber: (Arabic): precious jewel, yellow-brown color
Beryl: (Greek & English): green jewel

Jewel & Gemma

Jewel: (English & French): precious gem
Gemma: (French & Italian): jewel

Names from Weather, Seasons, Nature & Animals

Summer & Stormy

Summer: (American): the summer season
Stormy: (English): tempest; (American): impetuous nature

Autumn & Winter

Autumn: (English & Latin America): the fall season
Winter: (American): the season

Brooke & Spring

Brooke: (English): lives by the stream
Spring: (English): the spring season

April & May

April: (English): opening buds of spring; (Latin America): opening, fourth month
May: (English): name of month; (Hebrew & Latin America): from Mary

June & Luna

June: (Dominican Republic): born in June
Luna: (Latin & Latin America): the moon

River & Ridge

River: (English): from the river
Ridge: (English): from the ridge

Thorne & Fawn

Thorne: (English): from the thorn bush
Fawn: (French & English): young deer

Sailor & Bay

Sailor: (American): sailor
Bay: (Vietnam): born on a Saturday

Clay & Fern

Clay: (English): clay maker, immortal
Fern: (English): the fern plant

Flora & Forrest

Flora: (English): flower: (Latin): flowering
Forrest: (English & French): from the woods

Heath & Heather

Heath: (English): from the heath wasteland
Heather: (English): a flowering plant

Holly & Laurel

Holly: (French, English & Germany): shrub
Laurel: (English & French): crowned with laurel, from the laurel tree

Lake & Lark

Lake: (American): body of water, from the lake
Lark: (English): a lark; (American): songbird

Marina & Lavender

Marina: (Greek & Slovakian): from the sea
Lavender: (English): a purple flowering plant

Leaf/Leif & Meadow

Leif: (Scandinavian): beloved descendent
Meadow: (American): beautiful field

Willow & Sky(e)

Willow: (English): willow tree
Skye: (English): sky

Brock & Colt

Brock: (English): badger
Colt: (American): baby horse; (English): from the dark town

Coral & Ivory

Coral: (English): a reef formation
Ivory: (English & Latin America): white, pure

Drake & Fox

Drake: (English): male duck, dragon
Fox: (English): fox

Raven & Robin

Raven: (English): to be black, blackbird
Robin: (English): a small bird

Star & Rain

Starr: (English & American): star
Rain/Raine: (American): blessings from above; (French & Latin): ruler; (English): lord, wise

Una & Ursula

Una: (Welsh & Celtic): white wave; (Native America): remember; (English): one
Ursula: (Danish & Scandinavian): female bear

Wolf & Wren

Wolf: (English): the animal, wolf
Wren: (Welsh): ruler; (English): small bird

Chapter 10: Last Names as First Names

In the past decade, one of the most popular trends is the use of last names as first names. This approach offers parents a creative way to honor a cherished surname or to give their child a gender neutral (unisex) moniker that will be easy to remember. Alternatively, these choices also make excellent middle names.

In this chapter, we have included the most popular pairs of last names as first names. Use the list to narrow your search - or as inspiration for your own unique choices.

Abbott & Alton

Abbott: (Hebrew): father
Alton: (English): from the old town

Ames & Ashton

Ames: (French): friend
Ashton: (Hebrew): shining light; (English): ash tree settlement

Avery & August

Avery: (English): counselor, sage, wise
August: (German): revered

Addison & Anderson

Addison: (English): son of Adam
Anderson: (Scottish): son of Andrew

Bailey & Brown

Bailey: (English): bailiff, steward, public official
Brown: (English): brown color, dark-skinned

Bellamy & Bowen

Bellamy: (French): handsome
Bowen: (Gaelic): small son; (Irish): archer

Black & Blake

Black: (English): dark-skinned
Blake: (English): pale, fair

Brooks & Brogan

Brooks: (English): running water, son of Brooke
Brogan: (Gaelic & Irish): from the ditch

Brady & Blair

Brady: (Irish): a large-breasted woman
Blair: (Irish & Celtic): from the plain, (Gaelic): child of the fields; (Scottish): peat moss

Campbell & Cullen

Campbell: (Gaelic): crooked mouth; (French): from the beautiful field
Cullen: (Irish & Gaelic): handsome; (Celtic): cub; (English): city in Germany

Chase & Curran

Chase: (English): hunter
Curran: (Celtic): hero

Casey & Cameron

Casey: (Celtic & Gaelic): brave; (Irish): observant, alert, brave; (Spanish): honorable
Cameron: (Irish & Gaelic): crooked nose

Carson & Cain

Carson: (English): son who lives in the swamp
Cain: (Israel): craftsman; (Hebrew): spear; (Welsh): clear water; (Irish): archaic

Carter & Chen

Carter: (English): cart driver
Chen: (Chinese): great, dawn

Cramer & Crosby

Cramer: (English): full
Crosby: (English): town crossing

Drew & Davis

Drew: (English): courageous, valiant
Davis: (English & Scottish): David's son

Drake & Dixon

Drake: (English): male duck, dragon
Dixon: (English): power, brave ruler

Emerson & Elliott

Emerson: (English): brave, powerful
Elliott: (Israel): close to God; (English): the Lord is my God

Easton & Ennis

Easton: (English): from east town
Ennis: (Irish): island; (Gaelic): the only choice

Ford & Franklin

Ford: (English): river crossing
Franklin: (English): free man

Foster & Gallagher

Foster: (English & French): one who keeps the forest
Gallagher: (Irish & Gaelic): eagle helper

Fletcher & Fleming

Fletcher: (English): one who makes arrows
Fleming: (English): from Denmark

Fitzgerald & Fitzpatrick

Fitzgerald: (English): the son of Gerald
Fitzpatrick: (English): son of Patrick

Flynn & Ford

Flynn: (Irish): ruddy complexion
Ford: (English): from the river crossing

Grant & Gannon

Grant: (Latin): great
Gannon: (Irish & Gaelic): fair-skinned

Grayson & Graham

Grayson: (English): son of the bailiff
Graham: (Scottish): from the gray home

Haines & Hayden

Haines: (English): from the vine-covered cottage
Hayden: (English & Welsh): in the meadow or valley

Hilton & Henderson

Hilton: (English): town on a hill
Henderson: (Scottish): son of Henry

Hunter & Holt

Hunter: (English): one who hunts
Holt: (English): wood, by the forest

Hogan & Howard

Hogan: (Irish & Gaelic): young, young at heart
Howard: (English): guardian of the home

Jordan & Jensen

Jordan: (Hebrew): to flow down; (Israel): descendant
Jensen: (Scandinavian): God is gracious

Jackson & Johnson

Jackson: (English): son of Jack; (Scottish): God has been gracious
Johnson: (Scottish & English): son of John

Jagger & Jefferson

Jagger: (English): a carter, to carry
Jefferson: (English): son of Jeffrey, which means divine peace

Kane & Keaton

Kane: (Welsh): beautiful; (Gaelic): little warrior
Keaton: (English): from the town of hawks

Kendall & Kennedy

Kendall: (English & Celtic): from the bright valley
Kennedy: (Scottish): ugly head; (Irish & Gaelic): helmeted

Kirkland & Kramer

Kirkland: (English): from the church's land
Kramer: (German): shopkeeper

Landon & Lawrence

Landon: (English): grassy plain; from the long hill
Lawrence: (Latin America): crowned with laurel

Lincoln & Logan

Lincoln: (English): Roman colony at the pool; (Latin America): village
Logan: (Irish): small cove; (Scottish): Finnian's servant; (Gaelic): from the hollow

London & Lewis

London: (English): fortress of the moon
Lewis: (German): famous warrior

MacKenzie & Meyer

Mackenzie: (Irish & Scottish): fair, favored one
Meyer: (Jewish & Hebrew): shining

Morgan & Marlowe

Morgan: (Celtic): lives by the sea; (Welsh): bright sea
Marlowe: (English): from the hill by the lake

Macdonald & Malloy

Macdonald: (Scottish): son of Donald
Malloy: (Irish): noble chief

Madison & Monroe

Madison: (English): son of Matthew
Monroe: (Gaelic): from the red swamp; (Scottish & Irish): near the river roe

Marshall & Martin

Marshall: (French): caretaker of horses; (English): a steward
Martin: (Latin): dedicated to Mars, the god of war

Miller & Maxwell

Miller: (English): one who works at the mill
Maxwell: (English): capable, great spring

Nash & North

Nash: (American): adventurer
North: (English): from the north

Moore & Murphy

Moore: (French): dark-skinned; (Irish & French): surname
Murphy: (Gaelic): warrior of the sea

Nolan & Nelson

Nolan: (Irish & Gaelic): famous; (Celtic): noble
Nelson: (English, Celtic, Irish & Gaelic): son of Neil

Nash & Newman

Nash: (American): adventurer
Newman: (English): a newcomer

Oliver & Osborne

Oliver: (French, English, Danish & Latin America): the olive tree; (German): elf army
Osborne: (Norse): a bear of God

Payton & Paxton

Payton: (English): village
Paxton: (English): from the peaceful farm; (Latin America): town of peace

Parker & Porter

Parker: (English): keeper of the park or forest
Porter: (French): gate keeper; (Latin America): door guard

Regan & Riley

Reagan: (Celtic): regal; (Irish): son of the small ruler
Riley: (Irish): a small stream

Ryan & Rowan

Ryan: (Gaelic): little king; (Irish): kindly, young royalty
Rowan: (Irish): red-haired; (English & Gaelic): from the rowan tree

Reese & Rylan

Reese: (Welsh): enthusiastic
Rylan: (English); dweller in the rye field

Quinn & Quentin

Quinn: (Celtic): wise; (Irish): fifth, counsel, intelligent
Quentin: (French, English & Latin America): fifth

Shea & Smith

Shea: (Irish): majestic, fairy place
Smith: (English): artisan, tradesman

Scully & Silver

Scully: (Irish): herald; (Gaelic): town crier
Silver: (English): the color silver

Sawyer & Sheldon

Sawyer: (English): one who works with wood
Sheldon: (English): from the steep valley

Tanner & Terrell

Tanner: (English & German): leather worker
Terrell: (German): thunder ruler

Tate & Tyler

Tate: (English): cheerful
Tyler: (English): maker of tiles

Taylor & Thomas

Taylor: (English & French): a tailor
Thomas: (Hebrew, Greek & Dutch): twin

West & Winter

West: (English): from the west
Winter: (American): the season

Wyatt & Wilson

Wyatt: (English): guide, wide, wood, famous bearer; (French): son of the forest guide
Wilson: (English & German): son of William

Chapter 11: Named After Famous Places

This chapter explores a fascinating trend that has emerged in the past two decades: the use of city, state, and country names for both boys and girls. Some of these choices are fairly common, such as Austin and Charlotte, while others are esoteric, such as Aiken and Fullerton. Nevertheless, the trend is real, the names are eclectic, and the variety can't be beat. So, sit back and explore the most popular twin names based on famous places.

Named After Famous Places - Boys

Austin & Ames

Austin: (English): from the name Augustin, which means revered
Ames: (French): friend

Alton & Aiken

Alton: (English): from the old town
Aiken: (English): sturdy, made of oak

Boston & Beaumont

Boston: (English): the city Boston
Beaumont: (French): beautiful mountain

Berkeley & Benson

Berkeley: (English & Irish): from the birch meadow
Benson: (English): son of Benedict

Bentley & Barrington

Bentley: (English): from the bent grass meadow
Barrington: (English): town of Barr

Chester & Clayton

Chester: (English): a rock fortress
Clayton: (English): mortal

Camden & Carlin

Camden: (Irish, Scottish, English & Gaelic): from the winding valley
Carlin: (Irish, Gaelic & Scottish): little champion

Clyde & Carlisle

Clyde: (Irish): warm
Carlisle: (English): from the walled city

Cody & Chandler

Cody: (Irish): helpful; (English): a cushion, helpful
Chandler: (French): candle maker

Colton & Columbus

Colton: (English): coal town, from the dark town
Columbus: (Greek): curious

Derby & Devon

Derby: (English): deer park; (Irish): from the village of dames
Devon: (English & Irish): a poet, a county in England

Diego & Dallas

Diego: (Spanish): Saint James
Dallas: (Irish & Gaelic): wise; (Scottish & Celtic): from the waterfall

Easton & Everett

Easton: (English): from east town
Everett: (English): hardy, brave, strong

Fairbanks & Fargo

Fairbanks: (English): from the bank along the path
Fargo: (American): jaunty

Frederick & Flint

Frederick: (German): peaceful ruler
Flint: (English): stream, hard quartz rock

Fremont & Fullerton

Fremont: (French): protector of freedom
Fuller/Fullerton: (English): from Fuller's town

Jordan & Jackson

Jordan: (Hebrew): to flow down; (Israel): descendant
Jackson: (English): son of Jack; (Scottish): God has been gracious

Hartley & Hadley

Hartley: (English): from the stage meadow
Hadley: (English & Irish): from the heath covered meadow

Holland & Houston

Holland: (American): from the Netherlands
Houston: (Gaelic): from Hugh's town: (English): from the town on the hill

Kent & Kingston

Kent: (English & Welsh): white; (Celtic): chief
Kingston: (English): from the king's village

Lincoln & Lawrence

Lincoln: (English): Roman colony at the pool; (Latin America): village
Lawrence: (Latin America): crowned with laurel

Logan & Landon

Logan: (Irish): small cove; (Scottish): Finnian's servant; (Gaelic): from the hollow
Landon: (English): grassy plain, from the long hill

London & Livingston

London: (English): fortress of the moon
Livingston: (English): Leif's town

Mitchell & Maxwell

Mitchell: (Hebrew): gift from God
Maxwell: (English): capable, great spring

Mason & Merrill

Mason: (French & English): stone worker
Merrill: (English): falcon, shining sea

Orlando & Oliver

Orlando: (Spanish): land of gold
Oliver: (French, English, Danish & Latin America): the olive tree; (German): elf army

Ramsey & Redford

Ramsey: (Scottish): island of ravens
Redford: (English): over the red river, from the reedy ford

Raleigh & Radcliff

Raleigh: (English): deer meadow
Radcliff/Radcliffe: (English): red cliff

Salem & Salisbury

Salem: (Hebrew): peace
Salisbury: (English): fort at the willow pool

Trenton & Tanner

Trenton: (English): town of Trent
Tanner: (English & German): leather worker

Texas & Tennessee

Texas: (Native American): one of many friends, from the state of Texas
Tennessee: (Native American): from the state of Tennessee

York & Vernon

York: (Celtic, English & Latin America): from the yew tree
Vernon: (Latin): youthful, young at heart; (French & English): alder tree grove

Warren & Wesley

Warren: (English): to preserve; (German): protector, loyal
Wesley: (English & Berman): from the west meadow

Named After Famous Places - Girls

Aurora & Augusta

Aurora: (Latin): dawn
Augusta: (Latin): venerable, majestic

Afton & Ada

Afton: (English): from the Afton River
Ada: (English): wealthy; (Hebrew): ornament; (German): noble; (African): first daughter

Asia & Arizona

Asia: (Greek & English): resurrection, rising sun
Arizona: (Native American): from the little spring, from the state of Arizona

Aspen & Alexandria

Aspen: (English): from the aspen tree
Alexandria: (Greek, English & Latin America): defender of mankind

Brooklyn & Bristol

Brooklyn: (English): water, stream
Bristol: (English): bridge

Catalina & Carolina

Catalina: (Spanish): pure
Carolina: (Mexican): beautiful woman; (French & English): song of happiness

Chelsea & Charlotte

Chelsea: (English): seaport
Charlotte: (French): feminine

Cheyenne & China

Cheyenne: (French): dog; (Native American): an Algonquin tribe
China: (Chinese): fine porcelain

Dakota & Darby

Dakota: (Native American): friend, ally
Darby: (Irish & Gaelic): free man; (English): deer park

Eden & Echo

Eden: (Hebrew): delight; (Israel): paradise
Echo: (Greek): sound returned

Florence & Fallon

Florence: (English): flowering; (Latin America): prosperous
Fallon: (Irish): of a ruling family

Georgia & Geneva

Georgia: (Greek & German): farmer
Geneva: (French): juniper berry: (German): of the race of woman

Helena & Hailey

Helena: (Greek): light
Hailey/Hailee/Haley: (English): hero, field of hay

Ireland & India

Ireland: (Irish): of a ruling family
India: (English): from India

Jordan & Logan

Jordan: (Hebrew): to flow down; (Israel): descendant
Logan: (Irish): small cove; (Scottish): Finnian's servant; (Gaelic): from the hollow

Kent & Kenya

Kent: (English & Welsh): white; (Celtic): chief
Kenya: (Israel): animal horn

Lincoln & Lane

Lincoln: (English): Roman colony at the pool; (Latin America): village
Lane: (English): narrow road, from the long meadow

Madison & Montana

Madison: (English): son of Matthew
Montana: (Latin America): mountainous

Nazareth & Nevada

Nazareth: (Hebrew): religion
Nevada: (English): covered in snow

Odessa & Octavia

Odessa: (Latin America): the odyssey
Octavia: (Latin America): eighth; (Italian): born eighth

Paris & Phoenix

Paris: (Persian): angelic face; (Greek): downfall; (French): the capital city of France
Phoenix: (Greek): rising bird

Regina & Racine

Regina: (Italian, Spanish & Latin America): queen
Racine: (French): root

Sierra & Savannah

Sierra: (Spanish): mountain; (Irish): dark
Savannah: (Spanish): open plain, field

Virginia & Vienna

Virginia: (English, Spanish, Italian & Latin America): pure
Vienna: (Latin America): from wine country

Sydney & Sahara

Sydney: (English): wide island
Sahara: (Arabian): wilderness

Victoria & Valencia

Victoria: (Latin America): winner
Valencia: (Spanish): brave

Chapter 12: Named After U.S. Presidents & First Ladies

The names of U.S. Presidents and First Ladies are favorites for many prospective parents. This is particularly true in election years, when the country "meets" the candidates' spouses and families. In this chapter, we will explore the presidential names that have stood the test of time - and are particularly popular with the parents of twins.

Abraham & Lincoln

Abraham: (Hebrew & Biblical): exalted father
Lincoln: (English): Roman colony at the pool; (Latin America): village

Carter & Clinton

Carter: (English): cart driver
Clinton: (English): town on a hill

Garfield & Grant

Garfield: (English): battlefield
Grant: (Latin): great

Harrison & Hayes

Harrison: (English): son of Harry
Hayes: (English): from the hedged place

Jackson & Jefferson

Jackson: (English): son of Jack; (Scottish): God has been gracious
Jefferson: (English): son of Jeffrey, which means divine peace

Kennedy & Johnson

Kennedy: (Scottish): ugly head; (Irish & Gaelic): helmeted
Johnson: (Scottish & English): son of John

Madison & Monroe

Madison: (English): son of Matthew
Monroe: (Gaelic): from the red swamp; (Scottish): from the river; (Irish): near the river roe

Quincy & Reagan

Quincy: (English): fifth; (French): estate belonging to Quintus
Reagan: (Celtic): regal; (Irish): son of the small ruler

Taylor & Truman

Taylor: (English & French): a tailor
Truman: (English): loyal, trusted man; (German): faithful man

Tyler & Theodore

Tyler: (English): maker of tiles
Theodore: (Greek): divine gift

Wilson & Woodrow

Wilson: (English & German): son of William
Woodrow: (English): forester, row of houses

Ulysses & Zachary

Ulysses: (Latin) : hateful
Zachary: (Hebrew & Israel): remembered by God

First Ladies & Daughters

Abigail & Eleanor

Abigail: (Hebrew): father rejoiced; (Biblical): source of joy
Eleanor: (English): torch

Chelsea & Claudia

Chelsea: (English): seaport
Claudia: (Spanish & Latin America): lame

Caroline & Rosalind

Caroline: (Spanish): beautiful woman; (French & English): song of happiness
Rosalind: (Spanish): beautiful one

Jenna & Julia

Jenna: (English): small bird
Julia: (French): youthful; (Latin America): soft-haired, youthful

Malia & Sasha

Malia: (American): calm, peaceful
Sasha: (English): defender of mankind

Dolly & Hillary

Dolly: (American): cute child
Hillary: (English & Greek): joyous, cheerful

Jacqueline & Michelle

Jacqueline: (French): to protect
Michelle: (French & Hebrew): like God, close to God

Chapter 13: Named after Famous Couples & Twins

In our celebrity-driven culture, famous couples often serve as the inspiration for the names of opposite sex twins. This chapter presents the most common names that parents choose from history, movies, television, and literature.

Adam & Eve

Adam: (Hebrew): red; (Israel): man of the earth; (English): of the red earth
Eve: (Hebrew): to breathe

Bonnie & Clyde

Bonnie: (English): good; (French): sweet; (Scottish): pretty, charming
Clyde: (Irish): warm

Romeo & Juliet

Romeo: (Italian, Spanish, Latin America & African American): from Rome
Juliet: (French): youthful, soft-haired

Mickey & Minnie

Mickey: (Irish, English & Hebrew): diminutive of Michael, which means like God
Minnie: (Irish): bitter; (Hebrew): wished for a child

Ebony & Ivory

Ebony: (American): dark strength
Ivory: (English & Latin America): white, pure

Fred & Ginger

Fred: (German): peaceful ruler
Ginger: (English): the spice

Edward & Bella

Edward: (English): wealthy guardian; (German): strong as a boar
Bella: (Hebrew): devoted to God; (Spanish & Latin America): beautiful

Scarlett & Rhett

Scarlett: (English): red
Rhett: (English): stream

Nelson & Winnie

Nelson: (English, Celtic, Irish & Gaelic): son of Neil
Winnie: (Irish & Celtic): white, fair

Anthony & Cleopatra

Anthony: (English & Biblical): worthy of praise
Cleopatra: (Greek): glory to the father; (African American): queen

Napoleon & Josephine

Josephine: (French): God will add
Napoleon: (French): fierce one

Bart & Lisa

Bart: (Hebrew): ploughman; (English): from the barley farm
Lisa: (German): devoted to God; (Israel): consecrated to God

William & Hillary

William: (English, German & French): protector
Hillary: (English & Greek): joyous, cheerful

Frankie & Johnnie

Frankie: (English & French): diminutive of Frank, which means free
Johnnie: (French, English & Hebrew): diminutive of John, which means God is gracious

Hansel & Gretel

Hansel: (Hebrew): gift from God; (Scandinavian): God is gracious
Gretel: (German & Scandinavian): pearl

Jack & Jill

Jack: (English): God is gracious; (Hebrew): supplanter
Jill: (English): girl, sweetheart

Lancelot & Guinevere

Lancelot: (English & French): servant
Guinevere: (Celtic): white lady; (English): white wave

Linus & Lucy

Linus: (Latin America): flaxen
Lucy: (Latin America): bringer of light

Monica & Ross

Monica: (Greek & Spanish): advisor
Ross: (Scottish): from the peninsula

Ned & Stacy

Ned: (English & French): diminutive of Edward, which means wealthy guardian
Stacy: (English): productive, resurrection

Celebrity Twins

Barbara & Jenna (George & Barbara Bush)

Barbara: (Latin America): stranger
Jenna: (English): small bird

Vivienne & Knox (Angelina Jolie & Brad Pitt)

Knox: (English): from the hills
Vivienne: (English): the lady of the lake

Hazel & Phinnaeus (Julia Roberts)

Hazel: (English & Irish): the hazel tree
Phinneaus: (Hebrew): oracle; (Israel): loudmouth

Hudson & Julitta (Marcia Gay Harden)

Hudson: (English): son of the hooded man
Julietta: (French): youthful, young at heart

Gideon & Harper (Neil Patrick Harris)

Gideon: (Hebrew & Israel): great warrior
Harper: (English): musician, harp player

Max & Emme (Jennifer Lopez & Marc Anthony)

Emme: (Latin America): industrious, striving
Max: (English): greatest

Ryan & Rodney, Jr. (Holly Robinson-Peete)

Ryan: (Gaelic): little king; (Irish): kindly, young royalty
Rodney: (English): land near the water, island of reeds

Slater & Bronwyn (Angela Bassett)

Slater: (English): one who works with slate
Bronwyn: (Welsh): dark and pure; (English): white-skinned

Max & Kate (Joan Lunden)

Max: (English): greatest
Kate: (Irish, English & French): diminutive of Katherine, which means pure, virginal

Kimberly & Jack (Joan Lunden)

Kimberly: (English): ruler
Jack: (English): God is gracious; (Hebrew): supplanter

Hunter & Jake (Niki Taylor)

Hunter: (English): one who hunts
Jake: (Hebrew): he grasps the heel

Dane & Trey (Lee Majors)

Dane: (Hebrew & Scandinavian): God will judge; (English): brook
Trey: (English & Latin America): three

Christian & Edward (Mel Gibson)

Christian: (English & Irish): follower of Christ
Edward: (English): blesses guardian

Matthew & Gregory (Ray Romano)

Gregory: (English & Greek): vigilant
Matthew: (Hebrew & Biblical): gift of the Lord

Julian & Aaron (Robert De Niro)

Julian: (Spanish, French & Greek): youthful
Aaron: (Jewish): enlightened; (Hebrew): lofty, exalted

Henry & Rufus (James Taylor)

Henry: (English, German & French): rules his household
Rufus: (Latin America): redhead

Kristopher & John (Jane Seymour)

Kristopher: (Biblical): Christ-bearer; (English): he who holds Christ in his heart
John: (Israel): God is gracious; Jehovah has been gracious

Gus & John (Julie Bowen)

Gus: (German): revered
John: (Israel): God is gracious; Jehovah has been gracious

Matteo & Valentino (Ricky Martin)

Matteo: (Italian): gift of God
Valentino: (Italian): brave or strong; (Latin America): health or love

Moroccan & Monroe (Mariah Carey & Nick Cannon)

Moroccan: (African): one from Morocco
Monroe: (Gaelic): from the red swamp; (Scottish): from the river; (Irish): near the river roe

Chapter 14: One Syllable Names

When I speak to prospective parents, I tend to hear the same question over and over again: "Why aren't there any great one-syllable names?" This chapter answers that question in a fairly conclusive way: there are literally *hundreds* of excellent names for twins that are short, sweet, and just one syllable. A better question - how can you choose just two?

One Syllable Names - Boys

Abe & Ace

Abe: (Jewish): father of nations
Ace: (Latin): unity

Bart & Beau

Bart: (Hebrew): ploughman; (English): from the barley farm
Beau: (French): handsome, beautiful

Ben & Black

Ben: (English): son of my right hand
Black: (English): dark-skinned

Blade & Blake

Blade: (English): wielding a sword or knife
Blake: (English): pale, fair

Blaze & Boone

Blaze: (Latin): one who stammers; (English): flame
Boone: (French): good

Boyd & Brant

Boyd: (Celtic): blond-haired
Brant: (English): steep, tall

Brent & Brett

Brent: (English): from the hill
Brett: (French, English & Celtic): a native of Brittany

Brice & Brock

Brice: (Welsh): alert, ambitious
Brock: (English): badger

Brooks & Brown

Brooks: (English): running water, son of Brooke
Brown: (English): brown color, dark-skinned

Bruce & Bryce

Bruce: (French & English): woods, thick brush
Bryce: (Scottish): speckled

Buck & Bud

Buck: (German & English): male deer
Bud: (English): brotherly

Burke & Byrd

Burke: (German): birch tree
Byrd: (English): bird-like

Cade & Cain

Cade: (American): pure
Cain: (Israel): craftsman; (Hebrew): spear; (Welsh): clear water; (Irish): archaic

Carl & Cash

Carl: (English): man; (German): strong one
Cash: (Latin): money

Chad & Chance

Chad: (English): battle
Chance: (English & French): good luck, keeper of records

Charles & Chase

Charles: (English): strong, manly
Chase: (English): hunter

Clark & Claude

Clark: (English): cleric, scholar, clerk
Claude: (English): lame

Claus & Clay

Claus: (Greek): people's victory
Clay: (English): clay maker, immortal

Cliff & Clive

Cliff: (English): from the ford near the cliff
Clive: (English): one who lives near the cliff

Cole & Colt

Cole: (Irish): warrior; (English): having dark features
Colt: (American): baby horse; (English): from the dark town

Craig & Creed

Craig: (Scottish): dwells at the crag; (Welsh): rock
Creed: (English): belief, guiding principle

Dale & Dane

Dale: (German): valley; (English): lives in the valley
Dane: (Hebrew & Scandinavian): God will judge; (English): brook

Dax & Dean

Dax: (English & French): water
Dean: (English): head, leader

Dell & Dierks

Dell: (English): from the small valley
Dierks: (Danish): ruler of the people

Dirk & Dobbs

Dirk: (German): a diminutive form of Derek, which means gifted ruler
Dobbs: (English): fiery

Dolph & Doyle

Dolph: (German): diminutive form of Adolph, which means noble wolf
Doyle: (Irish): dark river

Drake & Drew

Drake: (English): male duck, dragon
Drew/Dru: (English): courageous, valiant

Duane & Dwight

Duane: (Gaelic): a dark and swarthy man
Dwight: (English): a diminutive form of DeWitt, which means blond hair

Earl & Fenn

Earl: (Irish): pledge; (English): nobleman
Fenn: (English): from the marsh

Finn & Fitch

Finn: (English): blond
Fitch: (English): resembling an ermine

Flynn & Ford

Flynn: (Irish): ruddy complexion
Ford: (English): from the river crossing

Fox & Frank

Fox: (English): fox
Frank: (English): free man

Fred & Fynn

Fred: (German): peaceful ruler
Fynn: (Russian): the Offin River

Gabe & Gage

Gabe: (English): strength of God
Gage/Gaige: (French): a pledge or pawn

Garth & Gene

Garth: (Scandinavian): keeper of the garden
Gene: (English): a well-born man

George & Giles

George: (English): farmer
Giles: (Greek): resembling a young goat

Gill & Glenn

Gill: (Gaelic): servant
Glenn: (Scottish): glen, valley

Grant & Gray

Grant: (Latin): great
Gray: (English): gray-haired

Gus & Guy

Gus: (German): revered
Guy: (French): guide; (Hebrew): valley; (Celtic): sensible; (Latin America): living spirit

Haines & Hal

Haines: (English): from the vine-covered cottage
Hal: (English): ruler of the army

Hank & Hans

Hank: (Dutch & German): rules his household
Hans: (German & Hebrew): gift from God; (Scandinavian): God is gracious

Heath & Holt

Heath: (English): from the heath wasteland
Holt: (English): wood, by the forest

Hoyt & Hugh

Hoyt: (Irish): mind, spirit
Hugh: (English): intelligent

Hurst & Hyde

Hurst: (Irish): dense grove, thicket
Hyde: (English): animal hide

Ike & Ives

Ike: (Hebrew): full of laughter
Ives: (Scandinavian): the archer's bow

Jack & Jake

Jack: (English): God is gracious; (Hebrew): supplanter
Jake: (Hebrew): he grasps the heel

James & Jan

James: (English); supplant, replace; (Israel): supplanter
Jan: (Dutch): a form of John, which means God is gracious

Jax & Jay

Jax: (American): son of Jack
Jay: (German): swift; (French): blue jay; (English): to rejoice; (Latin America): a crow

Jean & Jess

Jean: (French): a form of John, which means God is gracious
Jess: (Israel): wealthy

Jett & Jobe

Jett: (English): resembling the black gemstone
Jobe: (Hebrew): afflicted

Joel & John

Joel: (Hebrew): Jehovah is God; (Israel): God is willing
John: (Israel): God is gracious; Jehovah has been gracious

Juan & Jules

Juan: (Hebrew): gift from God; (Spanish): God is gracious
Jules: (French): youthful, downy-haired

Kai & Kale

Kai: (American): ocean; (Welsh): keeper of the keys; (Scottish): fire
Kale: (English): manly and strong

Kane & Karl

Kane: (Welsh): beautiful; (Gaelic): little warrior
Karl: (English & Icelandic): man; (French): strong, masculine; (Danish): one who is free

Keefe & Keene

Keefe: (Irish): handsome, loved
Keene: (German): bold, sharp; (English): smart

Keith & Kent

Keith: (Scottish): wood; (Irish): warrior descending; (Welsh): dwells in the woods
Kent: (English & Welsh): white; (Celtic): chief

King & Kirk

King: (English): royal ruler
Kirk: (Norse): a man of the church

Knight & Knox

Knight: (English): noble soldier
Knox: (English): from the hills

Kris & Kurt

Kris: (Swedish): Christ-bearer
Kurt: (German): brave counselor

Kipp & Kyle

Kipp: (English): from the small pointed hill
Kyle: (Gaelic): young; (Irish): young at heart

Lane & Laird

Lane: (English): narrow road
Laird: (Scottish): lord; (Irish): head of household

Lance & Lear

Lance: (German): spear; (French): land
Lear: (English): Shakespearean king

Lee & Leif

Lee/Leigh: (English): meadow
Leif: (Scandinavian): beloved descendent

Lloyd & Locke

Lloyd: (Celtic, Welsh & English): gray
Locke: (English): forest

Luke & Lyle

Luke: (Greek & Latin America): light
Lyle: (French & English): from the island

Lynch & Lynn

Lynch: (Irish): mariner
Lynn: (English): waterfall

Mark & Max

Mark: (Latin): dedicated to Mars, the god of war
Max: (English): greatest

Mead & Merle

Mead: (English): meadow
Merle: (French): blackbird; (English): falcon

Miles & Moore

Miles: (German): merciful; (Latin): a soldier
Moore: (French): dark-skinned; (Irish & French): surname

Nash & Neal

Nash: (American): adventurer
Neal/Neil: (Irish, English & Celtic): a champion

Ned & Niles

Ned: (English & French): diminutive of Edward, which means wealthy guardian
Niles: (English): champion

Noel & North

Noel: (French): Christmas
North: (English): from the north

Oz & Puck

Oz: (Hebrew): having great strength
Puck: (English): elf

Pace & Paine

Pace: (English): a peaceful man
Paine/Payne: (Latin): a peasant

Paul & Pax

Paul: (English & French): small, apostle in the Bible
Pax: (English): peaceful

Pell & Penn

Pell: (English): a clerk
Penn: (Latin): pen, quill

Pierce & Platt

Pierce: (English): rock
Platt: (French): flatland

Ponce & Prince

Ponce: (Spanish): fifth
Prince: (Latin): chief, prince

Quinn & Royce

Quinn: (Gaelic): one who provides counsel
Royce: (Irish & French): king, regal; (Scottish, Gaelic & Scottish): red, red-haired

Rafe & Raine

Rafe: (Irish): a tough man
Rain/Raine: (American): blessings from above; (French & Latin): ruler; (English): lord, wise

Ralph & Rand

Ralph: (English): wolf counsel
Rand: (German): the wolf shield

Raul & Ray

Raul: (French): a form of Ralph, which means wolf counsel
Ray: (French): regal: (Scottish): grace; (English): wise protector

Reed & Rex

Reed/Reid: (English & French): red-haired
Rex: (Latin): king

Rhett & Rhys

Rhett: (English): stream
Rhys/Reese/Reece: (English & Welsh): ardent, fiery, enthusiastic

Rhodes & Ridge

Rhodes: (Greek): where roses grow
Ridge: (English): from the ridge

Roan & Roark

Roan: (English): from the Rowan tree
Roark: (Gaelic): champion

Rolf & Ross

Rolf: (German): wolf counsel
Ross: (Scottish): from the peninsula

Saige & Saul

Saige/Sage: (English & French): wise one; (English): from the spice
Saul: (Israel): borrowed: (Hebrew & Spanish): asked for

Scott & Sean

Scott: (Scottish): wanderer
Sean/Shawn: (Irish): God is gracious

Seth & Shane

Seth: (Hebrew): anointed; (Israel): appointed
Shane: (Hebrew): gift from God; (Irish): God is gracious

Shea & Slade

Shea: (Irish): majestic, fairy place
Slade: (English): child of the valley

Sloan & Smith

Sloan: (English): raid; (Irish, Celtic, Scottish & Gaelic): fighter, warrior
Smith: (English): artisan, tradesman

Stern & Stony

Stern: (English): austere
Stony: (English): stone

Storm & Sven

Storm: (English): tempest; (American): impetuous nature
Sven: (Scandinavian): youth

Taft & Thor

Taft: (French): from the homestead
Thor: (Norse): god of thunder

Thorne & Todd

Thorne: (English): from the thorn bush
Todd: (Scottish): fox

Trent & Trey

Trent: (Welsh): dwells near the rapid stream
Trey: (English & Latin): third-born child

Trigg & Tripp

Trigg: (Norse): truthful
Tripp: (English): traveler

Troy & True

Troy: (French): curly haired; (Irish): foot soldier
True: (English): loyal

Twain & Ty

Twain: (English): divided in two
Ty: (English): from the fenced-in pasture

Vance & Vaughn

Vance: (English): windmill dweller
Vaughn: (Celtic): small

Wade & Wayne

Wade: (English): ford, cross the river
Wayne: (English): craftsman, wagon maker

Webb & West

Webb: (English): weaver
West: (English): from the west

Whit & Wolf

Whit: (English): white-skinned
Wolf: (English): the animal, wolf

Yale & Yan

Yale: (Welsh): from the fertile upland
Yan/Yann: (Russian): a form of John, which means God is gracious

York & Yves

York: (Celtic, English & Latin America): from the yew tree
Yves: (French): a young archer

Zale & Zane

Zale: (Greek): having the strength of the sea
Zane: (Hebrew): gift from God; (Arabian): beloved

Zeke & Zeus

Zeke: (English): strengthened by God
Zeus: (Greek): powerful one

One Syllable Names - Girls

Anne & Bea

Anne: (Hebrew & Israel): favor or grace
Bea: (America): blessed

Belle & Bess

Belle: (French): beautiful
Bess: (English): my God is bountiful

Beth & Blair

Beth: (Scottish): lively
Blair: (Irish & Celtic): from the plain, (Gaelic): child of the fields; (Scottish): peat moss

Blaine & Blake

Blaine: (Gaelic, Irish & Celtic): thin
Blake: (English): pale blond or dark; (Scottish): dark-haired

Bliss & Blue

Bliss: (English): joy, happiness
Blue: (English): the color blue

Blythe & Brea

Blythe: (English): happy
Brea: (French): champion

Bree & Bryce

Bree: (Celtic): broth; (Irish): hill, strong one
Bryce: (Welsh): alert, ambitious

Brie & Britt

Brie: (French): from the northern region of France
Britt: (Swedish): high goddess

Brooke & Brynn

Brooke: (English): lives by the stream
Brynn: (Welsh): hill

Cate & Cher

Cate: (English): blessed, pure, holy
Cher: (English): beloved

Clove & Cree

Clove: (German): spice
Cree: (Native American): name of tribe

Dale & Dawn

Dale: (English): valley
Dawn: (English): aurora; (Greek): sunrise

Cove & Drew

Dove: (American): bird of peace
Drew: (Greek): courageous, strong

Dule & Fran

Dulce: (Latin): very sweet
Fran/Francine: (Latin America): free

Eve & Faith

Eve: (Hebrew): to breathe
Faith: (English): faithful; (Latin America): to trust

Fawn & Faye

Fawn: (French & English): young deer
Faye: (French): fairy; (Irish): raven; (English): faith, confidence

Fern & Fleur

Fern: (English): the fern plant
Fleur: (French): flower

Flynn & Gayle:

Flynn: (Irish): heir to the red-headed
Gayle: (English): merry, lively

Gay & Grace

Gay: (English): merry, happy
Grace: (Latin America): grace of God; (American): land of grace

Greer & Gwen

Greer: (Scottish): alert, watchful
Gwen: (Celtic): mythical son of Gwastad

Hope & Jade

Hope: (English): trust, faith
Jade: (Spanish): jewel, green gemstone

Jayne & Jean

Jayne: (Indian): victorious; (Hebrew): gift from God; (English): Jehovah has been gracious
Jean: (Hebrew): God is gracious

Jill & Joan

Jill: (English): girl, sweetheart
Joan: (Hebrew): gift from God; (English): God is gracious

Joy & June

Joy: (French, English & Latin America): rejoicing
June: (Dominican Republic): born in June

Kate & Kay

Kate: (Irish, English & French): diminutive of Katherine, which means pure, virginal
Kay: (Greek): rejoice; (Scottish & Welsh): fiery

Kent & Kim

Kent: (English & Welsh): white; (Celtic): chief
Kim: (Welsh): leader

Kyle & Lane

Kyle: (Irish): attractive
Lane: (English): narrow road, from the long meadow

Lake & Lark

Lake: (American): body of water, from the lake
Lark: (English): a lark; (American): songbird

Leigh & Liv

Leigh: (English): from the meadow
Liv: (Norwegian): protector

Love & Lynn

Love: (English): full of affection
Lynn(e): (English): woman of the lake, waterfall

Madge & Maeve

Madge: (English): pearl
Maeve: (Irish): intoxicating, joyous

Maude & Mauve

Maude: (French): strong in war; (Irish): strong battle maiden
Mauve: (American): purplish color

May & Nell

May: (English): name of month; (Hebrew & Latin America): from Mary
Nell: (English): torch

Neve & Noor

Neve: (Irish): radiant; (Hebrew): life
Noor: (Aramaic): light

Paige & Pearl

Paige: (French): assistant, attendant
Pearl: (English): gemstone

Queen & Quinn

Queen: (English): queen
Quinn: (Celtic): queenly

Rae & Rain

Rae: (Scottish): grace; (German): wise protection
Rain/Raine: (American): blessings from above; (French & Latin): ruler; (English): lord, wise

Reese & Rose

Reese: (Welsh): enthusiastic
Rose: (English, French & Scottish): flower, a rose; (German): horse, fame

Rue & Ruth

Rue: (Greek): herb of grace
Ruth: (Hebrew & Israel): companion, friend

Saige & Scout

Saige/Sage: (English): sage
Scout: (French): scout

Shane & Shawn

Shane: (Hebrew): gift from God; (Irish): God is gracious
Shawn: (Irish): a form of Sean, which means God is gracious

Skye & Sloane

Skye: (English): sky
Sloan: (English): raid; (Irish, Celtic, Scottish & Gaelic): fighter, warrior

Starr & Tess

Starr: (English & American): star
Tess: (English): harvester

Tish & Tyne

Tish: (Latin): joy
Tyne: (English): of the river Tyne

Vail & Wren

Vail: (English): valley
Wren: (Welsh): ruler; (English): small bird

Chapter 15: Four-Syllable Names

On a practical basis, this chapter is the flip side of Chapter 14, which presents hundreds of one syllable names for twins. Here, we will focus on the longest, most elegant and sophisticated names that are at least four syllables. Why, you may ask, would someone choose this type of name for their child, which is hard to pronounce and spell? Many times, a long name is the best fit for a short and simple last name, such as Smith, Tom, Wu, or Lee. Other times, the parents are seeking a formal name that the child can "grow into," such as Alexander. In the meantime, they will call the child one of many possible nicknames, such as Al, Alex, Alec or Zander.

Two things are fascinating about these lists. First, there are far fewer four syllable names for boys than girls, because male names tend to be shorter and simpler. Second, many of these longer names are older, from other cultures, and not particularly common (with a few notable exceptions, such as Alexander, Elizabeth, and Olivia). Nevertheless, for parents seeking elegant, sophisticated, and mature names that are also somewhat unusual, these lists have several hidden gems.

Boys Names with Four Syllables

Alejandro & Alexander

Alejandro: (Spanish): defender of mankind
Alexander: (Greek): protector of mankind

Aloysuius & Amadeus

Aloysius: (German): famous warrior
Amadeus: (Latin): loves God

Amerigo & Arsenio

Amerigo: (Teutonic): industrious
Arsenio: (Greek): masculine, virile

Archimedes & Aristotle

Archimedes: (Greek): to think about first
Aristotle: (Greek): thinker with a great purpose

Aurelius & Azariah

Aurelius: (Latin): golden
Azariah: (Hebrew & Israel): God helps

Barththolomew & Bonaventure

Bartholomew: (English, Hebrew & Biblical): son of a farmer
Bonaventure: (Latin): one who undertakes a blessed venture

Cornelius & Ezekiel

Cornelius: (Irish): strong willed, wise; (Latin America): horn-colored
Ezekiel: (Hebrew & Israel): strength of God

Deangelo & Demetrius

Deangelo: (Italian): a combination of De and Angelo; little angel
Demetrius: (Greek): goddess of fertility, one who loves the earth

Ebenezer & Emmanuel

Ebenezer: (Hebrew & Israel): rock of help
Emmanuel: (Hebrew): God with us

Fabrizio & Galileo

Fabrizio: (Italian): craftsman
Galileo: (Hebrew): one who comes from Galilee

Genovese & Geronimo

Genovese: (Italian): from Genoa, Italy
Geronimo: (Greek & Italian): a famous chef

Giovanni & Horatio

Giovanni/Gian: (Italian); God is gracious
Horatio: (French): hour, time

Indiana & Macallister

Indiana: (English): from the land of the Indians, the state of Indiana
Macallister: (Gaelic): the son of Alistair

Jedidiah & Jeremiah

Jedidiah: (Hebrew): one who is loved by God
Jeremiah: (Hebrew): may Jehovah exalt; (Israel): sent by God

Maximilian & Montgomery

Maximilian: (Latin): greatest
Montgomery: (French): rich man's mountain

Napoleon & Nehemiah

Napoleon: (French): fierce one
Nehemiah: (Hebrew): compassion of Jehovah

Octavius & Odyssues

Octavius: (Latin): eighth
Odysseus: (Greek): wrathful

Olivier & Onofrio

Olivier: (French, English, Danish & Latin America): the olive tree; (German): elf army
Onofrio: (Italian): a defender of peace

Santiago & Valentino

Santiago: (Spanish): named for Saint James
Valentino: (Italian): brave or strong; (Latin America): health or love

Zachariah & Michelangeo*

Zachariah: (Hebrew): Jehovah has remembered; (Israel): remembered by the Lord
Michelangelo*: (Italian): a combination of Michael and Angelo

Girls Names with Four Syllables

Adelina & Alejandra

Adelina: (French & Spanish): of the nobility
Alejandra: (Spanish): defender of mankind

Adriana & Alexandria

Adriana: (Spanish, Greek & Italian): woman with dark and rich features
Alexandria: (Greek, English & Latin America): defender of mankind

America & Anastasia

America: (English): ruler of the home
Anastasia: (Greek): resurrection

Angelina & Anjelica

Angelina: (Italian): little angel
Anjelica: (Greek): a diminutive form of Angela, which means angel

Antonia & Appollonia*

Antonia: (Greek): flourishing or flowering
Apollonia*: (Greek): strength

Aphrodite & Arabella

Aphrodite: (Greek): beauty, love goddess
Arabella: (Latin): answered prayer, beautiful altar

Arianna & Arizona

Arianna: (Greek & Italian): holy
Arizona: (Native American): from the little spring, from the state of Arizona

Belisama & Davinia

Belisama: (Celtic): goddess of rivers and lakes
Davina: (Scottish): feminine form of David, which means beloved one

Carolina & Catalina

Carolina: (Mexico): beautiful woman; (French & English): song of happiness
Catalina: (Spanish): pure

Caledonia & Calliope

Caledonia: (Latin): woman of Scotland
Calliope: (Greek): beautiful voice

Cleopatra & Concordia

Cleopatra: (Greek): glory to the father; (African American): queen
Concordia: (Latin): peace

Corinthia & Eliana

Corinthia: (Greek): woman of Clorinth
Eliana: (Hebrew): the Lord answers our prayers

Elizabeth & Eloisa

Elizabeth: (English): my God is bountiful; (Hebrew & Biblical): consecrated to God
Eloisa: (Latin): famous warrior

Emmanuelle & Epiphany

Emmanuelle: (Hebrew): God is with us
Epiphany: (Greek): manifestation

Ernestina & Esmerelda

Ernestina: (German): determined, serious
Esmeralda: (Spanish): resembling a prized emerald

Eugenia & Evangeline

Eugenia: (Greek): well-born
Evangeline: (Greek): like an angel

Fabiana & Felicity

Fabiana: (Latin): bean grower
Felicity: (French, English & Latin America): happiness

Fidelity & Frederica

Fidelity: (Latin): faithful, true
Frederica: (German): peaceful ruler

Gabriella & Gardenia

Gabriella: (Israel & Hebrew): God gives strength; (Italian): woman of God
Gardenia: (English): a sweet-smelling flower

Giovanna & Guadalupe

Giovanna: (Italian): God is gracious
Guadalupe: (Spanish): from the valley of wolves

Henrietta & Ileana

Henrietta: (German): ruler of the house
Ileana: (Roman): torch; (Greek): from the city of lion

Isabella & Isadora

Isabella: (Hebrew): devoted to God; (Spanish): God is bountiful; (Biblical): consecrated to God
Isadora: (Greek): gift from the goddess Isis

Javiera & Josephina

Javiera: (Spanish): owner of a new house
Josephina: (Hebrew): God will add

Julietta & Lavinia

Julietta: (French): youthful, young at heart
Lavinia: (Latin): purified

Magdalena & Mahogany

Magdalena: (Hebrew): from the tower; (Spanish): bitter
Mahogany: (Spanish): rich, strong

Mariana & Marietta

Mariana: (Spanish): star of the sea; (French): bitter
Marietta: (French): star of the sea

Nefertiti & Parthenia

Nefertiti: (Egyptian): queenly
Parthenia: (Greek): virginal

Octavia & Okalani

Octavia: (Latin America): eighth; (Italian): born eighth
Okalani: (Hawaiian): from the heavens

Olivia & Olympia

Olivia: (Spanish & Italian): olive; (Biblical): peace of the olive tree
Olympia: (Greek): from Mount Olympus

Orabella & Oriana

Orabella: (Latin): a form of Arabella, which means answered prayer
Oriana: (Latin): born at sunrise

Penelope & Pheodora

Penelope: (Greek): weaver
Pheodora: (Greek): supreme gift

Philomena & Pollyanna

Philomena: (Greek): friend of strength
Pollyanna: (American): overly optimistic

Seraphina & Serenity

Seraphina: (Latin): a winged angel
Serenity: (Latin & English): peaceful

Tatiana & Tayanita

Tatiana: (Slavic): fairy queen
Tayanita: (Cherokee): beaver

Theodora & Thomasina

Theodora: (English): gift of God
Thomasina: (Hebrew): a twin

Tijuana & Timothea

Tijuana: (Spanish): border town in Mexico
Timothea: (English): honoring God

Valentina & Venecia

Valencia: (Spanish & Italian): brave; (Latin America): health or love
Venecia: (Italian): from Venice

Veronica & Victoria

Veronica: (Latin): displaying a true image
Victoria: (Latin America): winner

Virgilia & Wilhelmina

Virgilia: (Latin): staff bearer
Wilhelmina: (German): resolute protector

*****Note**: The names Michelangelo and Appolonia are five-syllables, rather than four

Chapter 16: Gender Neutral (Unisex) Names

Throughout this book, you have probably stopped at least once or twice and thought: "Wow, I didn't know *that* was a girl's name." To me, that is the most distinctive trend that is worth noting - the fact that few names are reserved for only one sex.

Fifty years ago, that wasn't the case. If you asked someone to suggest a gender neutral name, they would probably say Pat, Lee, Dale, or Frances - and then draw a blank. Now, there are dozens of popular names that are equally used by both sexes. We've included this chapter for two reasons:

1. to offer suggestions for parents who want a gender neutral name

2. to note the names that truly **are** unisex, for prospective parents who might not be aware of this trend. Sadly, I have met several parents who chose a name on this list, thinking that it was exclusively male. A few years later, they were stunned to learn that there were three little girls in their son's kindergarten class with the exact same name.

And, that, ultimately, is the only pitfall of unisex names - they don't "announce" your child's gender the way most conventional names do. Nevertheless, these names are definitely hot and trendy - and well worth a second look.

Addison & Alpha

Addison: (English): son of Adam
Alpha: (Greek): first-born child

Aspen & Avery

Aspen: (English): from the aspen tree
Avery: (English): wise ruler

Bailey & Blair

Bailey: (English): bailiff, steward, public official
Blair: (Irish & Celtic): from the plain, (Gaelic): child of the fields; (Scottish): peat moss

Blaine & Blake

Blaine: (Gaelic, Irish & Celtic): thin
Blake: (English): pale blond or dark; (Scottish): dark-haired

Blue & Brady

Blue: (English): the color blue
Brady: (Irish): a large-breasted woman

Brett & Brice

Brett: (French, English & Celtic): a native of Brittany
Brice/Bryce: (Welsh): alert, ambitious

Camden & Cameron

Camden/Camdyn: (Irish, Scottish, English & Gaelic): from the winding valley
Cameron: (Irish & Gaelic): crooked nose

Campbell & Cary

Campbell: (Gaelic): crooked mouth; (French): from the beautiful field
Cary/Carey: (Greek): pure

Chris & Clancy

Chris: (English & Irish): follower of Christ
Clancy/Clancey: (Celtic): son of the red-haired warrior

Cleo & Coby

Cleo/Clio: (Greek): to praise, acclaim
Coby/Koby/Kobe: (Hebrew): supplanter

Cody & Cory

Cody: (English): cushion
Corey/Cory: (Irish): from the hollow, of the churning waters

Dale & Drew

Dale: (German): valley; (English): lives in the valley
Drew: (Greek): courageous, valiant

Derry & Dakota

Derry: (English, Irish, German & Gaelic): red-haired, from the oak grove
Dakota: (Native American): friend to all

Easton & Ellison

Easton: (English): from east town
Ellison: (English): son of Elias

Ellory & Emerson

Ellory/Ellery: (Cornish): resembling a swan
Emerson: (English): brave, powerful

Emery & Gale

Emery: (German): industrious
Gale/Gail/Gayle: (English): merry, lively

Finley & Flynn

Finley: (Irish): blond-haired soldier
Flynn: (Irish): heir to the red-head; ruddy complexion

Garnet & Gentry

Garnet: (English): gem, armed with a spear; (French): keeper of grain
Gentry: (English): gentleman

Hadley & Hagen

Hadley: (English & Irish): from the heath covered meadow
Hagen: (Gaelic): youthful

Halsey & Harlow

Halsey: (English): Hal's island
Harlow: (English): from the army on the hill

Harper & Haven

Harper: (English): one who plays or makes harps
Haven: (English): safe place

Hayden & Hunter

Hayden: (English): from the hedged valley
Hunter: (English): hunter

Jai & Jamie

Jai: (Tai): heart
Jamie: (Spanish): supplanter

Jensen & Jordan

Jensen: (Scandinavian): God is gracious
Jordan: (Hebrew): to flow down; (Israel): descendant

Kacey & Keaton

Kacey/Casey: (Irish): brave
Keaton: (English): from the town of hawks

Kelsey & Kendall

Kelsey: (English): from the island of ships
Kendall: (English & Celtic): from the bright valley

Kent & Kennedy

Kent: (English & Welsh): white; (Celtic): chief
Kennedy: (Gaelic): a helmeted chief

Kerry & Kim

Kerry: (Irish): dark-haired
Kim: (Vietnamese): as precious as gold; (Welsh): leader

Kimball & Kinsey

Kimball: (Greek): hollow vessel
Kinsey: (English): victorious prince

Kirby & Kyle

Kirby: (Scandinavian): church village
Kyle: (Irish): attractive

Lane & Lee

Laine/Lane: (English): narrow road
Lee/Leigh: (English): meadow

Landon & Linden

Landon: (English): from the long hill
Linden: (English): from linden hill

London & Lynn

London/Londyn: (English): capital of England; fortress of the moon
Lynn(e): (English): waterfall

Mackenzie & Marlowe

Mackenzie: (Scottish): son of Kenzie
Marlowe: (English): from the hill by the lake

McKenzie & McKinley

McKenzie: (Irish): fair, favored one
McKinley: (English): offspring of the fair hero

Mica & Monroe

Mika/Micah: (Finnish): like God; (Japanese): new moon
Monroe: (Gaelic): from the red swamp; (Scottish): from the river; (Irish): near the river roe

Morgan & Murphy

Morgan: (Celtic): lives by the sea; (Welsh): bright sea
Murphy: (Irish): sea warrior

O'Shea & Orion

O'Shea: (Irish): child of Shea
Orion: (Greek): a hunter in Greek mythology

Page & Parker

Page/Paige: (French): youthful assistant
Parker: (English): keeper of the park

Paris & Pembroke

Paris: (Persian): angelic face; (Greek): downfall; (French): the capital city of France
Pembroke: (Welsh): headland

Peyton & Presley

Peyton: (English): from the village of warriors
Presley: (English): priest's land

Quincy & Quinn

Quincy: (English): fifth-born child; (French): estate belonging to Quintus
Quinn: (Celtic): queenly; (Gaelic): one who provides counsel

Rain & Reese

Rain: (American): blessings from above; (Latin): ruler; (English): lord, wise
Reese/Reece: (English &Welsh): ardent, fiery, enthusiastic

Randy & Remi

Randy: (German): the wolf shield
Remi/Remy: (French): oarsman or rower, from Rheims

Rene & Riley

Rene/Renee: (French): reborn
Riley: (English): from the rye clearing; (Irish): a small stream

Rio & River

Rio: (Spanish & Portuguese): river
River: (Latin & French): stream, water

Rory & Rowan

Rory: (Irish): famous brilliance, famous ruler; (Gaelic): red-haired
Rowan: (Irish): red-haired; (English & Gaelic): from the rowan tree

Rylan & Saige

Rylan/Ryland: (English): the place where rye is grown
Saige/Sage: (English & French): wise one; (English): from the spice

Sailor & Santana

Sailor: (American): sailor
Santana: (Spanish): saintly

Shane & Shawn

Shane: (Hebrew): gift from God; (Irish): God is gracious
Shawn: (Irish): a form of Sean, which means God is gracious

Sheridan & Shiloh

Sheridan: (Irish, English & Celtic): untamed; (Gaelic): bright, a seeker
Shiloh: (Hebrew): he who was sent, God's gift, the one to whom it belongs; (Israel): peaceful

Silver & Sloan

Silver: (English): precious metal, the color silver
Sloan: (English): raid; (Irish, Celtic, Scottish & Gaelic): fighter, warrior

Spencer & Stormy

Spencer/Spenser: (English): dispenser of provisions
Storm/Stormy: (English): tempest; (American): impetuous nature

Sydney & Tai

Sydney: (English): wide island
Tai: (Chinese): large; (Vietnamese): prosperous

Teagen & Toby

Teagan: (Gaelic): handsome, attractive
Toby: (Hebrew): God is good

Unique & Whitley

Unique: (Latin): only one; (American): unlike others
Whitley: (English): from the white meadow

Chapter 17. Popular Names for African-American Twins

In a country as large and diverse as the United States, parents often choose baby names that honor their cultural heritage and family traditions. By doing so, they bring a depth and richness to our society that is fresh and exciting. We will explore these trends in this chapter by presenting the most popular names for twins in African-American households (in states that break down this information by race).

The Most Popular Names for African American Twins - Boys

Anel & Elon

Anel: (Greek): messenger of God, angel
Elon: (Biblical & African American): spirit, God loves me

Alonzo & Anthony

Alonzo: (Spanish & American): ready for battle
Anthony: (English & Biblical): worthy of praise

Demarco & Dion

Demarco: (African American): of Mark: (South African): warlike
Dion: (Greek & French): mountain of Zeus; (African American): God

Darius & Demond

Darius: (Greek): kingly, wealthy; (American): pharaoh
Demond: (African American): of man

Caleb & Cameron

Caleb: (Israel): faithful; (Hebrew): dog or bold
Cameron: (Irish & Gaelic): crooked nose

Christian & Chikae

Christian: (English & Irish): follower of Christ
Chikae: (African American): God's power

Christopher & Lamar

Christopher: (Biblical): Christ-bearer; (English): he who holds Christ in his heart
Lamar: (German): famous land; (French): of the sea

Daniel & David

Daniel: (Hebrew & Biblical): God is my judge; (Irish & Welsh): attractive
David: (Hebrew, Scottish & Welsh): beloved

Elijah & Ethan

Elijah: (Biblical): the Lord is my God; (Hebrew): Jehovah is God
Ethan: (Hebrew & Biblical): firm, strong

Gabriel & Isaiah

Gabriel: (Israel): hero of God; (Hebrew): man of God; (Spanish): God is my strength
Isaiah: (Hebrew): the Lord is generous; (Israel): salvation by God

James & Jordan

James: (English): supplant, replace; (Israel): supplanter
Jordan: (Hebrew): to flow down; (Israel): descendant

Jayden & Jaylen

Jayden: (American): God has heard
Jaylen: (English); to rejoice

Jeremiah & Josiah

Jeremiah: (Hebrew): may Jehovah exalt; (Israel): sent by God
Josiah: (Hebrew): Jehovah has healed; (Israel): God has healed

Joseph & Joshua

Joseph: (Biblical): God will increase; (Hebrew): may Jehovah add/give
Joshua: (Hebrew & Biblical): Jehovah saves

Justin & Kevin

Justin: (English & French): just, true; (Irish): judicious
Kevin: (Irish & Gaelic): handsome, beautiful; (Celtic): gentle

Malik & Nathan

Malik: (African & Arabic): king, master
Nathan: (Hebrew & Israel): gift of God

Taye & Tyler

Taye: (Ethiopian): one who has been seen
Tyler: (English): maker of tiles

Matthew & Michael

Matthew: (Hebrew & Biblical): gift of the Lord
Michael: (Biblical & Hebrew): like God

William & Xavier

William: (English, German & French): protector
Xavier: (Basque): owner of a new house; (Arabic): one who is bright

The Most Popular Names for African American Twins - Girls

Aisha & Aaliyah

Aisha/Aiesha: (African): womanly, lively; (Muslim): life, lively
Aaliyah/Aliyah: (Arabic): an ascender; (Muslim): exalted; (American): immigrant to a new home

Alexandra & Alexis

Alexandra: (Greek, English & Latin America): defender of mankind
Alexis: (English): helper, defender; (Biblical): protector of mankind

Aniyah & Amaya

Aniyah: (Polish & Hebrew): God has shown favor
Amaya: (Japanese & Arabic): night rain

Alyssa & Angel

Alyssa: (Greek): logical
Angel: (Spanish & Greek): angelic

Brianna & Beyonce

Brianna: (Irish): strong; (Celtic & English): she ascends
Beyonce: (English & American): one who surpasses others

Destiny & Diamond

Destiny: (English): fate
Diamond: (English): bridge protector; (Greek): unbreakable

Gabrielle & Chloe

Gabrielle: (French): strength of God
Chloe: (Greek): verdant, blooming

Hannah & Haylee

Hannah: (English & Hebrew): favor, grace; (Biblical): grace of God
Haylee: (English): from the hay meadow, hero

Imani & Isis

Imani: (Kenya): faith
Isis: (Egyptian): most powerful goddess

Jayla & Jada

Jayla: (Arabia): charity; (African American): one who is special
Jada: (Israel): wise

Jasmine & Jordan

Jasmine: (Persian): a climbing plant; (English): a fragrant flower
Jordan: (Hebrew): to flow down; (Israel): descendant

Kayla & Layla

Kayla: (Irish & Greek): pure and beloved
Layla: (Arabic): beauty of the night

Kennedy & Kiara

Kennedy: (Gaelic): a helmeted chief
Kiara: (Irish): small and dark

Madison & Makayla

Madison: (English): son of Matthew
Makayla: (English & Irish): like God

Nevaeh & Davina

Nevaeh: (American): gift from God, heaven spelled backwards
Davina: (Scottish): feminine form of David, which means beloved one

Tamara & Tiana

Tamara: (Hebrew): palm tree; (Israel): spice
Tiana: (Greek): princess

Taylor & Trinity

Taylor: (English & French): a tailor
Trinity: (Latin): the holy three

Sydney & Serena

Sydney: (French): from Saint Denis
Serena: (Latin): peaceful disposition; (African American): calm, tranquil

Zakiyyah & Lakeisha

Zakiyyah: (Muslim): sharp, intellectual, pious, pure
Lakeisha: (American): joyful, happy

Chapter 18. Popular Names for Hispanic Twins

On a practical basis, this chapter continues the theme that we started in Chapter 17 - it presents the most popular names for twins in Hispanic households (in states that break down this information by race). The selections include a fascinating mix of old and new favorites that blend the richness of the Spanish culture with a decidedly American flair.

The Most Popular Names for Hispanic Twins - Boys

Alonzo & Alejandro

Alonzo: (Spanish & American): ready for battle
Alejandro: (Spanish): defender of mankind

Agustin & Alexander

Agustin: (Spanish): majestic dignity
Alexander: (Greek): protector of mankind

Angel & Andres

Angel: (Spanish & Greek): angelic
Andres: (Spanish): manly, courageous

Aaron & Adrian

Aaron: (Jewish & Hebrew): enlightened
Adrian: (German, Spanish & Italian): dark

Alex & Axel

Alex: (Greek): protector of mankind
Axel: (German & Hebrew): father of peace; (German): source of all life

Alan & David

Alan: (English & Irish): handsome; (Celtic): harmony, stone or noble
David: (Hebrew, Scottish & Welsh): beloved

Benjamin & Nicolas

Benjamin: (English, Hebrew & Biblical): son of my right hand
Nicolas: (Greek): victorious people

Bruno & Bautista

Bruno: (German): brown-haired
Bautista: (Italian): John the Baptist

Carlos & Christopher

Carlos: (Spanish): a free man
Christopher: (Biblical): Christ-bearer; (English): he who holds Christ in his heart

Dante & Dylan

Dante: (Latin): enduring, everlasting
Dylan: (English & Welsh): born from the ocean, son of the wave; (Gaelic): faithful

Damian & Diego

Damian: (Greek): one who tames others
Diego: (Spanish): Saint James

Emmanuel & Esteban

Emmanuel: (Hebrew): God with us
Esteban: (Spanish): crowned in victory

Emiliano & Leonardo

Emiliano: (Italian & Latin): rival, industrious
Leonardo: (German): brave as a lion

Fernando & Francisco

Fernando: (Spanish): daring, adventurous
Francisco: (Spanish): a man from France, free

Facundo & Felipe

Facundo: (Spanish): significant, eloquent
Felipe: (Spanish): one who loves horses

Gabriel & Geronimo

Gabriel: (Israel): hero of God; (Hebrew): man of God; (Spanish): God is my strength
Geronimo: (Greek & Italian): a famous chef

Gael & Iker

Gael: (English): merry, lively
Iker: (Spanish): visitation

Ian & Isaac

Ian: (Scottish): gift from God
Isaac: (Biblical): he will laugh

Javier & Jesus

Javier: (Spanish): owner of a new house
Jesus: (Hebrew): God is my salvation

Julian & Joaquin

Julian: (Spanish, French & Greek): youthful
Joaquin: (Hebrew): God will establish

Juan & Pablo

Juan: (Hebrew): gift from God; (Spanish): God is gracious
Pablo: (Spanish): borrowed

Juan Jose & Juan Pablo

Juan Jose: (Spanish): God has given/God shall add
Juan Pablo: (Spanish): God is gracious/borrowed

Lucas & Lorenzo

Lucas: (Gaelic, English & Latin America): light
Lorenzo: (Italian & Spanish): crowned with laurel

Maximiliano & Matias

Maximiliano: (Italian): greatest
Matias: (Spanish & Hebrew): gift of God

Martin & Mateo

Martin: (Latin): dedicated to Mars, the god of war
Mateo: (Italian): gift of God Nicolas:

Manuel & Miguel

Manuel: (Spanish): God is with us
Miguel: (Spanish): like God

Rodrigo & Rafael

Rodrigo: (Spanish): famous ruler
Rafael: (Spanish): one who is healed by God

Sebastian & Santiago

Sebastian: (Greek): the revered one
Santiago: (Spanish): named for Saint James

Santino & Samuel

Santino: (Italian): little angel
Samuel: (Israel): God hears; (Hebrew): name of God

Tomas & Thiago

Tomas: (German): a form of Thomas, which means twin
Thiago: (Spanish, Portuguese & Brazilian): Saint James

Valentino & Emilio

Valentino: (Italian): brave or strong; (Latin America): health or love
Emilio: (Spanish): flattering

The Most Popular Names for Hispanic Twins - Girls

Ariana & Antonella

Ariana: (Greek & Italian): holy
Antonella: (Latin America): praiseworthy

Alma & Alexa

Alma: (Latin & Italian): nurturing, kind
Alexa: (Greek, English & Latin America): defender of mankind

Andrea & Alejandra

Andrea: (Greek & Latin): courageous, strong
Alejandra: (Spanish): defender of mankind

Antonia & Agustina

Antonia: (Greek): flourishing or flowering
Agustina: (Latin America): majestic, grand

Abigail & Amanda

Abigail: (Hebrew): father rejoiced; (Biblical): source of joy
Amanda: (Latin): much loved

Ana & Abril

Ana: (Hebrew): favor or grace; (Native American): mother; (Israel): gracious
Abril: (Spanish): April

Allison & Zoe

Allison: (English): noble, truthful, strong character
Zoe: (Greek): life, alive

Bianca & Camila

Bianca: (Italian): white, fair
Camila: (Italian): a noble virgin, a ceremonial attendant

Catalina & Constanza

Catalina: (Spanish): pure
Constanza: (American): strong-willed

Carla & Clara

Carla: (Portuguese & Latin America): strong one
Clara: (French & Catalonia): clear, bright

Danna & Daniela

Danna: (Indian): gift
Daniela: (Hebrew & Spanish): God is my judge

Emilia & Elisa

Emilia: (Spanish): flattering
Elisa: (Hebrew): my God is bountiful

Emily & Elena

Emily: (Latin America): admiring
Elena: (Spanish): the shining light

Emma & Julia

Emma: (English, Danish & German): whole, complete, universal
Julia: (French): youthful; (Latin America): soft-haired, youthful

Fabiana & Fiorella

Fabiana: (Latin): bean grower
Fiorella: (Italian): little flower

Fernanda & Guadalupe

Fernanda: (Spanish): adventurous
Guadalupe: (Spanish): from the valley of wolves

Gabriella & Isabella

Gabriella: (Israel & Hebrew): God gives strength; (Italian): woman of God
Isabella: (Hebrew): devoted to God; (Spanish): God is bountiful; (Biblical): consecrated to God

Ivana & Luciana

Ivana: (Slavic): God is gracious
Luciana: (Latin America): bringer of light

Julieta & Jazmin

Julieta: (French): youthful, young at heart
Jazmin: (Japanese): the flower

Juliana & Josephina

Juliana: (Spanish): soft-haired
Josefina: (Hebrew): God will add

Lucia & Luna

Lucia: (Latin America): bringer of light
Luna: (Latin & Latin America): the moon

Monserrat & Magdalena

Monserrat: (Latin): jagged mountain
Magdalena: (Hebrew): from the tower; (Spanish): bitter

Maite & Mia

Maite: (Spanish): loved
Mia: (Italian): my; (Biblical): mine

Michelle & Maria

Michelle: (French & Hebrew): like God, close to God
Maria: (Latin): bitter

Mariana & Martina

Mariana: (French): bitter
Martina: (Latin America): warlike

Noa & Natalia

Noa: (Israel): movement
Natalia: (French): to be born at Christmas; (Slovakian): to be born

Nicole & Olivia

Nicole: (French): victory of the people
Olivia: (Spanish & Italian): olive; (Biblical): peace of the olive tree

Paola & Paula

Paola: (Italian): little
Paula: (Latin America): small

Regina & Renata

Regina: (Italian, Spanish & Latin America): queen
Renata: (French): a form of Renee, which means reborn

Romina & Rafaella

Romina: (Arabian): from the Christian land
Rafaella: (Hebrew): healed by God

Sofia & Salome

Sofia: (Greek & Biblical): wisdom
Salome: (Hebrew): peace and tranquility

Sara & Samantha

Sara(h): (Hebrew, Spanish & Biblical): princess
Samantha: (Hebrew & Biblical): listener of God

Ximena & Valery

Ximena: (Greek): heroine
Valery: (French): brave, fierce one; (English): strong, valiant

Victoria & Valentina

Victoria: (Latin America): winner
Valentina: (Spanish & Italian): brave; (Latin America): health or love

Violeta & Valeria

Violeta: (Bulgarian): violet
Valeria: (French): brave, fierce one; (English): strong, valiant

Chapter 19. Popular Names for Asian Twins

In this chapter, we present the most popular names for Asian twins in the last decade (in states that break down this information by race). These eclectic choices, which reflect the amazing history and culture of China, Japan, and Korea, are intriguing options for parents who seek distinctive names from a traditional part of the world.

The Most Popular Chinese Names for Twins - Boys

An & Chung

An: (Chinese): peaceful
Chung: (Chinese): intelligent

Dai & Fai

Dai: (Chinese): sword technique
Fai: (Chinese): beginning to fly

Fa & Feng

Fa: (Chinese): setting off
Feng: (Chinese): sharp blade

Gan & Gen

Gan: (Chinese): dare, adventure
Gen: (Chinese): root

Geming & Guang

Geming: (Chinese): revolution
Guang: (Chinese): light

He & Heng

He: (Chinese): yellow river
Heng: (Chinese): eternal

Hong & Hop

Hong: (Chinese): wild swan
Hop: (Chinese): agreeable

Huan & Hung

Huan: (Chinese): happiness
Hung: (Chinese): brave

Jin & Jiang

Jin: (Chinese): gold
Jiang: (Chinese): fire

Lei & Li

Lei: (Chinese): thunder
Li: (Chinese): having great strength

Liang & Liu

Liang: (Chinese): good man
Liu: (Chinese): one who is quiet and peaceful

Park & Ping

Park: (Chinese): the cypress tree
Ping: (Chinese): stable

Qiang & Qiu

Qiang: (Chinese): strong
Qiu: (Chinese): autumn

Shan & Shen

Shan: (Chinese): mountain
Shen: (Chinese): deep spiritual thought

Xiu & You

Xiu: (Chinese): cultivated
You: (Chinese): friend

Zhen & Zian

Zhen: (Chinese): astonished
Zian: (Chinese): peace

The Most Popular Chinese Names for Twins - Girls

Bo & Chun

Bo: (Chinese): precious
Chun: (Chinese): springtime

Fang & Far

Fang: (Chinese): fragrant
Far: (Chinese): flower

Hua & Huan

Hua: (Chinese): flower
Huan: (Chinese): happiness

Jia & Jiao

Jia: (Chinese): beautiful
Jiao: (Chinese): dainty

Jing & Lan

Jing: (Chinese): stillness, luxurious
Lan: (Chinese): orchid

Li & Lien

Li: (Chinese): upright
Lien: (Chinese): lotus

Lin & Ling

Lin: (Chinese): resembling jade
Ling: (Chinese): dainty

Meili & Mingzhu

Meili: (Chinese): beautiful
Mingzhu: (Chinese): bright pearl

Nuo & Ping

Nuo: (Chinese): graceful
Ping: (Chinese): peaceful

Qi & Qiang

Qi: (Chinese): fine jade
Qiang: (Chinese): beautiful rose

Qing & Ting

Qing: (Chinese): dark blue
Ting: (Chinese): graceful and slim

Rong & Song

Rong: (Chinese): martial
Song: (Chinese): pine tree

Xiang & Xiu

Xiang: (Chinese): pleasant fragrance
Xiu: (Chinese): grace

Wen & Yin

Wen: (Chinese): refinement
Yin: (Chinese): silver

The Most Popular Japanese Names for Twins - Boys

Aki & Amida

Aki: (Japanese): autumn, bright
Amida: (Japanese): Buddha

Dai & Daiki

Dai: (Japanese): sword technique
Daiki: (Japanese): of great value

Hiro & Hiromi

Hiro: (Japanese): widespread
Hiromi: (Japanese): widespread beauty; wide-seeing

Isamu & Isas

Isamu: (Japanese): courageous
Isas: (Japanese): meritorious

Jiro & Jo

Jiro: (Japanese): second son
Jo: (Japanese): God will increase

Jun & Kiyoshi

Jun: (Japanese): truthful
Kiyoshi: (Japanese): quiet one

Kuo & Kuro

Kuo: (Japanese): approval
Kuro: (Japanese): ninth son

Naoki & Naoko

Naoki: (Japanese): honest tree
Naoko: (Japanese): honest

Nobu & Norio

Nobu: (Japanese): faith
Norio: (Japanese): man of principles

Raiden & Ringo

Raiden: (Japanese): god of thunder and lightning
Ringo: (Japanese): peace be with you

Ronin & Tama

Ronin: (Japanese): samurai without a master
Tama: (Japanese): jewel

Shin & Shiro

Shin: (Japanese): truth
Shiro: (Japanese): fourth-born son

The Most Popular Japanese Names for Twins - Girls

Aki & Aika

Aki: (Japanese): born in autumn
Aika: (Japanese): love song

Ame & Anka

Ame: (Japanese): rain, heaven
Anka: (Japanese): color of the dawn

Fujita & Fuyu

Fujita: (Japanese): field
Fuyu: (Japanese): born in winter

Hachi & Haya

Hachi: (Japanese): eight, good luck
Haya: (Japanese): quick, light

Kama & Kana

Kama: (Japanese): one who loves and is loved
Kana: (Japanese): dexterity and skill

Kayo & Kenja

Kayo: (Japanese): beautiful
Kenja: (Japanese): a sage

Kin & Kita

Kin: (Japanese): golden
Kita: (Japanese): north

Ko & Kono

Ko: (Japanese): filial piety
Kono: (Japanese): dexterity and skill

Kuma & Kosame

Kuma: (Japanese): bear, mouse
Kosame: (Japanese): fine rain

Mako & Mana

Mako: (Japanese): truth, grateful
Mana: (Japanese): truth

Midori & Mizuki

Midori: (Japanese): green
Mizuki: (Japanese): beautiful moon

Nami & Naoki

Nami: (Japanese): wave
Naoki: (Japanese): honest tree

Nishi & Noriko

Nishi: (Japanese): west
Noriko: (Japanese): child of principles

Raeden & Rippina

Raeden: (Japanese): thunder and lightning
Rippina: (Japanese): brilliant light

Sada & Sato

Sada: (Japanese): pure
Sato: (Japanese): sugar

Sayo & Shima

Sayo: (Japanese): born at night
Shima: (Japanese): true intention

Taka & Tama

Taka: (Japanese): borrowed
Tama: (Japanese): precious stone

Tomoko & Tomiko

Tomoko: (Japanese): two friends
Tomiko: (Japanese): wealthy

Yumiko & Yukiko

Yumiko: (Japanese): beautiful and helpful child
Yukiko: (Japanese): happy child

The Most Popular Korean Names for Twins - Boys

Bae & Dae

Bae: (Korean): inspiration
Dae: (Korean): great

Chin & Cho

Chin: (Korean): precious
Cho: (Korean): beautiful

Eui & Eun

Eui: (Korean): righteousness
Eun: (Korean): silver

Hea & Hee

Hea: (Korean): grace
Hee: (Korean): brightness

Dong & Nam

Dong: (Korean): the east
Nam: (Korean): south

Hyo & Hyun

Hyo: (Korean): filial duty
Hyun: (Korean): wisdom

Ki & Kwan

Ki: (Korean): arise
Kwan: (Korean): bold character

Kyong & Kyu

Kyong: (Korean): brightness
Kyu: (Korean): standard

Mee & Min

Mee: (Korean): beauty
Min: (Korean): cleverness

Joo & Soo

Joo: (Korean): jewel
Soo: (Korean): excellent, long life

Yeo & Young

Yeo: (Korean): mildness
Young: (Korean): forever, unchanging

The Most Popular Korean Names for Twins - Girls

Hae & Hye

Hae: (Korean): ocean
Hye: (Korean): graceful

Ja & Ki

Ja: (Korean): attractive, fiery
Ki: (Korean): arisen

Yeo & Yon

Yeo: (Korean): mild
Yon: (Korean): lotus blossom

Chapter 20: The Evolution of Names Since 1900

While reading this book, you have probably wondered how (and why) names have evolved over time - and why some of your choices sound really strange to your parents and grandparents. In Chapter 2, we listed the most popular names for twins in the United States in 2014. In this chapter, we will take a look back at the same data for three separate generations: those born in 1900, 1950, and 2000.

This exercise is fun for several reasons. First, it will allow you to see the types of names that were popular when your parents and grandparents were making the same decisions that you are making today (when no one, and I mean, *no one*, named their baby Axel). Second, it reveals the names that are truly timeless - and those that only stayed popular for a few years. Third, it may spark your interest in names that you might otherwise not have considered, either for your twins' first or middle names. Finally, at the end of this chapter, we offer a brief glimpse into the latest naming trends for 2014, which could possibly become the next generation's "traditional" names. You've come this far on your search for the perfect names - it's worth taking a few moments to look back at some genuine classics.

Most Popular Turn-of-the-Century Twin Names (1900) - Boys

John & James

John: (Israel): God is gracious; Jehovah has been gracious
James: (English); supplant, replace; (Israel): supplanter

Charles & Clarence

Charles: (English): strong, manly
Clarence: (English & Latin America): clear, luminous

Arthur & Albert

Arthur: (English): bear, stone
Albert: (English & German): noble, bright

Richard & Robert

Richard: (English, French & German): a strong and powerful ruler
Robert: (English, French, German & Scottish): famed, bright, shining

William & Walter

William: (English, German & French): protector
Walter: (German): army general, rules the people

Henry & Harry

Henry: (English, German & French): rules his household
Harry: (German): home or house ruler

Edward & Ernest

Edward: (English): wealthy guardian; (German): strong as a boar
Ernest: (German): serious, determined, truth

Frank & Fred

Frank: (Latin America): free
Fred: (German): peaceful ruler

David & Joseph

David: (Hebrew, Scottish & Welsh): beloved
Joseph: (Biblical): God will increase; (Hebrew): may Jehovah add/give

George & Thomas

George: (English): farmer
Thomas: (Greek & Hebrew): a twin

Samuel & Louis

Samuel: (Israel): God hears; (Hebrew): name of God
Louis: (French): famous warrior

Roy & Roger

Roy: (Irish & French): king, regal; (Scottish, Gaelic & Scottish): red, red-haired
Roger: (German): renowned spearman

Most Popular Turn-of-the-Century Twin Names (1900) - Girls

Anna/Annie & Alice

Anna/Ana: (Hebrew): favor or grace; (Native American): mother; (Israel): gracious
Alice: (Spanish): of the nobility

Mary & Margaret

Mary: (Biblical, English & Slovakian): bitter
Margaret: (Greek & Latin America): a pearl

Clara & Cora

Clara: (French & Catalonia): clear, bright
Cora: (Greek & English): maiden; (Scottish): seething pool

Carrie & Grace

Carrie: (American): melody, song
Grace/Gracie: (Latin America): grace of God; (American): land of grace

Emma & Elizabeth

Emma: (English, Danish & German): whole, complete, universal
Elizabeth: (English): my God is bountiful; (Hebrew & Biblical): consecrated to God

Bertha & Ethel

Bertha: (German): bright
Ethyl: (English): noble

Minnie & Mabel

Minnie: (Irish): bitter; (Hebrew): wished for a child
Mabel: (English): lovable, beautiful

Florence & Ida

Florence: (English): flowering; (Latin America): prosperous
Ida: (English): hardworking

Martha & Helen

Martha: (Israel): lady
Helen: (Greek): light

Sarah & Ella

Sara(h): (Hebrew, Spanish & Biblical): princess
Ella: (English); beautiful fairy; (Spanish): she

Bessie & Nellie

Bessie: (Hebrew, English & Israel): oath of God, God is satisfaction
Nellie: (English): torch

Laura & Maude

Laura: (English, Spanish & Latin America): crowned with laurel, from the laurel tree
Maude: (French): strong in war; (Irish): strong battle maiden

Most Popular Mid-Century Twin Names (1950) - Boys

James & John

James: (English); supplant, replace; (Israel): supplanter
John: (Israel): God is gracious; Jehovah has been gracious

Jeffrey & Joseph

Jeffrey: (French, Germany & English): divine peace
Joseph: (Biblical): God will increase; (Hebrew): may Jehovah add/give

Gary & George

Gary: (German & English): spear
George: (English): farmer

Robert & Richard

Robert: (English, French, German & Scottish): famed, bright, shining
Richard: (English, French & Germany): a strong and powerful ruler

David & Daniel

David: (Hebrew, Scottish & Welsh): beloved
Daniel: (Hebrew & Biblical): God is my judge; (Irish & Welsh): attractive

Donald & Dennis

Donald: (Celtic & Gaelic): dark stranger; (Irish, Scottish & English): mighty leader
Dennis: (Greek): wild, frenzied

Thomas & Timothy

Thomas: (Hebrew, Greek & Dutch): twin
Timothy: (Greek & English): to honor God

Mark & Michael

Mark: (Latin America): warlike
Michael: (Biblical & Hebrew): like God

William & Charles

William: (English, German & French): protector
Charles: (English): strong, manly

Stephen & Kenneth

Stephen: (English & Greek): crowned one
Kenneth: (Celtic, Scottish & Irish): handsome; (English): royal obligation

Paul & Edward

Paul: (English & French): small, apostle in the bible
Edward: (English): wealthy guardian; (German): strong as a boar

Ronald & Larry

Ronald: (English, Gaelic & Scottish): rules with counsel
Larry: (Dutch & Latin America): laurels

Most Popular Mid-Century Twin Names (1950) - Girls

Mary & Margaret

Mary: (Biblical, English & Slovakian): bitter
Margaret: (Greek & Latin America): a pearl

Karen & Kathy

Karen: (Greek): pure
Kathy: (English, Irish & French): diminutive of Katherine, which means pure

Barbara & Brenda

Barbara: (Latin America): stranger
Brenda: (Gaelic): little raven; (Scandinavian): sword

Deborah & Donna

Deborah: (Hebrew & Israel): honey bee
Donna: (Italian): lady

Cheryl & Carolyn

Cheryl: (English): beloved
Carolyn: (English): joy, song of happiness

Susan & Sharon

Susan: (Israel): lily
Sharon: (Hebrew & Israel): a flat clearing

Sandra & Cynthia

Sandra: (Greek): helper of humanity; (English): unheeded prophetess
Cynthia: (Greek): moon

Patricia & Pamela

Patricia: (Spanish & Latin America): noble
Pamela: (Greek, English & Indian): honey

Janet & Janice

Janet: (Hebrew & English): gift from God
Janice: (Hebrew): gift from God; (Israel): God is gracious

Linda & Nancy

Linda: (Spanish): pretty; (English): lime tree; (German): snake, lime tree
Nancy: (Hebrew & English): grace

Carol & Diane

Carol: (French): melody, song
Diane: (Greek): divine, goddess of the moon

Ann & Elizabeth

Anne: (Hebrew & Israel): favor or grace
Elizabeth: (English): my God is bountiful; (Hebrew & Biblical): consecrated to God

Most Popular Turn-of-the-Century Twin Names (2000) - Boys

Michael & Matthew

Michael: (Biblical & Hebrew): like God
Matthew: (Hebrew & Biblical): gift of the Lord

Joshua & Jacob

Joshua: (Hebrew & Biblical): Jehovah saves
Jacob: (Biblical): supplanter; (Hebrew): he grasps the heel

John & Joseph

John: (Israel): God is gracious; Jehovah has been gracious
Joseph: (Biblical): God will increase; (Hebrew): may Jehovah add/give

Christopher & Nicholas

Christopher: (Biblical): Christ-bearer; (English): he who holds Christ in his heart
Nicholas: (Greek): victorious people

Alexander & Andrew

Alexander: (Greek): protector of mankind
Andrew: (English, Scottish & Biblical): manly; brave

Daniel & David

Daniel: (Hebrew & Biblical): God is my judge; (Irish & Welsh): attractive
David: (Hebrew, Scottish & Welsh): beloved

James & Justin

James: (English); supplant, replace; (Israel): supplanter
Justin: (English & French): just, true; (Irish): judicious

Tyler & Thomas

Tyler: (English): maker of tiles
Thomas: (Hebrew, Greek & Dutch): twin

Jason & Jonathan

Jason: (Greek): to heal
Jonathan: (Hebrew): Jehovah has given: (Israel): gift of God

Brandon & Dylan

Brandon: (Irish): little raven
Dylan: (English & Welsh): born from the ocean, son of the wave

Ryan & Ethan

Ryan: (Gaelic): little king; (Irish): kindly, young royalty
Ethan: (Hebrew & Biblical): firm, strong

Christian & Cameron

Christian: (English & Irish): follower of Christ
Cameron: (Irish & Gaelic): crooked nose

William & Anthony

William: (English, German & French): protector
Anthony: (English & Biblical): worthy of praise

Zachary & Benjamin

Zachary: (Hebrew & Israel): remembered by God
Benjamin: (English, Hebrew & Biblical): son of my right hand

Austin & Noah

Austin: (English): from the name Augustin, which means revered
Noah: (Biblical): rest, peace; (Hebrew): comfort, long-lived

Nathan & Hunter

Nathan: (Hebrew): he gives; (Israel): gift of God
Hunter: (English): one who hunts

Kevin & Robert

Kevin: (Irish & Gaelic): handsome, beautiful; (Celtic): gentle
Robert: (English, French, German & Scottish): famed, bright, shining

Samuel & Jordan

Jordan: (Hebrew): to flow down; (Israel): descendant
Samuel: (Israel): God hears; (Hebrew): name of God

Kyle & Logan

Kyle: (Gaelic): young; (Irish): young at heart
Logan: (Irish): small cove; (Scottish): Finnian's servant; (Gaelic): from the hollow

163

Most Popular Turn-of-the-Century Twin Names (2000) - Girls

Hannah & Emily

Hannah: (English & Hebrew): favor, grace; (Biblical): grace of God
Emily: (Latin America): admiring

Sarah & Alexis

Sara(h): (Hebrew, Spanish & Biblical): princess
Alexis: (English): helper, defender; (Biblical): protector of mankind

Madison & Brianna

Madison: (English): son of Matthew
Brianna/Breanna: (Irish): strong; (Celtic & English): she ascends

Kaylee & Kaitlyn

Kaylee: (American): pure
Kaitlyn: (Irish): pure

Ashley & Lauren

Ashley: (English & Biblical): lives in the ash tree
Lauren: (French): crowned with laurel

Elizabeth & Katherine

Elizabeth: (English): my God is bountiful; (Hebrew & Biblical): consecrated to God
Katherine/Kathryn: (Irish): clear; (English): pure; (Greek): pure, virginal

Hailey & Taylor

Hailey/Hailee/Haley/Haylee: (English): hero, field of hay
Taylor: (English & French): a tailor

Jessica & Jasmine

Jessica: (Israel): God is watching; (Hebrew): rich, God beholds
Jasmine: (Persian): a climbing plant; (English): a fragrant flower

Madeline & Makayla

Madeline: (Greek): high tower
Makayla: (English & Irish): like God

Anna & Abigail

Anna/Ana: (Hebrew): favor or grace; (Native American): mother; (Israel): gracious
Abigail: (Hebrew): father rejoiced; (Biblical): source of joy

Samantha & Brittany

Samantha: (Hebrew & Biblical): listener of God
Brittany: (English & Celtic): from Britain

Kayla & Alyssa

Kayla: (Irish): pure and beloved
Alyssa: (Greek): logical

Olivia & Nicole

Olivia: (Spanish & Italian): olive; (Biblical): peace of the olive tree
Nicole: (French): victory of the people

Meagan & Mackenzie

Meagan: (Irish): soft and gentle; (Greek): strong and mighty
Mackenzie/Mackinsey: (Irish & Scottish): fair, favored one

Destiny & Jennifer

Destiny: (English): fate
Jennifer: (English & Welsh): fair one; (English & Celtic): white wave

Emma & Rachel

Emma: (English, Danish & German): whole, complete, universal
Rachel: (Hebrew): ewe; (Israel): innocent lamb

Sydney & Megan

Sydney: (English): wide island
Megan: (Irish): soft and gentle; (Greek): strong and mighty

Looking ahead: Names that are Expected to Emerge in 2014

Angel & Bliss

Angel: (Spanish & Greek): angelic
Bliss: (English): joy, happiness

Charity & Deacon

Charity: (English): kindness, generous, goodwill
Deacon: (American): pastor; (English): dusty one, servant

Dharma & Ever

Dharma: (Indian): ultimate law of all things
Ever: (English): strong as a boar

Eden & Essence

Eden: (Hebrew): delight; (Israel): paradise
Essence: (English): scent

Peace & Genesis

Peace: (English): peaceful
Genesis: (Hebrew): origin, birth; (Israel): beginning

Harmony & Haven

Harmony: (Latin America): a beautiful blending
Haven: (English): safe place

Heaven & Honor

Heaven: (American): from the heavens
Honor: (Spanish & Irish): honor; (Latin America): integrity

Mercy & Paxton

Mercy: (English): compassion; (French): merciful
Paxton: (English): from the peaceful farm; (Latin America): town of peace

Pax & Serenity

Pax: (English): peaceful
Serenity: (English): peaceful disposition

Trinity & True

Trinity: (Latin): the holy three
True: (English): loyal

Chapter 21: Names with Similar Meanings

Throughout this book, we have listed the meaning of every name we have presented; we have also presented the same information for each of the 5,000 names in the appendix.

In this chapter, we have summarized a portion of that information for readers who are trying to select two names that have the same meaning. Bear in mind, translations vary widely among languages, which is why we encourage readers to further investigate their top choices, if meanings are important to them. With that in mind, these tables are a general guide to groupings of names that have similar - if not identical - meanings.

Boys Names That Mean "Strong"

Amos & Armstrong	Arnold & Barrett	Bernard & Bogart
Bjorn & Bryan	Carl & Charles	Carlo & Connor
Cornelius & Edward	Ethan & Everett	Harvey & Hartman
Kale & Ken	Jarrett & Malin	Pedro & Ricardo
Quinlan & Richard	Rico & Taurean	Valentino & Virgil

Girls Names That Mean "Strong"

Abira & Allison	Andres & Bree	Brianna & Bridget
Carla & Costanza	Carly & Drew	Ever & Isana
Mahogany & Miriam	Maude & Mena	Megan & Nina
Ondrea & Osita	Plato & Richelle	Valerie & Viveca

Boys Names That Mean "Brave"

Amos & Andre	Andrew & Bryan	Baldwin & Brendan
Conrad & Devlin	Dixon & Dre	Emerson & Everett
Garcia & Harding	Hardwin & Hillard	Hung & Kurt
Polo & Prewitt		

Girls Names That Mean "Brave"

Casey & Tracy	Emerson & Bernadette	Valentina & Valerie

Boys Names That Mean "Warrior"

Aloysius & Boris	Clancy & Cole	Duncan & Dustin
Gideon & Gunther	Hillard & Keelan	Kane & Keith
Kelly & Lewis	Ludwig & Luigi	Luis & Polo
Mackinley &Malin	Marcel & Murphy	Owen & Sloan

Girls Names That Mean "Warrior"

Eloise & Fiana	Gertrude & Imelda	Katniss & Kimball
Kelly & Murphy	Lois & Louise	Sloan & Trudy

Boys Names That Mean "Noble"

Adolph & Albert	Alan & Alvin	Alphonso & Ansel
Brian & Elgin	Dolph & Earl	Ellsworth & Elmer
Kareen & Knight	Grady & Nolan	Hirum & Odwin
Malloy & Patrick		

Girls Names That Mean "Noble"

Ada & Adelaide
Alison & Audrey
Elsa & Ethyl
Marquis & Patricia

Adele & Akela
Camille & Della
Heidi & Trisha

Alberta & Alicia
Earlene & Elmira
Lyra & Lecia

Boys Names That Mean "Bright"

Akiko & Albert
Englebert & Fulbright
Wilbur & Xavier

Bertram & Colbert
Robert & Robin
Zavier & Minh

Delbert & Elbert
Samson & Sheridan

Girls Names That Mean "Bright"

Alanis & Alberta
Claudette & Bertha
Shirley & Roberta

Candy & Clara
Electra & Phoebe
Ziva & Zahara

Claire & Clarise
Sheridan & Shula

Boys Names That Mean "Dark"

Adrian & Blackwell
Delaney & Dolan
Duff & Dugan
Maurice & Morrell

Black & Brown
Delano & Donal
Finias & Kerry
Morris & Sullivan

Cole & Dwayne
Douglas & Doyal
Kerwin & Kieran

Girls Names That Mean "Dark"

Blake & Bronwyn
Ebony & Keara
Adriana & Orin

Ciara & Maura
Keri & Layla

Darcy & Delaney
Maura & Melanie

Boys Names That Mean "Light"

Abner & Akiko
Finian & Izod
Lucas & Luka

Alvin & Ashton
Lambert & Lucian
Orly & Uri

Barak & Bertram
Luke & Lux

Girls Names That Mean "Light"

Aileen & Chiara
Ellen & Evelyn
Kenzie & Lucile
Lucy & Ming
Olena & Orle
Yitta & Zia

Eileen & Elaine
Helen & Helena
Lacretia & Letitia
Neriah & Nirel
Rhonwyn & Uriel

Elena & Elani
Helene & Ilene
Lucile & Lucinda
Noor & Nora
Yalena & Yelena

Boys Names That Mean "Enlightened or Wise"

Aaron & Aryn
Cato & Cornelius
Hakin & Rashad

Aldo & Alvin
Dallas & Reynold
Raymond & Thaddeus

Aldrich & Avery
Eldridge & Elvis
Sage & Socrates

Girls Names That Mean "Enlightened or Wise"

Athena & Avery	Freda & Jada	Medora & Minerva
Monique & Ophelia	Rae & Rain	Ramona & Rayna
Sage & Ulima		

Boys Names That Mean "Beautiful or Handsome"

Adonis & Beauregard	Kane & Keefe	Kevin & Kenneth
Naveen & Jamal	Alan & Bellamy	Hasani & Hussein
Jamar & Japheth	Cullem & Kitoko	McKenna & Teagen

Girls Names That Mean "Beautiful or Handsome"

Adina & Alaina	Alanna & Ayanna	Annabella & Arabella
Belinda & Bella	Callie & Calla	Calliope & Calista
Carolina & Carrington	Ella & Inga	Jacinta & Jaffa
Kaelyn & Keely	Lydia & Mabel	Maribel & Maybelline
Meadow & Miyo	Naveen & Neena	Rosalind & Sapphire
Shaina & Shakila	Siri & Serlina	Yaffah & Zaynah

Boys Names That Mean "Peace"

Amani & Axel	Geoffrey & Godfrey	Frederick & Humphrey
Ingram & Jefferson	Pax & Pace	Jeffrey & Manfred
Liu & Noah	Paxton & Salem	Shiloh & Siegfried
Solomon & Wilfred	Zigfred & Ziggy	

Girls Names That Mean "Peace"

Dove & Erin	Fia & Frida	Concordia & Fredericka
Irena & Lana	Malia & Irene	Olivia & Tully
Peace & Ping	Saloma & Serena	Serenity & Shiloh
Winetta & Xerena		

Names That Mean "Red"

Adam & Auburn	Clancy & Crimson	Derry & Flynn
Flann & Flynn	Redford & Ridley	Scarlett & Sienna
Reed & Roden	Rooney & Rory	Rowan & Rufus
Russell & Roja	Rusty & Monroe	Omri & Phoenix

Names That Mean "Fiery"

Aiden & Dobbs	Egan & Edana	Flame & Reese
Ignacious & Seraphina	Kagen & Keegan	McKenna & McKayla

Names That Mean "Bitter"

Mario & Annmarie	Magdalena & Marianna	Mali & Mara
Maria & Mariah	Marianne & Mariel	Marina & Marissa
Marlie & Marita	Marlene & Maureen	Mary & Meli
Minnie & Mitzi	Moira & Molly	Polly & Romy

Boys Names That Mean "Gift from God"

Hans & Ian
Juan & Matteo
Nathaniel & Theodore

Hansel & Jonas
Lathan & Nathan
Shane & Shiloh

Johann & Jonathan
Matthew & Mitchell
Thierry & Zane

Girls Names That Mean "Gift from God"

Dita & Dora
Jane & Joan
Neveah & Pheodora
Shona & Shonda

Dorothea & Eudora
Janice & Janine
Shea & Shane
Siobhan & Theodora

Dorothy & Isadora
Joanna & Juanita
Sheena & Shiloh

Boys Names That Mean "(God is) Gracious"

Chan & Hans
Ioan & Ivan
Jock & John
Sean & Shane

Elian & Giovanni
Jackson & Johann
Juan & Yan

Hansel & Jenson
Jan & Jean
Nino & Terrance

Girls Names That Mean "(God is) Gracious"

Anais & Anita
Gia & Gianna
Jana & Janae
Jane & Jean
Nanette & Shana

Anna & Annette
Giovanna & Jeanette
Janelle & Janessa
Jeannette & Joann
Shane & Shawn

Annika & Elisha
Ivana & Ivanka
Janice & Jeanne
Jensen & Jonna
Sheena & Winola

Names That Mean "Protector"

Alexander & Alistair
Lex & Liam
Sacha & Sigmund
Ramona & Xantara

Edmund & Elmo
Odon & Ramon
Warren & William
Liv & Willa

Fremont & Guillermo
Raymond & Zander
Alexis & Meredith

Names That Mean "Champion or Victorious"

Carlin & Carroll
Ajay & Vijay
Seigfried & Sigmund,
Brea & Jane
Eunice & Victoria

Kendrick & Neal
Kinsey & Nicholas
Victor & Vincent
Tori & Nia
Sigourney& Collette

Nigel & Roark
Niles & Nicolai
Zigfred & Ziggy
Neela & Nikita

Names That Mean "Joy or Happy"

Alaire & Asher
Abigail & Beatrice
Edith & Jovi
Merry & Rona
Blythe & Bunny

Winston & Denton
Joy & Bliss
Jovita & Jubilee
Tatum & Tisha
Felicia & Jocelyn

Felix & Sayed
Carolyn & Hillary
Lakeisha & Ranita
Olina & Rowena
Nara & Gay

Boys Names Relating "To The Sea"

Hurley & Lamar
Merrill & Morgan
Ocean & Seaman

Marlon & Marvin
Mortimer & Murdoch
Seaton & Zale

Merlin & Merrick
Murphy & Neptune

Girls Names Relating "To The Sea"

Bela & Chelsea
Ionia & Mariah
Marianne & Marika
Meredith & Muriel
Narelle & Narissa

Cordelia & Delores
Mali & Marin
Marina & Marissa
Meryl & Morgan
Pasha & Sula

Doris & Galilee
Mariana & Marietta
Maris & Maureen
Ula & Umiko

Names That Mean "Sun"

Asia & Dawn
Liane & Roxanne
Surya & Zelene
Ravi & Samson

Eldora & Kalina
Oriana & Sunshine
Zelia & Zora

Helene & Kira
Solana & Sorina
Apollo & Helio

Names That Mean "Queen"

Cleopatra & Dionne
Nefertiti & Quintana
Regina & Reina
Thelma & Tonia

Juno & Latanya
Queen & Quinn
Reya & Thema
Quinn & Quentin

Malika & Nala
Raine & Rani
Tania & Tatiana

Names That Mean "Supplanter"

Coby & Jack
James & Kobe

Iago & Jacques
Kemo & Seamus

Jacob & Jamie

Names That Mean Defender

Alejandro & Azim
Warner & Zander
Sandrine & Sasha

Eli & Hero
Alejandra & Alexi
Shura & Sandra

Titus & Onofrio
Alexandria & Alexis

Names That Mean Intelligent

Akira & Chung
Hobart & Hubert
Tomo & Trang

Hakin & Hewitt
Fulbright & Akilah

Hugh & Keene
Zakia & Narella

Names That Mean "Star"

Altair & Astra
Hester & Spica

Danica & Vega
Quarralia & Vespera

Estelle & Esther
Star & Stella

Names That Mean "Consecrated to God"

Elian & Enoch
Lisa & Liza

Bettina & Elizabeth

Isabella & Talisa

Appendix A: Alphabetical List of Boys Names

Aaron: (Jewish): enlightened; (Hebrew): lofty, exalted
Abbott: (Hebrew): father
Abdul: (Arabic): servant of God
Abe: (Jewish): father of nations
Abel: (Hebrew & Biblical): breathe, son
Abner: (Israel & Hebrew): father is light, father of light
Abraham: (Hebrew & Biblical): exalted father
Abram: (Hebrew): high father; (Israel): father of nations
Abu: (African): father
Ace: (Latin): unity
Achilles: (Greek): hero of the Trojan War
Ackerly: (English): meadow of oak trees
Adair: (Scottish): oak tree ford
Adam: (Hebrew): red; (Israel): man of the earth; (English): of the red earth
Adamson: (English): the son of Adam
Addison: (English): son of Adam
Adler: (German): eagle
Adolf/Adolph: (German): noble wolf
Adonis: (Greek): beautiful
Adrian: (German, Spanish & Italian): dark; (Greek): rich
Adriel: (Hebrew): from God's flock
Ahmad: (Arabic): one who thanks God
Ahmet: (Turkish): worthy of praise
Aidan/Aiden/Adan: (Irish, Celtic & Gaelic): fire, fiery
Aiken: (English): sturdy, made of oak
Ainsley: (Scottish): my own meadow
Ainsworth: (English): from Ann's estate
Ajay: (Punjabi): victorious, undefeatable
Ajit: (Indian): invincible
Akeem: (Hebrew): a form of Joachim, which means God will establish
Aki: (Japanese): autumn, bright
Akiko: (Japanese): surrounded by bright light
Akira: (Japanese): intelligent
Aladdin: (Arabian): faithful
Alaire: (French): filled with joy
Alan/Allan/Allen: (English & Irish): handsome; (Celtic): harmony, stone or noble
Alastair: (Scottish): a form of Alexander, which means protector of mankind
Albert/Alberto: (English & German): noble, bright
Alden: (English): old, wise protector
Aldo: (German): old and wise
Aldrich: (English): wise counselor
Alejandro: (Spanish): defender of mankind
Alexander/Alex/Alek/Alexi/Alexis: (Greek): protector of mankind
Alfonso/Alfonzo: (Italian): ready for battle
Alfred: (English): elf counselor
Alistair/Allister: (English): a form of Alexander, which means protector of mankind
Alon: (Hebrew): of the oak tree
Alonzo/Alonso: (Spanish & American): ready for battle
Aloysius: (German): famous warrior
Alpha: (Greek): first-born child
Alphonso/Alphonse: (Italian & German): noble and eager
Altair: (Greek): star

Alton: (English): from the old town
Alvin: (German): light skin, noble friend; (English): wise friend
Amadeus: (Latin): loves God
Amal: (Hebrew): worker; (Arabic): hopeful
Amani: (African): peaceful
Amber: (French): amber
Ambrose: (Greek): immortal
Amerigo: (Teutonic): industrious
Ames: (French): friend
Amida: (Japanese): Buddha
Amil: (Hindu): invaluable
Amir: (Arabic): prince
Amit: (Arabic): highly praised
Amory: (German): ruler
Amos: (Hebrew): strong, carried, brave: (Israel): troubled
An: (Chinese & Vietnamese): peaceful
Anders: (Scandinavian): a courageous, valiant man
Anderson: (Scottish): son of Andrew
Andre: (French): manly, brave
Andrei: (Italian): manlike
Andres: (Spanish): manly, courageous
Andrew: (English, Scottish & Biblical): manly; brave
Anel: (Greek): messenger of God, angel
Angel: (Spanish & Greek): angelic
Angelo: (Italian): angel
Angus: (Irish): vigorous one
Anil: (Hindu): wind god
Ansel: (French): follower of a nobleman
Anson: (German): divine
AnthonyAntony: (English & Biblical): worthy of praise
Antoine/Anton: (French): a flourishing man
Antonio: (Italian): a flourishing man
Antwan/Antwaun/Antwoine/Antwon/Antwone: (Arabic): worthy of praise
Anwar: (Arabic): luminous
Apollo: (Latin): strength, sun god
Apollos: (Israel): one who destroys
Archer: (Latin): a skilled bowman
Archibald: (German): bold
Archimedes: (Greek): to think about first
Arden: (Latin): passionate
Aristotle/Ari: (Greek): thinker with a great purpose
Arlen: (Irish): pledge
Arlo: (Spanish): barberry
Armand/Armando: (French): of the army
Armani/Armon: (Hebrew): high fortress
Armstrong: (English): strong arm
Arne/Arnie/Arnold: (German): strong as an eagle
Arsenio: (Greek): masculine, virile
Arthur/Art/Artur/Arturo: (English): bear, stone
Ary: (Hebrew): lion of God
Aryn: (Hebrew & Arabic): a form of Aaron, which means enlightened
Asa: (Hebrew): physician; Japan: born at dawn
Ashby: (Scandinavian): ash tree farm
Asher: (Hebrew & Israel): happy, blessed
Ashley: (English & Biblical): lives in the ash tree
Ashton: (Hebrew): shining light; (English): ash tree settlement

Atlas: (Greek): lifted, carried
Atticus: (Latin): a man from Athens
Attila: (Gothic): little father
Atwell: (English): one who lives at the spring
Aubrey: (English): one who rules with elf-wisdom
Auburn: (Latin): reddish-brown
Augustine/August/Augie/Augustus: (German): revered
Aurelius: (Latin): golden
Austin/Austen: (English): from the name Augustin, which means revered
Avery: (English): wise ruler
Avi: (Hebrew): my God, father; (Latin America): Lord of mine
Axel/Axl: (German & Hebrew): father of peace; (German): source of all life
Azariah: (Hebrew & Israel): God helps
Azim: (Arabic): defender

Baden: (German): bather
Bae: (Korean): inspiration
Bailey: (French): bailiff, steward
Bain: (Irish): fair-haired
Bainbridge: (Irish): fair bridge
Baird: (Irish): traveling minstrel
Baldwin: (German): brave friend
Balthazar: (English): the comedy of errors a merchant
Bancroft: (English): from the bean field
Barak: (Hebrew & Israel): flash of lightening
Barclay: (Scottish & English): birch tree meadow
Barlow: (English): bare hillside
Barnabus: (Hebrew & Israel): comfort
Barnett: (English): of honorable birth
Barney: (English): comfort
Baron: (English): a title of nobility
Barr: (English): a lawyer
Barrett: (German): strong as a bear
Barrington: (English): fenced town
Barry: (English & Irish): fair-haired; (Celtic); marksman; (Gaelic): spear
Bart: (Hebrew): ploughman; (English): from the barley farm
Bartholomew: (English, Hebrew & Biblical): son of a farmer
Bartlett: (French): son of the father
Barton: (English): from the barley town
Basil: (Greek & Latin): royal, kingly
Bautista: (Italian): John the Baptist
Baxter: (English): baker
Bay: (Vietnamese): born on a Saturday; (American): a natural body of water
Beacan: (Irish): small
Beau: (French): handsome, beautiful
Beaufort: (French): beautiful fort
Beaumont: (French): beautiful mountain
Beauregard: (French): handsome, beautiful
Beckett/Beck: (English) : brook
Beethoven: (German): music
Bellamy: (French): handsome
Ben: (English): son of my right hand
Benedict: (Latin): Blessed
Benito: (Italian): blessed
Benjamin: (English, Hebrew & Biblical): son of my right hand
Bennett: (English): one who is blessed

Benoit: (French): bland
Benson: (English): son of Benedict
Bentley: (English): from the bent grass meadow
Beresford: (English): from the barley ford
Bergen: (German): hill lover
Berkeley: (English & Irish): from the birch meadow
Bernard: (German): strong as a bear
Bertram/Bert: (German & English): bright light
Bevis: (Teutonic): an archer
Bing: (German): kettle-shaped hollow
Birch: (English): white, shining
Birkitt: (English): birch-tree coast
Birney: (English): from the island with the brook
Bjorn: (Scandinavian): a form of Bernard, which means strong as a bear
Black: (English): dark-skinned
Blackwell: (English): from the dark spring
Blade: (English): wielding a sword or knife
Blaine: (Gaelic, Irish & Celtic): thin
Blair: (Irish): plain, field
Blaise: (French & English): stutter, stammer
Blake: (English): pale, fair
Blaze: (Latin): one who stammers; (English): flame
Bodhi: (Indian): awakens
Bogart: (French): strong with a bow
Bonaventure: (Latin): one who undertakes a blessed venture
Booker: (English): bible, book maker
Boone: (French): good
Boris: (Slavic): warrior
Boston: (English): the city Boston
Bowen: (Gaelic): small son; (Irish): archer
Bowie: (Celtic): yellow-haired
Boyd: (Celtic): blond-haired
Bracken: (English): resembling a large fern
Braden/Brayden/Braiden: (Irish & English): broad hillside; (Scottish): salmon
Braddock: (English); from the broadly spread oak
Bradford: (English): from the wide ford
Brady: (Gaelic & Irish): spirit; (Irish): broad-shouldered
Brandon: (Irish): little raven
Branson/Bransen: (English): the son of Brandon
Brant/Brantley: (English): steep, tall
Braxton: (English): from Brock's town
Breck: (Irish): freckled
Brendan: (Irish): prince; (Gaelic): brave; (Celtic & Irish): raven; (German): flame
Brennan: (Gaelic): teardrop
Brent: (English): from the hill
Bret/Brett: (French, English & Celtic): a native of Brittany
Brian: (Gaelic): noble birth; (Celtic): great strength
Brice: (Welsh): alert, ambitious
Brigham: (English): covered bridge
Britt/Britton/Brittan: (Scottish): from Britain
Brock: (English): badger
Broderick: (English): from the wide ridge
Brody: (Irish): brother, from the muddy place; (Scottish): second son
Brogan: (Gaelic & Irish): from the ditch
Bronson: (English): son of Brown
Brooks: (English): running water, son of Brooke

Brown: (English): brown color, dark-skinned
Bruce: (French & English): woods, thick brush
Bruno: (German): brown-haired
Brutus: (Latin): course, stupid
Bryan: (Irish): strong one; (Celtic): brave
Bryce: (Scottish): speckled
Buck: (German & English): male deer
Buckley: (English): deer meadow
Bud: (English): brotherly
Budha: (Hindu): the planet Mercury
Buford: (English): ford near the castle
Burgess: (English): town dweller, shopkeeper
Burke: (German): birch tree
Burton: (English): from the fortified town
Butler: (English): keeper of the bottles
Byrd: (English): bird-like
Byron: (French & English): barn or cottage

Cade: (American): pure
Caden: (Welsh): spirit of battle
Caesar: (Latin): emperor
Caiden/Caden: (American): friend, companion
Cain: (Israel): craftsman; (Hebrew): spear; (Welsh): clear water; (Irish): archaic
Caleb: (Israel): faithful; (Hebrew): dog or bold
Callan/Callen: (Australian): sparrow hawk
Callum: (Gaelic): resembling a dove
Calvin: (English & Latin America): bald
Camden: (Irish, Scottish, English & Gaelic): from the winding valley
Cameron: (Irish & Gaelic): crooked nose
Campbell: (Gaelic): crooked mouth; (French): from the beautiful field
Carey: (Greek): pure
Carl/Carle: (English): man; (German): strong one
Carlin: (Irish, Gaelic & Scottish): little champion
Carlisle: (English): from the walled city
Carlo: (French): strong; (Italian): manly
Carlos: (Spanish): a free man
Carlsen: (Scandinavian): son of Carl
Carlton/Carleton: (English): town of Charles
Carlyle: (English): Carl's island
Carmelo: (Hebrew & Israel): fruit orchard
Carmine: (Latin): beautiful song
Carroll: (Irish): champion
Carson: (English): son who lives in the swamp
Carter: (English): cart driver
Carver: (English): sculptor
Cary: (Celtic): from the river; (Welsh): from the fort on the hill
Cash: (Latin): money
Casper: (Persian): treasurer; (German): imperial
Cassius: (Latin): empty, hollow, vain
Cato: (Latin): sagacious, wise one, good judgment
Caton: (Spanish): knowledgeable
Cayden: (Scotland): fighter
Ceasar/Caesar: (Latin): long-haired
Cecil: (Latin): blind
Cedric: (English): battle chieftain
Chad: (English): battle

Chadwick: (English): from Chad's dairy farm
Chai: (Hebrew): giver of life
Chan: (Spanish): God is gracious
Chance: (English & French): good luck, keeper of records
Chancellor/Chancelor/Chancey: (English): record keeper
Chandler: (French): candle maker
Channing: (French): church official; (English): resembling a young wolf
Charles: (English): strong, manly
Chase: (English): hunter
Chauncey: (Latin): chancellor
Chavez: (Spanish): a surname
Che: (Spanish): a derivative of Jose, which means God will add
Chen: (Chinese): great, dawn
Chester: (English): a rock fortress
Chevy: (French): a diminutive form of Chevalier, which means horseman, knight
Chico: (Spanish): boy
Chikae: (African American): God's power
Chin: (Korean): precious
Cho: (Korean): beautiful
Christian: (English & Irish): follower of Christ
Christopher/Christoff: (Biblical): Christ-bearer; (English): he who holds Christ in his heart
Chun: (Chinese): spring
Chung: (Chinese): intelligent
Cicero: (Latin): chickpea
Ciro: (Italian): a diminutive form of Cyril, which means lordly
Cisco: (Spanish): a diminutive form of Francisco, which means free
Clancy/Clancey: (Celtic): son of the red-haired warrior
Clarence: (English & Latin America): clear, luminous
Clark: (English): cleric, scholar, clerk
Claud/Claude: (English): lame
Claudius: (English): lame
Claus: (Greek): people's victory
Clay: (English): clay maker, immortal
Clayborne: (English): brook near the clay pit
Clayton: (English): mortal
Cleavon: (English): cliff
Clement: (French): compassionate
Cleo: (Greek): to praise, acclaim
Cletus: (Greek): illustrious
Cliff/Clifford/Clifton: (English): from the ford near the cliff
Clinton: (English): town on a hill
Clive: (English): one who lives near the cliff
Clyde: (Irish): warm
Coburn: (English): meeting of streams
Coby: (English): supplanter
Cody: (Irish): helpful; (English): a cushion, helpful
Colbert: (French): famous and bright
Cole: (Irish): warrior; (English): having dark features
Colin/Collin: (Irish & Gaelic): young; (Scottish): young dog; (English): of a triumphant people
Colt: (American): baby horse; (English): from the dark town
Colton: (English): coal town, from the dark town
Columbus: (Greek): curious
Conan: (English): resembling a wolf; (Gaelic): high and mighty
Cong: (Chinese): clever
Conlan: (Irish): hero
Connery: (Scottish): daring

177

Connor/Conner: (Irish): strong willed, much wanted
Conrad: (German): brave counselor
Constantine: (Latin): steadfast, firm
Cooper: (English): barrel maker
Corbett: (French): resembling a young raven
Cordero: (Spanish): little lamb
Cornelius: (Irish): strong willed, wise; (Latin America): horn-colored
Cory/Corey: (English & Irish): hill, hollow
Cosimo: (Italian): the order of the universe
Cosmo: (Greek): the order of the universe
Covington: (English); from the town near the cave
Coy/Coye/Coyt: (English): woods
Craig: (Scottish): dwells at the crag; (Welsh): rock
Cramer: (English): full
Crandall: (English): from the valley of cranes
Crawford: (English): from the crow's ford
Creed: (English): belief, guiding principle
Creighton: (Scottish): from the border town
Crispin: (Latin): curly-haired
Cromwell: (English): winding spring
Crosby: (English): town crossing
Cruz: (Spanish): of the cross
Cuba: (Spanish): tub
Cullen: (Irish & Gaelic): handsome; (Celtic): cub; (English): city in Germany
Culley: (Irish): woods
Culver: (English): dove
Cunningham: (Gaelic): descendant of the chief
Curran/Curry: (Celtic): hero
Curtis: (Latin): enclosure
Cutter: (English): tailor
Cyrano: (Greek): from Cyrene
Cyril: (English & Greek): master, lord
Cyrus: (English): far-sighted

Dack: (English): from the French town of Dax
Dae: (Korean): great
Daegan: (Irish): black-haired
Dai: (Chinese): sword technique
Daiki: (Japanese): of great value
Dakota: (Native American): friend to all
Dale: (German): valley; (English): lives in the valley
Dallas: (Irish & Gaelic): wise; (Scottish & Celtic): from the waterfall
Dalton: (English): from the town in the valley
Damian: (Greek): one who tames others
Damon: (English): calm, tame
Dane: (Hebrew & Scandinavian): God will judge; (English): brook
Daniel: (Hebrew & Biblical): God is my judge; (Irish & Welsh): attractive
Dante: (Latin): enduring, everlasting
Darian: (Irish): from the name Darren, which means great
Dario: (Spanish): affluent
Darius: (Greek): kingly, wealthy; (American): pharaoh
Darnel/Darnell: (English): hidden
Darren/Darrin/Darin/Darron/Darryn: (English, Irish & Gaelic): great
Darvell: (French): from the eagle town
Darwin/Derwin: (English): dear friend
Daryl/Darrell: (French): darling, beloved

Dashawn: (English): God is willing
David: (Hebrew, Scottish & Welsh): beloved
Davis: (English & Scottish): David's son
Dawayne/Dwayne: (Irish): dark, small
Dawson: (English): son of David
Dax: (English & French): water
De: (Chinese): virtuous
Deacon: (American): pastor; (English): dusty one, servant
Dean: (English): head, leader
Deangelo: (Italian): a combination of De and Angelo, which means little angel
Decker: (German): one who prays: (Hebrew): piercing
Declan: (Irish): saint
Dedrick: (German): ruler of the people
Deepak: (Hindu): little lamp
Deion/Dion/Deiondre: (Greek & French): mountain of Zeus
Delaney: (Irish): dark challenger
Delano: (English): nut tree; (Irish): dark
Delbert: (English): proud, bright as day
Dell: (English): from the small valley
Delroy: (French): belonging to the king
Demarco: (African American): of Mark: (South African): warlike
Demetrius: (Greek): goddess of fertility, one who loves the earth
Demond: (African American): of man
Dennis: (Greek): wild, frenzied
Dennison: (English): son of Dennis
Denton: (English): happy home
Denzel: (English): fort; (African): wild
Derby: (English): deer park; (Irish): from the village of dames
Derek: (German & English): gifted ruler
Dermot: (Irish): free from envy
Derry: (English, Irish, German & Gaelic): red-haired, from the oak grove|
Deshawn/Deshaun: (American): a combination of De and Shawn, which means God is gracious
Desi: (Latin): desiring
Desmond: (Gaelic): a man from South Munster
Destin: (French): fate
Devin/Devaughn/Devon: (Irish): poet
Devlin: (Gaelic): fierce bravery
Dewayne: (American): a combination of De and Wayne, which means wagon maker
Dewey: (Welsh): prized
DeWitt: Flemish: blond hair
Dexter: (Latin): right-handed, skillful; (Latin America): flexible
Diego: (Spanish): Saint James
Dierks: (Danish): ruler of the people
Diesel: (American): having great strength
Dietrich: (German): ruler of the people
Dijon: (French): a city in France
Dimitri/Demetrius: (Russian): lover of the earth
Dino: (Italian): one who wields a great sword
Dirk: (German): a diminutive form of Derek, which means gifted ruler
Dixon: (English): power, brave ruler
Dobbs: (English): fiery
Dolan: (Irish): dark-haired
Dolph: (German): diminutive form of Adolph, which means noble wolf
Domingo: (Spanish): born on a Sunday
Dominic: (Spanish): born on a Sunday
Donal/Donald: (Celtic & Gaelic): dark stranger; (Irish, English & Scottish): great leader

Dong: (Korean): the east
Donovan: (Irish): brown-haired chief
Doug/Dougal/Douglas: (Scottish): dark river
Doyle: (Irish): dark river
Drake: (English): male duck, dragon
Draper: (English): fabric maker
Dre: (American): a diminutive form of Andre, which means manly, brave
Drew/Dru: (English): courageous, valiant
Driscoll: (Celtic): mediator
Drummond: (Scottish): one who lives near the ridge
Drury: (French): loving
Dryden: (English): dry valley
Duane: (Gaelic): a dark and swarthy man
Dudley: (English): common field
Duff: (Scottish): dark
Dugan: (Irish): dark
Duke: (English): leader
Duncan/Dunn: (Scottish): brown warrior
Dustin/Dusty: (English): fighter, warrior
Dwayne: (Irish): dark
Dwight: (English): a diminutive form of DeWitt, which means blond hair
Dylan/Dillon/Dilan: (English & Welsh): born from the ocean, son of the wave; (Gaelic): faithful

Eagle: (Native American): resembling the bird
Eamon: (Irish): blessed guardian
Earl: (Irish): pledge; (English): nobleman
Earnest: (English): industrious
Eastman: (English): a man from the east
Easton: (English): from east town
Eben: (Hebrew): rock
Ebenezer: (Hebrew & Israel): rock of help
Edgar: (English): powerful and wealthy spearman
Edison: (English): son of Edward
Edmund/Edmond: (English): wealthy protector
Edward: (English): wealthy guardian; (German): strong as a boar
Edwin: (English): wealthy friend
Efrain/Ephraim: (Hebrew): fruitful
Egan/Egin/Egen/Egyn: (Irish): ardent, fiery
Elan: (Hebrew): tree
Elbert: (English): a well-born man; (German): a bright man
Eldon: (English): from the sacred hill
Eldridge: (German & English): wise ruler
Elgin: (English) & Celtic): noble, white
Eli/Ely: (Hebrew): ascended, uplifted, high; (Greek): defender of man
Elian: (Spanish): consecrated to the gracious God
Elias: (Latin & Hebrew): the Lord is my God
Elijah: (Biblical): the Lord is my God; (Hebrew): Jehovah is God
Elliott: (Israel): close to God; (English): the Lord is my God
Ellison: (English): son of Elias
Ellory/Ellery: (Cornish): resembling a swan
Ellsworth: (English): from the nobleman's estate
Elmer: (English): famous, noble
Elmo: (English): protector; (Latin): amiable
Elmore: (English): moor where the elm trees grow
Elon: (Biblical & African American): spirit, God loves me
Elroy: (French, English & African American): king; (Irish): red-haired youth

Elton: (English): old town
Elvin: (Irish): friend of elves
Elvis: (Scandinavian): wise
Elwood: (English): old forest
Emerson: (English): brave, powerful
Emery: (German): industrious leader
Emil/Emile: (Latin): eager, industrious
Emiliano: (Italian & Latin): rival, industrious
Emilio: (Spanish): flattering
Emmanuel: (Hebrew): God with us
Emmett/Emmitt: (English): whole, universal
Engelbert: (German): bright as an angel
Ennis: (Irish): island; (Gaelic): the only choice; (Greek): mine
Enoch: (Hebrew): dedicated, consecrated
Enos: (Hebrew): man
Enrique: (Spanish): ruler of the estate
Enzo: (Italian): ruler of the estate
Ephraim: (Hebrew & Israel): fruitful
Eric/Erik/Erich: (Scandinavian): honorable ruler
Ernest: (German): serious, determined, truth
Errol: (Latin): wanderer
Esau: (Hebrew): hairy, famous bearer; (Israel): he that acts or finishes
Esme: (French): esteemed
Esteban: (Spanish): crowned in victory
Ethan: (Hebrew & Biblical): firm, strong
Eugene: (Greek): well-born man
Eui: (Korean): righteousness
Eun: (Korean): silver
Evan: (English): God is good; (Welsh): young; (Celtic): young fighter
Evander: (Greek): benevolent ruler
Everett: (English): hardy, brave, strong
Ewan: (Celtic, Scotch & Irish): young
Ezekiel: (Hebrew & Israel): strength of God
Ezra: (Hebrew & Israel): helper

Fa: (Chinese): setting off
Fabian/Faber/Fabio: (Latin): bean grower
Fabrizio/Fabrice: (Italian): craftsman
Facundo: (Spanish): significant, eloquent
Fagan/Fagin: (Gaelic): ardent; (Irish): eager
Fai: (Chinese): beginning to fly
Fairbanks: (English): from the bank along the path
Faisal: (Arabic): decisive
Falkner: (English): trainer of falcons
Fargo: (American): jaunty
Farley: (English): bull meadow
Farnell: (English): fern-covered hill
Farrell/Ferrell: (Irish): heroic, courageous
Farrow: (English): piglet
Faust: (Latin): fortunate
Felipe: (Spanish): one who loves horses
Felix: (Latin): happy and prosperous
Felton: (English): from the town near the field
Feng: (Chinese): sharp blade
Fenn: (English): from the marsh
Fenton: (English): from the farm on the fens

Ferdinand: (German): courageous voyager
Fergus: (Gaelic): first and supreme choice
Fernando: (Spanish): daring, adventurous
Ferris: (Irish): small rock
Fidel: (Latin) faithful
Fielding: (Irish): from the field
Filbert: (English): brilliant
Finch: (Irish): resembling the small bird
Fineas/Phineas: (Egyptian): dark-skinned
Finian/Phinian: (Irish): light-skinned, white
Finlay/Findlay/Finian/Finley: (Irish): blond-haired soldier
Finn: (English): blond
Finnegan: (Irish): fair-haired
Fisher: (English): fisherman
Fitch: (English): resembling an ermine
Fitzgerald: (English) the son of Gerald
Fitzpatrick: (English): son of Patrick
Flann: (Irish): redhead
Fleming: (English): from Denmark
Fletcher: (English): one who makes arrows
Flint: (English): stream, hard quartz rock
Flynn: (Irish): ruddy complexion; heir to the red-head
Fogarty: (Irish): exiled
Foley: (English): creative
Fontaine: (French): from the water source
Ford: (English): from the river crossing
Forrest: (English & French): from the woods
Forster: (American & French): from the woods
Foster: (English & French): one who keeps the forest
Fox: (English): fox
Francis/Franco: (Latin): a man from France
Francisco: (Spanish): a man from France, free
Frank/ Frankie/Franklin: (English): free man
Franz/Frantz: (German): a man from France
Fraser: (Scottish): strawberry flowers
Frasier: (French): strawberry, curly-haired
Fred: (German): peaceful ruler
Frederick/Frederique/Frederico/Freidrich: (German): peaceful ruler
Freeborn: (English): child of freedom
Freeman: (English): free
Fremont: (French): protector of freedom
Frey: (English): lord
Frick: (English): bold
Fulbright: (English): brilliant
Fuller/Fullerton: (English): from Fuller's town
Fyfe: (Scottish): a man from Fifeshire
Fynn: (Russian): the Offin River

Gabe: (English): strength of God
Gabriel: (Israel): hero of God; (Hebrew): man of God; (Spanish): God is my strength
Gaetan: (French & Italian): from Italy
Gage/Gaige: (French): a pledge or pawn
Galbraith: (Scottish): a foreigner
Gale/Galen: (Gaelic): tranquil; (English): festive party: (Greek): healer, calm
Galileo: (Hebrew): one who comes from Galilee
Gallagher: (Irish & Gaelic): eagle helper

Galt: (English): from the wooded land
Gan: (Chinese): dare, adventure
Gannon: (Irish & Gaelic): fair-skinned
Garcia: (Spanish): one who is brave in battle
Gared: (English): mighty with a spear
Garen/Garin/Garren/Garrin: (English): mighty spearman
Garfield: (English): battlefield
Garnet: (English): gem, armed with a spear; (French): keeper of grain
Garrett: (Irish): to watch
Garrick: (English): oak spear
Garrison: (French): prepared
Garroway: (English): spear fighter
Garry/Gary: (English): mighty spearman
Garson: (English): the son of Gar
Garth: (Scandinavian): keeper of the garden
Gaston: (French): a man from Gastony
Gavin: (English): little hawk; (Welsh): hawk of the battle
Gaylord: (French): merry lord, jailer
Geming: (Chinese): revolution
Gen: (Chinese): root
Gene: (English): a well-born man
Genovese/Geno: (Italian): from Genoa, Italy
Gentry: (English): gentleman
Geoffrey/Geffrey/Jeffrey/Geoff/Geff/Jeff: (English): a man of peace
George: (English): farmer
Gerald/Gerry: (German): one who rules with the spear
Gerard: (French): one who is mighty with the spear
Geronimo: (Greek & Italian): a famous chef
Gervaise: (French): honorable
Gibson: (English): son of Gilbert
Gideon: (Hebrew & Israel): great warrior
Gilbert/Gil: (French): bright promise: (English): trustworthy
Giles: (Greek): resembling a young goat
Gill: (Gaelic): servant
Gilmore: (Irish): devoted to the Virgin Mary
Gilroy: (Irish): devoted to the king
Gino: (Greek): a diminutive form of Eugene, which means well-born man
Giovanni/Gian: (Italian); God is gracious
Guiseppe: (Italian): God will add
Gizmo: (American): playful
Glade: (English): from the clearing in the woods
Glendon: (Scottish): fortress in the glen
Glenn: (Scottish): glen, valley
Glover: (English): one who makes gloves
Goddard: (German): divinely firm
Godfrey: (German): God is peace
Godric: (English): power of God
Goldwin: (English): a golden friend
Goliath: (Hebrew): exiled
Gomer: (Hebrew): completed, finished
Gomez: (Spanish): man
Goode: (English): upstanding
Gordon: (Gaelic): from the great hill, hero
Grady: (Gaelic): famous, noble
Graham: (Scottish): from the gray home
Granger: (English): farmer

Grant: (Latin): great
Granville: (French): from the large village
Gray: (English): gray-haired
Grayson: (English): son of the bailiff
Gregory/Greg: (English & Greek): vigilant
Griffin: (Latin): hooked nose
Griffith: (Welsh): mighty chief
Grover: (English): grove
Guang: (Chinese): light
Guido: (Italian): guide
Guillermo: (Spanish): a form of William, which means protector
Gunner/Gunther: (Scandinavian): warrior
Gus: (German): revered
Gustav: (Scandinavian): of the staff of the gods
Guthrie: (German): war hero
Guy: (French): guide; (Hebrew): valley; (Celtic): sensible; (Latin America): living spirit

Hackett/Hackman: (German & French): little wood cutter
Hadley: (English & Irish): from the heath covered meadow
Hagen: (Gaelic): youthful
Haig: (English): enclosed with hedges
Haim: (Hebrew): giver of life
Haines: (English): from the vine-covered cottage
Hakin: (Arabic): wise and intelligent
Hal: (English): ruler of the army
Hallan: (English): dweller at the hall
Halley: (English): from the hall near the meadow
Halliwell: (English): from the holy spring
Halsey: (English): Hal's island
Hamid: (Arabic): praised
Hamilton: (English): from the flat-topped hill
Hamlet: (English): home
Hammond: (English): village
Hancock: (English): one who owns a farm
Hanford: (English): from the high ford
Hank: (Dutch & German): rules his household
Hanley: (English): from the high meadow
Hannibal: (Phoenician): grace of god
Hans: (German & Hebrew): gift from God; (Scandinavian): God is gracious
Hansel: (Hebrew): gift from God; (Scandinavian): God is gracious
Harcourt: (French): fortified dwelling
Harding: (English): brave, manly
Hardwin: (English): brave friend
Harim: (Arabic): superior
Harlan: (English): hare's land
Harley: (English): hare's meadow
Harlow: (English): from the army on the hill
Harold: (Scandinavian): ruler of the army
Harper: (English): one who plays or makes harps
Harrington: (English): from the herring town
Harrison: (English): son of Harry
Harry/Harris: (German): home or house ruler
Hartford: (English): from the stag's ford
Hartley: (English): from the stage meadow
Hartman: (German): hard, strong
Hartwell: (English): deer well

Harvey: (English): strong, ready for battle
Hasam: (Turkish): reaper, harvester
Hasani: Swahili: handsome
Hasim: (Arabic): decisive
Hasin: (Hindu): laughing
Haven: (Dutch): safe harbor or port
Hawk: (English): hawk
Hawkins: (English): resembling a small hawk
Hawthorne: (English): from the hawthorn tree
Hayden: (English & Welsh): in the meadow or valley
Hayes: (English): from the hedged place
He: (Chinese): yellow river
Hea: (Korean): grace
Heath: (English): from the heath wasteland|
Heathcliff: (English): cliff near the heath
Heaton: (English): from the town on high ground
Hector: (Greek): steadfast, the prince of Troy
Hedley: (English): heather-filled meadow
Hee: (Korean): brightness
Heinrich: (German): a form of Henry, which means rules his household
Helio: (Greek): god of the sun
Henderson: (Scottish): son of Henry
Heng: (Chinese): eternal
Henley: (English): from the high meadow
Henry: (English, German & French): rules his household
Herbert: (German): glorious soldier
Hercules: (Greek): son of Zeus
Herman: (German): soldier
Hermes: (Greek): stone pile
Hero: (Greek): great defender
Hershel: (Hebrew): resembling a deer
Hewitt: (English): little smart one
Hillard: (German): brave warrior
Hilton: (English): town on a hill
Hiro: (Japanese): widespread
Hiromi: (Japanese): widespread beauty; wide-seeing
Hirum: (Hebrew): noblest, exalted
Hobart: (American): having a shining intellect
Hobson: (English): son of Robert
Hoffman: (German): influential
Hogan: (Irish & Gaelic): young, young at heart
Holbrook: (English): brook in the hollow
Holcomb: (English): from the deep valley
Holden: (English): from a hollow in the valley
Holland: (American): from the Netherlands
Hollis: (English): from the holly tree
Holt: (English): wood, by the forest
Homer: (Greek & English): pledge, promise
Hong: (Chinese): wild swan
Hop: (Chinese): agreeable
Horace/Horatio: (French): hour, time
Horton: (English): garden estate
Houghton: (English): settlement on the headland
Houston: (Gaelic): from Hugh's town: (English): from the town on the hill
Howard: (English): guardian of the home
Howe: (German): high

Howell: (Welsh): remarkable
Hoyt: (Irish): mind, spirit
Hu: (Chinese): tiger
Huan: (Chinese): happiness
Hubert: (German): having a shining intellect
Hud: (Arabic): religion, a Muslim prophet
Hudson: (English): son of the hooded man
Hugh/Hugo: (English): intelligent
Humbert/Humberto: (German): brilliant strength
Humphrey: (German): peaceful strength
Hung: (Vietnamese): brave
Hunter: (English): one who hunts
Huntley: (English): hunter's meadow
Hurley: (Irish): sea tide
Hurst: (Irish): dense grove, thicket
Hussein: (Arabic): little, handsome
Hutton: (English): house on the jutting ledge
Huxley: (English): Hugh's meadow
Huy: (Vietnamese): glorious
Hy: (Vietnamese): hopeful
Hyatt: (English): high gate
Hyde: (English): animal hide
Hyo: (Korean): filial duty
Hyun: (Korean): wisdom

Iago: (Welsh & Spanish): supplanter
Ian: (Scottish): gift from God
Ibsen: (German): archer's son
Ichabod: (Hebrew): the glory has gone
Ignatius/Iggy: (Latin): fiery
Igor: (Scandinavian): hero; (Russian): soldier
Ike: (Hebrew): full of laughter
Iker: (Spanish): visitation
Ilias: (Greek): form of Elijah, which means the Lord is my God
Indiana: (English): from the land of the Indians, the state of Indiana
Ingo: (Scandinavian): lord; (Danish): from the meadow
Ingram: (Scandinavian): a raven of peace
Ioan: (Greek, Bulgarian & Romanian): a form of John, which means God is gracious
Ira: (Hebrew & Israel): watchful
Irv/Irvin/Irving: (Irish): handsome
Irwin: (English): friend of the wild boar
Isaac: (Biblical): he will laugh
Isaiah: (Hebrew): the Lord is generous; (Israel): salvation by God
Isamu: (Japanese): courageous
Isas: (Japanese): meritorious
Isham: (English): from the iron one's estate
Ishmael: (Hebrew, Israel & Spanish): God listens, God will hear
Isidore: (Greek): a gift of Isis
Israel: (Israel): prince of God; (Hebrew): may God prevail
Ivan: (Slavic): God is gracious
Ives: (Scandinavian): the archer's bow
Izod: (Irish): light haired

Jabari: (African): valiant
Jabbar: (Indian): one who consoles others
Jabin: (Hebrew): God has built

Jabo: (American): feisty
Jacinto: (Spanish): resembling a hyacinth
Jack: (English): God is gracious; (Hebrew): supplanter
Jackson: (English): son of Jack; (Scottish): God has been gracious
Jacob: (Biblical): supplanter; (Hebrew): he grasps the heel
Jacques: (French): supplanter
Jaden: (American): God has heard
Jafar: (Hindu): little stream
Jagger: (English): a carter, to carry
Jai: (Tai): heart
Jaime/Jamie: (Spanish): supplanter
Jake: (Hebrew): he grasps the heel
Jaleel/Jalen: (American): one who heals others
Jamal/Jamaal/Jamall/Jamaul: (Arabic): handsome
Jamar: (American): handsome
James: (English): supplant, replace; (Israel): supplanter
Jameson/Jamieson: (English): son of James
Jan: (Dutch): a form of John, which means God is gracious
Janson/Jansen: (Dutch): son of Jan
Japheth: (Hebrew): handsome
Jared: (Hebrew): descending
Jarek: (Slavic): born in January
Jaron: (Hebrew): he will sing
Jarrett/Jerritt: (English): one who is strong with a spear
Jarvis: (German): skilled with a spear
Jasdeep: (Sikh): the lamp radiating Gods' glories
Jason: (Greek): to heal
Jasper/Jaspar: (Hebrew, French & English): precious stone
Javier/Xavier: (Spanish): owner of a new house
Jax: (American): son of Jack
Jay: (German): swift; (French): blue jay; (English): to rejoice; (Latin America): a crow
Jayce/Jace: (American): God is my salvation
Jayden: (American): God has heard
Jaylen: (English); to rejoice
Jazz: (American): jazz
Jean: (French): a form of John, which means God is gracious
Jeb/Jed/Jebidiah/Jedidiah: (Hebrew): one who is loved by God
Jefferson: (English): son of Jeffrey, which means divine peace
Jeffrey: (French, German & English): divine peace
Jensen: (Scandinavian): God is gracious
Jerald: (English): one who rules with the spear
Jeremiah: (Hebrew): may Jehovah exalt; (Israel): sent by God
Jeremy: (Israel): God will uplift
Jericho: (Arabic): city of the moon
Jermaine: (French): a man from Germany; (Latin): brotherly
Jerome: (Greek): of the sacred name
Jess: (Israel): wealthy
Jesse: (Hebrew): wealthy; (Israel): God exists; (English): Jehovah exists
Jesus: (Hebrew): God is my salvation
Jethro: (Hebrew & Israel): excellence
Jett: (English): resembling the black gemstone
Jiang: (Chinese): fire
Jim: (English): supplanter
Jin: (Chinese): gold
Jiro: (Japanese): second son
Jo: (Japanese): God will increase

Joab: (Israel): paternity, voluntary
Joachim/Joaquin: (Hebrew): God will establish
Job/Jobe: (Hebrew): afflicted
Jock: (Scottish): God is gracious
Jody: (Hebrew): a diminutive form of Joseph, which means God will increase
Joel: (Hebrew): Jehovah is God; (Israel): God is willing
Johann: (German): God's gracious gift
John: (Israel): God is gracious; Jehovah has been gracious
Johnnie: (French, English & Hebrew): diminutive of John, which means God is gracious
Johnson: (Scottish & English): son of John
Jonah: (Hebrew & Israel): a dove
Jonas: (Hebrew): gift from God; (Spanish): dove; (Israel): accomplishing
Jonathan: (Hebrew): Jehovah has given: (Israel): gift of God
Joo: (Korean): jewel
Jordan: (Hebrew): to flow down; (Israel): descendant
Jorell: (American): he saves
Jorge: (Spanish): farmer
Jose: (Spanish): God will add
Joseph/Josef/Jozef: (Biblical): God will increase; (Hebrew): may Jehovah add/give
Joshua: (Hebrew & Biblical): Jehovah saves
Josiah: (Hebrew): Jehovah has healed; (Israel): God has healed
Journey: (American): one who likes to travel
Jovan: (Latin): majestic
Juan: (Hebrew): gift from God; (Spanish): God is gracious
Juan Jose: (Spanish): God has given/God shall add
Juan Pablo: (Spanish): God is gracious/borrowed
Judah/Judas/Jude/Judd: (Hebrew & Israel): praised
Jules: (French): youthful, downy-haired
Julian/Julius/Julio: (Spanish, French & Greek): youthful
Jun: (Chinese): truthful; (Japanese): obedient, pure
Jung: (Korean): a righteous man
Justice/Justus: (English): fair and moral
Justin: (English & French): just, true; (Irish): judicious

Kacey: (Irish): vigilant
Kadeem: (Arabic): servant
Kaden/Kade/Kadin/Caden: (Arabic): beloved companion
Kagen: (Irish): fiery
Kai: (American): ocean; (Welsh): keeper of the keys; (Scottish): fire
Kale: (English): manly and strong
Kaleb/Caleb: (Hebrew): resembling an aggressive dog
Kalil/Khalil/Kali: (Arabic): friend
Kamil/Kamal: (Arabic & Hindu): lotus
Kana: (Japanese): powerful
Kane: (Welsh): beautiful; (Gaelic): little warrior
Kang: (Korean): healthy
Kano: (Japanese): powerful
Kareem: (Arabic): noble, distinguished
Karl: (English & Icelandic): man; (French): strong, masculine; (Danish): one who is free
Kavi: (Hindu): poet
Keanu: (Hawaiian): of the mountain breeze
Keaton: (English): from the town of hawks
Kedrick: (English): a form of Cedric, which means battle chieftain
Keefe: (Irish): handsome, loved
Keegan/Kaegan/Keigan: (Gaelic): small and fiery
Keelan/Keilan: (Irish): mighty warrior

Keenan: (Irish): little Keene

Keene: (German): bold, sharp; (English): smart

Keith: (Scottish): wood; (Irish): warrior descending; (Welsh): dwells in the woods

Kellen/Kallen: (Gaelic): slender; (German): from the swamp

Kelley/Kelly: (Celtic): warrior; (Gaelic): one who defends

Kelsey: (English): from the island of ships

Kelvin: (Irish): narrow river

Ken: (Welsh): clear water; (English): royal obligation; (Irish): handsome; (Japanese): strong

Kendall: (English & Celtic): from the bright valley

Kendrick: (English): royal ruler; (Gaelic): champion

Kenley: (English): from the king's meadow

Kennedy: (Scottish): ugly head; (Irish & Gaelic): helmeted

Kenneth: (Celtic, Scottish & Irish): handsome; (English): royal obligation

Kent: (English & Welsh): white; (Celtic): chief

Kenton: (English): from the king's town

Kenyon: (Gaelic): blond-haired

Kermit: (Irish): free from envy

Kerrick: (English): king's rule

Kerry: (Irish): dark-haired

Kerwin: (Irish): little, dark

Kesler: (American): energetic and independent

Keung: (Chinese): a universal spirit

Kevin: (Irish & Gaelic): handsome, beautiful; (Celtic): gentle

Khouri: (Arabic): spiritual, a priest

Ki: (Korean): arise

Kidd: (English): resembling a young goat

Kiefer: (German): one who makes barrels

Kieran: (Gaelic): the little dark one

Kiley/Kile: (Gaelic): young; (Irish): young at heart

Kim: (Vietnamese): as precious as gold; (Welsh): leader

Kimball: (Greek): hollow vessel

Kimo: (Hawaiian): a form of James, which means supplant

Kin: (Japanese): golden

Kincaid: (Celtic): the leader during a battle

King: (English): royal ruler

Kingsley: (English): from the king's meadow

Kingston: (English): from the king's village

Kinsey: (English): victorious prince

Kioshi: (Japanese): quiet

Kip/Kipp: (English): from the small pointed hill

Kirby: (Scandinavian): church village

Kirk: (Norse): a man of the church

Kirkland: (English): from the church's land

Kirkley: (English): from the church's meadow

Kit: (English): one who bears Christ inside

Kitoko: (African): handsome

Kiyoshi: (Japanese): quiet one

Knight: (English): noble soldier

Knox: (English): from the hills

Kobe/Kobi/Koby: (African): supplanter; (American): from California

Kode: (English): helpful

Kojo: (African): born on a Monday

Kong: (Chinese): glorious, sky

Kramer: (German): shopkeeper

Kris/Kristian/Kristoff/Kristopher: (Swedish): Christ-bearer

Krishna: (Hindu): delightful, pleasurable

Kuo: (Japanese): approval
Kuro: (Japanese): ninth son
Kurt: (German): brave counselor
Kwame: (Akan): born on a Saturday
Kwan: (Korean): bold character
Kyle: (Gaelic): young; (Irish): young at heart
Kyong: (Korean): brightness
Kyu: (Korean): standard

Lafayette: (Israel): to God to the mighty
Laine/Lane: (English): narrow road
Laird: (Scottish): lord; (Irish): head of household
Laken: (American): man from the lake
Lamar: (German): famous land; (French): of the sea
Lambert: (Scandinavian): the light of the land
Lamont: (Scandinavian): lawyer
Lance: (German): spear; (French): land
Lancelot: (English & French): servant
Landon: (English): grassy plain; from the long hill
Langley: (English): long meadow
Langston: (English): from the tall man's town
Lanier: (French): one who works with wool
Larkin: (Irish): tough, fierce
Lars/Larry: (Dutch & Latin America): laurels
Larson: (Scandinavian): the son of Lars
LaSalle: (French): from the hall
Lashaun: (American): enthusiastic
Lathan: (American): gift from God
Latimer: (English): an interpreter
Laurent/Laurence: (French & African American): crowned with laurel
Lawford: (English): from the ford near the hill
Lawrence/Lawry: (Latin America): crowned with laurel
Lawson: (English): son of Lawrence, which means crowned with laurel
Lazarus/Lazaro: (Hebrew & Israel): God will help
Lear: (English): Shakespearean king
Leavitt: (English): a baker
Lee/Leigh: (English): meadow
Legend: (American): memorable
Lei: (Chinese): thunder
Leib: (Yiddish): roaring lion
Leif: (Scandinavian): beloved descendent
Leighton: (English): from the town near the meadow
Leland: (English): meadow land
Len: (Native American): one who plays the flute
Lenard: (French & German): lion, bold
Lenin: (Russian): one who belongs to the river Lena
Lennon: (English): son of love
Lennox: (Scottish): one who owns many elm trees
Leo: (Italian & English): a lion
Leon/Leonard: (Spanish, German, French & Latin America): lion
Leonardo: (German): brave as a lion
Leron: (French): round, circle
Leroy: (French): king
Les/Leslie/Lester: (Scottish): gray fortress
Levi/Levin: (Hebrew & Israel): attached, united as one
Levon: (Armenian): lion

Lew/Lewis: (German): famous warrior
Lewellyn: (Welsh): resembling a lion
Lex/Lexus: (English): a diminutive form of Alexander, which means protector of mankind
Li: (Chinese): having great strength
Liam: (Irish & Gaelic): determined protector
Liang : (Chinese): good man
Lilo: (Hawaiian): generous
Linc/Lincoln: (English): Roman colony at the pool; (Latin America): village
Lindberg: (German): mountain where linden grow
Linden/Lyndon: (English): linden hill
Lindley: (English): from the meadow of linden trees
Linley: (English): flax meadow
Linus: (Latin America): flaxen
Linwood: (English): flax wood
Lionel: (French): lion cub
Liu: (Asian); one who is quiet and peaceful
Livingston: (English): Leif's town
Lloyd: (Celtic, Welsh & English): gray
Locke: (English): forest
Logan: (Irish): small cove; (Scottish): Finnian's servant; (Gaelic): from the hollow
Lombard: (Latin): long-bearded
Lon/Lonnie: (Irish): fierce
London: (English): fortress of the moon
Lonzo: (Spanish): ready for battle
Lorcan: (Irish): the small fierce one
Lorenzo: (Italian & Spanish): crowned with laurel
Lot: (Hebrew): hidden covered
Loudon: (German): low valley
Louis: (French): famous warrior
Lovell/Lowell: (French & English): young wolf
Loyal: (English): faithful, loyal
Luc/Luca/Lucian/Lucius: (Latin): surrounded by light
Lucas: (Gaelic, English & Latin America): light
Ludwig: (German): famous warrior
Luigi: (Italian): famous warrior
Luis: (Spanish): famous warrior
Luka: (Latin America): light; (Russian): of Luciana
Luke: (Greek & Latin America): light
Luther: (German): soldier of the people
Lux: (Latin): man of the light
Lyle: (French & English): from the island
Lyman: (English): meadow
Lynch: (Irish): mariner
Lynn: (English): waterfall
Lysander: (Greek): liberator

Mac: (Gaelic): the son of Macarthur or Mackinley
Macallister: (Gaelic): the son of/ Alistair
Macarthur: (Gaelic): the son of Arthur
Macauley: (Scottish): son of righteousness
Macbride: (Scottish): son of a follower of Saint Brigid
Macdonald: (Scottish): son of Donald
Macdougall: (Scottish): son of Dougal
Macintosh: (Gaelic): the son of the thane
Mack/Mac: (Scottish): son
Mackenzie: (Scottish): son of Kenzie

Mackinley: (Gaelic): the son of the white warrior
Maclean: (Irish): son of Leander
Macon: (English): to make
Madden: (Pakistani): well organized
Maddox: (English): son of the Lord; (Celtic): beneficent
Magnus: (Latin): great
Maguire: (Gaelic): the son of the beige one
Mahmud/Mahmoud: (Arabic): one who is praiseworthy
Maitland: (English): from the meadow land
Major: (Latin): greater, military rank
Malachi/Malachy: (Hebrew): angel of God
Malcolm: (Gaelic): follower of St. Columbus
Malik: (African & Arabic): king, master
Malin: (English): strong, warrior
Mallory: (German): army counselor
Malloy: (Irish): noble chief
Manfred: (English): man of peace
Manley: (English): hero's meadow
Mann: (German): man
Manu: (African): the second-born child
Manuel: (Spanish): God is with us
Marcel: (French): little warrior
Marcelo: (Italian & Latin): hammer
Marcus/Marcellus/Marco: (Gaelic): hammer; (Latin America): warlike
Mario: (Hebrew): bitter, king-ruler
Mark/Marc: (Latin): dedicated to Mars, the god of war
Marlon: (French): falcon, of the sea fortress
Marlowe: (English): from the hill by the lake
Marquis: (French): nobleman
Marshall: (French): caretaker of horses; (English): a steward
Marston: (English): from the town near the marsh
Martin: (Latin): dedicated to Mars, the god of war
Marvin: (Welsh): friend of the sea
Mason: (French & English): stone worker
Matias: (Spanish & Hebrew): gift of God
Matisse: (French): one who is gifted
Matlock: (American): rancher
Mateo/Matteo: (Italian): gift of God
Matthew: (Hebrew & Biblical): gift of the Lord
Maurice: (Latin): dark-skinned
Maverick: (American): independent
Max: (English): greatest
Maximilian: (Latin): greatest
Maximiliano: (Italian): greatest
Maximus: (Greek): greatest
Maxwell: (English): capable, great spring
Maynard: (English): powerful, brave
McKenna: (Gaelic): the son of Kenna, to ascend; (English): handsome, fiery
McKenzie: (Irish): fair, favored one
McKinley: (English): offspring of the fair hero
Mead: (English): meadow
Mee: (Korean): beauty
Melton/Melville: (English): from the mill town
Melvin: (English): a friend who offers counsel
Mendel: (English): repairman
Mercer: (English): storekeeper

Meredith: (Welsh): guardian from the sea
Merle: (French): blackbird; (English): falcon
Merlin: (Welsh): of the sea fortress
Merrick: (English): ruler of the sea
Merrill: (English): falcon, shining sea
Meyer: (Jewish & Hebrew): shining
Micah: (Israel): like God
Michael: (Biblical & Hebrew): like God
Michelangelo: (Italian): a combination of Michael and Angelo
Mickey: (Irish, English & Hebrew): diminutive of Michael, which means like God
Miguel: (Portuguese & Spanish): who is like God
Mika/Micah: (Finnish): like God; (Japanese): new moon
Mikhail: (Greek & Russian): a form of Michael, which means like God
Miles: (German): merciful; (Latin): a soldier
Milford: (English): from the mill's forge
Miller: (English): one who works at the mill
Milo: (English): soldier
Milton: (English): mill town
Min: (Korean): cleverness
Minh: (Vietnamese): bright
Mitchell: (Hebrew): gift from God
Mohammed/Muhammad: (Arabic): one who is greatly praised
Monroe: (Gaelic): from the red swamp; (Scottish): from the river; (Irish): near the river roe
Montel: (Italian): mountain
Montgomery/Monty/Monte: (French): rich man's mountain
Mooney: (Irish): a wealthy man
Moore: (French): dark-skinned; (Irish & French): surname
Moran: (Irish): a great man
Morell: (French): dark
Morgan: (Celtic): lives by the sea; (Welsh): bright sea
Morley: (English): from the meadow on the moor
Moroccan: (African): one from Morocco
Morris: (Latin America): dark skinned; (English): son of More
Mortimer: (French): of the dead sea
Moses: (Hebrew & Biblical): saved from the water
Muir: (Scottish): moor
Murdoch: (Scottish): from the sea
Murphy: (Gaelic): warrior of the sea
Murray: (Scottish): sailor
Myles: (Latin): soldier
Myron: (Greek): fragrant oil

Nam: (Korean): south
Namir: (Hebrew): leopard
Naoki: (Japanese): honest tree
Naoko: (Japanese): honest
Napier: (French): a mover; (Spanish): new city
Napoleon: (French): fierce one
Narcissus: (Greek): self-love
Naresh: (Indian): king
Nash: (American): adventurer
Nathan/Nathaniel/Nate: (Hebrew & Israel): gift of God
Navarro: (Spanish): from the plains
Naveed: (Persian): our best wishes
Naveen: (Hindu): new; (Irish): beautiful, pleasant
Neal/Neil: (Irish, English & Celtic): a champion

Ned: (English & French): diminutive of Edward, which means wealthy guardian
Nehemiah: (Hebrew): compassion of Jehovah
Nelson: (English, Celtic, Irish & Gaelic): son of Neil
Nemo: (Greek): glen, glade
Neo: (Greek & American): new
Neptune: (Latin): sea ruler
Nero: (Latin & Spanish): stern
Nesbit: (English): nose-shaped bend in a river
Nevada: (Spanish): covered in snow
Neville: (French): from the new village
Nevin: (Irish): worshipper of the saint
Newman: (English): a newcomer
Newton: (English): new town
Ngu/Nguyen: (Vietnamese): sleep
Nicholas/Nicolas/Nico/Nicco: (Greek): victorious people
Nicol: (Scottish & English): victorious
Nicolai: Russian: victorious
Nigel: (English, Gaelic & Irish): champion; (American): ahead
Nikola: (Greek): victorious
Niles: (English): champion
Nino: (Italian): God is gracious; (Spanish): a young boy
Nixon: (English): son of Nick
Noah: (Biblical): rest, peace; (Hebrew): comfort, long-lived
Nobu: (Japanese): faith
Noel: (French): Christmas
Nolan: (Irish & Gaelic): famous; (Celtic): noble
Norbert/Norberto: (Scandinavian): brilliant hero
Norio: (Japanese): man of principles
Norris: (French): northerner
North: (English): from the north
Northcliff: (English): from the northern cliff
Norward: (English): guardian of the north
Noshi: (Native American): fatherly
Nuriel: (Hebrew): God's light
Nye: (English): one who lives on the island

O'Neal/O'Neil: (Irish): Son of Neil
O'Shea/O'Shay: (Irish): son of Shea
Oberon: (German): bear heart
Ocean/Oceanus: (Greek): a titan who rules the sea
Octavio/Octavius: (Latin): eighth
Oden/Odin: (Scandinavian): ruler
Odon: (Hungarian): wealthy protector
Odwin: (German): noble friend
Odysseus: (Greek): wrathful
Ogden: (English): oak valley
Oki: (Japanese): from the center of the ocean
Olaf/Olav/Ole: (Scandinavian): the remaining of the ancestors
Oleg: (Russian): one who is holy
Oliver/Olivier: (French, English, Danish & Latin America): the olive tree; (German): elf army
Olney: (English): from the loner's field
Omar: (Arabian): ultimate devotee; (Hebrew): eloquent speaker
Omega: (Greek): the last great one
Onofrio: (Italian): a defender of peace
Onslow: (Arabic): from the hill of the enthusiast
Oral: (Latin): verbal, speaker

Oram: (English): from the enclosure near the river bank
Ordell: (Latin): of the beginning
Ordway: (Anglo-Saxon): a fighter armed with a spear
Oren: (Hebrew): from the pine tree; (Gaelic): fair-skinned
Orion: (Greek): a hunter in Greek mythology
Orland: (English): from the pointed hill; (Spanish & German): renowned in the land
Orlando: (Spanish): land of gold: (German): famous throughout the land
Orly: (Hebrew): surrounded by light
Ormond: (English): one who defends with a spear
Orpheus: (Greek): an excellent musician
Orrin: (English): river
Orson: (Latin): resembling a bear
Orton: (English): from the settlement by the shore
Orville: (French): golden city; (English): spear-strength
Orwell: (Welsh): of the horizon
Osborn/Osbourne: (Norse): a bear of God
Oscar: (English): a spear of the gods; (Gaelic): a friend of deer
Oswald: (English): the power of God
Oswin: (English): a friend of God
Othello: (Spanish): rich
Otto: (German): wealthy or prosperous
Ovid: (Latin): a shepherd, egg
Owen: (English, Welsh & Celtic); young warrior; (Irish): born to nobility
Oz: (Hebrew): having great strength
Ozzy: (English): divine ruler

Pablo: (Spanish): a form of Paul, which means small
Pace: (English): a peaceful man
Paco: (Spanish): a man from France
Page/Paige: (French): youthful assistant
Paine/Payne: (Latin): a peasant
Palmer: (English): a pilgrim bearing a palm branch
Pancho: (Spanish): diminutive form of Francisco, which means free
Panya: (African): resembling a mouse
Panyin: (African): the first-born twin
Paolo: (Italian): a form of Paul, which means small
Paris: (Greek): downfall; (French): the capital city of France
Park: (Chinese): the cypress tree
Parker: (English): keeper of the park or forest
Parnell: (French): little Peter
Parry: (Welsh): the son of Harry
Pascal: (French): born at Easter
Patrick: (Latin): a nobleman
Patton: (English): from the town of warriors
Paul: (English & French): small, apostle in the bible
Pax: (English): peaceful
Paxton: (English): from the peaceful farm; (Latin America): town of peace
Pearce/Pierce: (English): a form of Peter, which means small rock
Pearson: (English): son of Peter
Pedro: (Spanish): solid and strong as a rock
Peeta/Peetamber: (Indian): yellow silk cloth
Peli: (Latin): happy
Pell: (English): a clerk
Pelton: (English): from the town by the lake
Pembroke: (Welsh): headland
Penley: (English): from the enclosed meadow

Penn: (Latin): pen, quill
Pepe: (Spanish): a diminutive form of Jose, which means God will add
Pepin: (German): determined
Percival: (French): one who can pierce the vale
Percy: (English): piercing the valley
Perez: (Hebrew): to break through
Perry: (English): a familiar form of Peter, which means a small stone or rick
Peter: (Greek & English): a small stone or rock, apostle in the Bible
Peterson: (English): son of Peter
Peyton: (English): from the village of warriors
Philip: (French, Greek & English): lover of horses
Phinean/Finian: (Irish): light-skinned, white
Phineas/ Phinneaus/Fineas: (Hebrew): oracle; (Israel): loudmouth; (Egyptian): dark-skinned
Phong: (Vietnamese): of the wind
Pierce: (English): rock
Pierre: (French): a rock
Ping: (Chinese): stable
Placido: (Spanish): serene
Plato: (Greek): broad-shouldered
Platt: (French): flatland
Pollock/Pollux: (Greek): crown
Polo: (Tibetan): brave warrior
Ponce: (Spanish): fifth
Porter: (French): gate keeper; (Latin America): door guard
Powell: (English): alert
Prentice: (English): a student
Prescott: (English): from the priest's cottage
Presley: (English): priest's land
Preston: (English): from the priest's farm
Prewitt: (French): brave little one
Primo: (Italian): first, premier quality
Prince: (Latin): chief, prince
Pryor: (Latin): head of the monastery
Puck: (English): elf
Pullman: (English): one who works on a train
Purnam: (English): dweller by the pond
Purvis: (French & English): providing food

Qiang: (Chinese): strong
Qiu: (Chinese): autumn
Quade: (Latin): fourth
Quiad: (Irish): the commander of the army
Quain: (French): clever
Quashawn: (American): tenacious
Quentin: (Latin): fifth
Quigley: (Irish): maternal side
Quillan: (Gaelic): resembling a cub
Quimby: (Scandinavian): woman's estate
Quincy: (English): fifth-born child; (French): estate belonging to Quintus
Quinlan: (Gaelic): strong and healthy man
Quinn: (Celtic): queenly; (Gaelic): one who provides counsel
Quinton/Quinten/Quintin: (Latin): from the queen's town

Radcliff/Radcliffe: (English): red cliff
Rafael/Raphael: (Spanish): one who is healed by God
Rafe: (Irish): a tough man

Rafferty: (Irish): prosperous

Raiden: (Japanese): god of thunder and lightning

Rain/Raine: (American): blessings from above; (Latin): ruler; (English): lord, wise

Rainer: (German): counsel

Raj/Rajan/Rajah: (Hindu): king

Raleigh/Rawley: (English): deer meadow

Ralph: (English): wolf counsel

Ram: (Hindu): god, god-like

Ramon: (Spanish): a wise or mighty protector

Ramsey: (Scottish): island of ravens

Rand/Randy/Randall/Randolph: (German): the wolf shield

Raoul: (French): wolf counsel

Rashad: (Arabic): wise counselor

Raul: (French): a form of Ralph, which means wolf counsel

Ravi: (Hindu): from the sun

Ray: (French): regal: (Scottish): grace; (English): wise protector

Rayburn: (English): deer brook

Raymond: (German): wise protector

Razi: (Aramaic): my secret

Rebel: (American): outlaw

Redford: (English): over the red river, from the reedy ford

Redmond: (German): protecting counselor

Reece/Reese: (English &Welsh): ardent, fiery, enthusiastic

Reed/Reid: (English & French): red-haired

Reeve: (English): a bailiff

Regan/Reagan: (Gaelic): born into royalty

Reginald/Reggie: (Latin): the king's advisor

Regis: (Latin): regal; (Latin America): rules

Reilly: (Gaelic): outgoing

Reinhart/Reynard/Reynold/Renaldo/Rey: (French): wise, bold, courageous

Remi/Remy: (French): oarsman or rower, from Rheims

Remington: (English): from the town of the raven's family

Rene/Renee: (French): reborn

Reuben/Ruben: (Hebrew): behold, a son

Rex: (Latin): king

Rhett: (English): stream

Rhodes: (Greek): where roses grow

Rhys: (Welsh): enthusiasm for life

Ricardo: (Spanish): strong and powerful ruler

Richard: (English, French & German): a strong and powerful ruler

Rico: (German): glory; (Spanish & Cuban): strong ruler

Ridge: (English): from the ridge

Ridley: (English): from the red meadow

Rigby: (English): ruler's valley

Riley: (English): from the rye clearing; (Irish): a small stream

Ringo: (Japanese): peace be with you

Rio: (Spanish & Portuguese): river

Ripley: (English): from the noisy meadow

Rishi: (Hindu): sage

River: (Latin & French): stream, water

Roan: (English): from the Rowan tree

Roark: (Gaelic): champion

Robert: (English, French, German & Scottish): famed, bright, shining

Robin: (English): a diminutive form of Robert, which means famed, bright, shining

Robinson: (English): son of Robin

Rocco: (Italian & German) rest

Rocket/Rockett/Rockitt: (English): fast
Rockford: (English): from the rocky ford
Rockwell: (English): rocky spring
Roden: (English): red valley
Roderick: (German): famous ruler
Rodney: (English): land near the water, island of reeds
Rodrigo: (Spanish): famous ruler
Roger: (German): renowned spearman
Roland/Rollo/Rolle: (French, German & English): renowned in the land
Rolf: (German): wolf counsel
Roman: (Spanish & Latin America): from Rome
Romeo: (Italian, Spanish, Latin America & African American): from Rome
Romulus: (Latin): citizen of Rome
Ronald: (English, Gaelic & Scottish): rules with counsel
Ronan: (Gaelic): resembling a little seal
Ronin: (Japanese): samurai without a master
Rooney: (Gaelic): red-haired
Roosevelt: (Danish): from the field of roses
Rory: (Irish): famous brilliance, famous ruler; (Gaelic): red-haired
Roscoe: (Norwegian): deer forest
Ross: (Scottish): from the peninsula
Roswell: (English): fascinating
Rowan: (Irish): red-haired; (English & Gaelic): from the rowan tree
Roy: (Irish & French): king, regal; (Scottish, Gaelic & Scottish): red, red-haired
Royce: (English): royal, son of the king: (German): famous
Rudolph: (German): a famous wolf
Rufus: (Latin America): redhead
Ruiz: (Spanish): a good friend
Rupert: (German): bright fame
Russell/Russ/Rush: (French): a little red-haired boy
Rusty: (English): one who has red hair or a ruddy complexion
Rutherford: (English): from the cattle's ford
Ryan: (Gaelic): little king; (Irish): kindly, young royalty
Ryder: (English): knight
Ryker: (Danish): a powerful ruler
Rylan/Ryland: (English): the place where rye is grown

Saber: (French): man of the sword
Sacha: (French): protector of mankind
Said/Sa'id/Sayed: (Arabic): happy
Saige/Sage: (English & French): wise one; (English): from the spice
Sailor: (American): sailor
Salem: (Hebrew): peace
Salisbury: (English): fort at the willow pool
Salmon: (Czech): a form of Solomon, which means peaceful
Salvador/Salvatore: (Spanish & Italian): savior
Samson/Sampson: (Hebrew & Israel): bright as the sun
Samuel: (Israel): God hears; (Hebrew): name of God
Sanborn: (English): sandy brook
Sandburg: (English): from the sandy village
Sandeep: (Punjabi): enlightened
Sanford: (English): from the sandy crossing
Sanjay: (American): a combination of Sanford and Jay
Santana: (Spanish): saintly
Santiago: (Spanish): named for Saint James
Santino: (Italian): little angel

Santo: (Italian): a holy man
Sargent: (French): army officer
Satchel: (French): Saturn
Saturn: (Latin): the god of agriculture
Saul: (Israel): borrowed: (Hebrew & Spanish): asked for
Sawyer: (English): one who works with wood
Saxon/Sax: (English): a swordsman
Sayid: (African): lord and master
Schaffer/Schaeffer: (German): a steward
Schuman: (German): shoemaker
Scott: (Scottish): wanderer
Scout: (French): scout
Scully: (Irish): herald; (Gaelic): town crier
Seaman: (English): a mariner
Seamus: (Irish): a form of James, which means supplant
Sean/Shawn: (Irish): God is gracious
Sebastian: (Greek): the revered one
Sergio/Sergei/Serge: (Latin, Italian & Russian): a servant
Seth: (Hebrew): anointed; (Israel): appointed
Seton/Seaton: (English): from the farm by the sea
Seung: (Korean): a victorious successor
Seven: (American): the number seven
Sexton: (English): church custodian
Seymour: (French): from the town of Saint Maur
Shade: (English): secretive
Shan: (Chinese): mountain
Shane: (Hebrew): gift from God; (Irish): God is gracious
Shannon: (Gaelic): having ancient wisdom
Sharif: (Arabic): noble
Shaw: (English): from the woodland
Shawn: (Irish): a form of Sean, which means God is gracious
Shea: (Irish): majestic, fairy place
Sheffield: (English): from the crooked field
Sheldon: (English): from the steep valley
Shelton: (English): from the farm on the ledge
Shen: (Chinese): deep spiritual thought
Shepherd: (English): one who herds sheep
Sheridan: (Irish, English & Celtic): untamed; (Gaelic): bright, a seeker
Sherlock: (English): fair-haired
Sherman: (English): one who cuts wool cloth
Sherwin: (English): swift runner
Shiloh: (Hebrew): he who was sent, God's gift, the one to whom it belongs; (Israel): peaceful
Shin: (Japanese): truth
Shiro: (Japanese): fourth-born son
Siddhartha: (Hindu): the original name of Buddha
Siegfried: (German): victorious peace
Sierra: (Spanish): from the jagged mountain range
Sigmund: (German): victorious protector
Silas: (Latin America): man of the forest
Silver: (English): precious metal, the color silver
Simba: (African): lion
Simmons: (Hebrew): the son of Simon
Simon: (Israel): it is heard
Simpson: (Hebrew): son of Simon
Sinclair: (English): man from Saint Clair
Singh: (Hindu): lion

Skelly: (Irish): storyteller
Skylar/Schuyler: (Dutch): sheltering
Slade: (English): child of the valley
Slater: (English): one who works with slate
Sloan: (English): raid; (Irish, Celtic, Scottish & Gaelic): fighter, warrior
Smith: (English): artisan, tradesman
Socrates: (Greek): wise, learning
Solomon: (Hebrew & Israel): peaceful
Soo: (Korean): excellent, long life
Spalding: (English): divided field
Speck: (German): bacon
Spence/Spencer: (English): dispenser, provider
Stanford: (English): from the stony ford
Stanley: (English): stony meadow
Stanton: (English): from the stony ford
Stavros: (Greek): one who is crowned
Steadman: (English): one who lives at the farm
Stefan: (German, Polish & Swedish): a form of Steven, which means crowned one
Stefano/Stephano: (Italian): a form of Steven, which means crowned one
Stephen/Steven: (English & Greek): crowned one
Sterling: (English): valuable
Stern: (English): austere
Stone/Stony: (English): stone
Storm/Stormy: (English): tempest; (American): impetuous nature
Striker: (American): aggressive
Stuart: (Scottish): steward; (English): bailiff; (Irish): keeper of the estate
Sullivan: (Gaelic): dark eyes
Sully: (English): from the southern meadow
Sven: (Scandinavian): youth
Sydney: (English): wide island
Sylvester/Sly: (Latin): man from the forest

Taft: (French): from the homestead
Taggart: (Gaelic): son of a priest
Tai: (Chinese): large; (Vietnamese): prosperous, talented
Taj: (Indian): one who is crowned
Tam: (Vietnamese): having heart, the number eight
Tama: (Japanese): jewel
Tanner: (English & German): leather worker
Tannon: (German): from the fir tree
Tao: (Chinese): one who has a long life
Tarek/Tarik/Tariq: (Arabic): conqueror
Tate/Tatum: (English): cheerful
Taurean: (Latin): strong
Tavor/Tavarus/Tavaris: (Aramaic): misfortune
Taye: *(Ethiopian):* one who has been seen
Taylor: (English & French): a tailor
Teagan: (Gaelic): handsome, attractive
Ted/Teddy: (English): a gift from God
Teller/Telly: (English & Greek): storyteller
Tennessee: (Native American): from the state of Tennessee
Tennyson: (English): a form of Dennison, which means son of Dennis
Terrell: (German): thunder ruler
Terrence/Terrance: (Latin America): tender, gracious
Tex: (English): of Texas
Texas: (Native American): one of many friends, from the state of Texas

Thaddeus: (Hebrew): valiant, wise: (Greek): praise, one who has courage
Thang: (Vietnamese): victorious
Thanh: (Vietnamese): finished
Thatcher: (English): one who repairs roofs
Theodore: (Greek): divine gift
Thiago: (Spanish, Portuguese & Brazilian): Saint James
Thierry: (French): a dorm of Theodore, which means divine gift
Thomas: (Hebrew, Greek & Dutch): twin
Thor: (Norse): god of thunder
Thorne: (English): from the thorn bush
Thurmond: (English): defended by Thor
Thurston: (English): Thor's town
Tien: (Chinese): heaven
Tiernan: (Gaelic): lord of the manor
Tiger: (English): powerful cat
Tilden: (English): tilled valley
Tilford: (English): prosperous ford
Timon: (Hebrew): honor
Timothy: (Greek & English): to honor God
Tito: (Italian): honor
Titus: (Greek): of the giants; (Latin): great defender
Tobias: (Hebrew & Israel): God is good
Toby: (English): God is good
Todd: (Scottish): fox
Tolbert: (English): tax collector
Tomas: (German): a form of Thomas, which means twin
Tong: (Vietnamese): fragrant
Torin: (Irish): chief
Torrence: (Irish): knolls
Travis: (French): to cross over
Trent: (Welsh): dwells near the rapid stream
Trenton: (English): town of Trent
Trevor: (Welsh): from the large village
Trey/Treat: (English & Latin): third-born child
Treyvon: (American): a form of Trevon, which is a combination of Trey and Von
Trigg: (Norse): truthful
Tripp: (English): traveler
Tristan: (English, Celtic & French): outcry, tumult; (Welsh): noisy; (Irish): bold
Trong: (Vietnamese): respected
Troy: (French): curly haired; (Irish): foot soldier
True: (English): loyal
Twain: (English): divided in two
Tybalt: (Latin): he who sees the truth
Tye/Ty: (English): from the fenced-in pasture
Tyler: (English): maker of tiles
Tyrone: (French): from Owen's land
Tyson: (French): explosive; (English): son of Tye

Udell: (English): from the valley of yew trees
Udi: (Hebrew): one who carries a torch
Ugo: (Italian): a great thinker
Ulmer: (German): having the fame of a wolf
Ulrich: (German): wolf ruler
Ulysses: (Latin): hateful
Unique: (Latin): only one; (American): unlike others
Unity: (English): unity, togetherness

Upton: (English): upper town
Uranus: (Greek): mythical father of the titans
Urban: (Latin): city dweller, courteous
Uri: (Hebrew): God is my light
Usher: (Latin): from the mouth of the river; (English): doorkeeper
Utah: (Native American): people of the mountains, the state of Utah
Uzi: (Hebrew): having great power
Uziel: (Hebrew): God is my strength

Vadim: (Russian): god looking
Valentine/Val: (Latin): strong and healthy
Valentino: (Italian): brave or strong; (Latin America): health or love
Vance: (English): windmill dweller
Vandyke: (Danish): from the dike
Vardon: (French): from the green hill
Varick: (German): a protective ruler
Vaughn: (Celtic): small
Vernon/Vern: (Latin): youthful, young at heart; (French & English): alder tree grove
Verrill: (German): masculine; (French): loyal
Vicente: (Spanish): a form of Vincent, which means winner
Victor: (Spanish & Latin America): winner
Vijay: (Hindu): victorious
Vikram: (Hindu): valorous
Vincent: (English & Latin America): conquering, victorious
Vinson: (English): son of Vincent
Virgil/Vergil: (English): flourishing; (Latin America): strong
Vito: (Latin): one who gives life
Vladimir: (Slavic): a famous prince
Vulcan: (Latin): the god of fire

Wade: (English): ford, cross the river
Wadley: (English): from the meadow near the ford
Wadsworth: (English): from the estate near the ford
Wagner: (German): wagoner
Wainwright: (English): one who builds wagons
Waite: (English): watchman
Walden: (English): wooded valley
Walker: (English): one who trods the cloth
Wallace: (Scottish): a man from the south
Walter: (German): the commander of the army
Walton: (English): walled town
Wane/Wayne: (English): craftsman, wagon maker
Wang: (Chinese): hope, wish
Warden: (English): guard
Warner/Werner: (German & English): defender
Warren: (English): to preserve; (German): protector, loyal
Warrick: (English): a protective ruler
Washington: (English): town near water
Watson: (English): the son of Walter
Waylon: (English): land by the road
Wayne/Wane: (English): craftsman, wagon maker
Webb: (English): weaver
Webster: (English): a weaver
Wei: (Chinese): a brilliant man, great strength
Weiss: (German): white
Welborne: (English): spring-fed stream

Wendall/Wendell: (German): a wanderer
Wentworth: (English): village, from the white one's estate
Wesley: (English & German): from the west meadow
West: (English): from the west
Weston: (English): west town
Wheatley: (English): wheat field
Whit: (English): white-skinned
Whitby: (English): from the white farm
Whitfield: (English): from the white field
Whitley/Whit: (English): from the white meadow
Whitman: (English): white-haired
Whitmore: (English): white moor
Whitney: (English): white island
Wickley: (English): village meadow
Wilbur: (English): bright willows, fortification
Wilder: (English): wilderness
Wiley: (English): crafty
Wilford: (English): from the willow ford
Wilfred: (German): determined peacemaker
William/Willem: (English, German & French): protector
Willis: (English): son of Willie, which is a diminutive form of William
Wilmer: (German): determined and famous
Wilson: (English & German): son of William
Windsor: (English): riverbank with a winch
Winston: (English): joy stone
Winter: (American): the season
Winthrop: (English): from the friendly village
Winton: (English): from the enclosed pastureland
Wolf: (English): the animal, wolf
Wolfgang: (German): wolf quarrel
Woodley: (English): wooded meadow
Woodrow: (English): forester, row of houses
Wyatt: (English): guide, wide, wood, famous bearer; (French): son of the forest guide
Wyndham: (English): from the windy village

Xander: (Greek): a diminutive form of Alexander, which means protector of mankind
Xannon: (American): from an ancient family
Xavier: (Basque): owner of a new house; (Arabic): one who is bright
Xiu: (Chinese): cultivated
Xoan: (Gaelic): God is gracious
Xue: (Chinese): studious

Yale: (Welsh): from the fertile upland
Yan/Yann: (Russian): a form of John, which means God is gracious
Yancy: (Native American): Englishman
Yang: (Chinese): people of goat tongue
Yao: (Ewe): born on a Tuesday
Yaphet: (Hebrew): handsome
Yardley: (English): from the fenced-in meadow
Yasir: (Arabic): well-off financially
Yeo: (Korean): mildness
Yeoman: (English): a man-servant
Yitzchak: (Hebrew): a form of Isaac, which means he will laugh
Yo: (Cambodian): honest
Yohan: (German): God is gracious
Yong: (Korean): courageous

York: (Celtic, English & Latin America): from the yew tree
Yosef: (Hebrew): a form of Joseph, which means God will increase
Yoshi: (Japanese): adopted son
You: (Chinese): friend
Young: (Korean): forever, unchanging
Yul/Yule: (English): born at Christmas
Yuri: (Russian & Ukrainian): a form of George, which means farmer
Yves: (French): a young archer

Zachariah/Zacarias/Zachary: (Hebrew): Jehovah has remembered; (Israel): remembered by the Lord
Zaden/Zayden: (Arabic & Dutch): a sower of seeds
Zale: (Greek): having the strength of the sea
Zander: (Slavic): helper and defender of mankind
Zane/Zain: (Hebrew): gift from God; (Arabian): beloved
Zared: (Hebrew): one who is trapped
Zarek: (Polish): may God protect the king
Zavier: (Arabic): a form of Xavier, which means bright
Zebulun/Zebulon/Zeb: (Hebrew & Israel): habitation
Zedekiah/Zed: (Hebrew): God is mighty and just
Zeke: (English): strengthened by God
Zeno: (Greek): cart, harness
Zephyr: (Greek): west wind
Zeus: (Greek): powerful one
Zhen: (Chinese): astonished
Zia: (Hebrew): trembling
Zian: (Chinese): peace
Zigfrid/Ziggy: (Latvian & Russian): a form of Siegfried, which means victorious peace
Zion: (Hebrew): from the citadel
Zoltan: (Hungarian): kingly

Appendix B: Alphabetical List of Girls Names

Aaliyah/Aliyah: (Arabic): an ascender; (Muslim): exalted; (American): immigrant to a new home
Abby/Abbey/Abby: (Hebrew): diminutive form of Abigail, which means father rejoiced
Abena: (African): born on a Tuesday
Abiela: (Hebrew): my father is Lord
Abigail: (Hebrew): father rejoiced; (Biblical): source of joy
Abira: (Hebrew): strong
Abra: (Hebrew): mother of many nations
Abril: (Spanish): April
Ada: (English): wealthy; (Hebrew): ornament; (German): noble; (African): first daughter
Addison: (English): son of Adam
Adelaide: (French & German): noble, kind
Adelina/Adeline: (French & Spanish): of the nobility
Adell/Adele: (German & French): noble, kind
Adina: (Israel): beautiful; (Hebrew): slender
Adriana/Adrianna: (Spanish, Greek & Italian): woman with dark and rich features
Afra: (Hebrew): young doe
Afton: (English): from the Afton River
Agatha: (Latin & Greek): pure, virtuous, good
Agnes: (Greek): pure
Agustina: (Latin America): majestic, grand
Aika: (Japanese): love song
Aileen: (Irish): light bearer, from the green meadow
Ainsley: (Scottish): one own's meadow
Aisha/Aiesha: (African): womanly, lively; (Muslim): life, lively
Aiyanna/Aiyana/Aianna: (Native American): forever flowering
Akela: (Hawaiian): noble
Aki: (Japanese): born in autumn
Akilah: (Arabic): intelligent
Akira: (Scottish): anchor
Alaina: (French): dear child, beautiful and fair woman
Alana: (Irish): beautiful, peaceful
Alanis: (English): attractive and bright
Alberta: (German & French): noble and bright
Alejandra: (Spanish): defender of mankind
Alexandria/Alessandra/Alexa: (Greek, English & Latin America): defender of mankind
Alexi: (English): helper, defender
Alexis: (English): helper, defender; (Biblical): protector of mankind
Ali: (Arabian): noble, sublime
Alice/Alyce: (Spanish): of the nobility
Alicia/Alysha: (English): of noble birth; (Spanish & German): sweet
Aline: (Dutch): alone; (Celtic & Irish): fair, good looking
Allegra: (Latin): cheerful
Allison/Alison: (English): noble, truthful, strong character
Alma: (Latin & Italian): nurturing, kind
Almira: (Arabic): aristocratic
Alpha: (Greek): first-born
Althea: (Greek): wholesome, healer
Alyssa: (Greek): logical
Amanda: (Latin): much loved
Amaranth: (Greek): an unfading flower
Amaya: (Japanese & Arabic): night rain
Amber: (Arabic): precious jewel, yellow-brown color
Ambra: (French): jewel; (Italian): Amber color

Ambrosia: (Greek): immortal
Ame: (Japanese): rain, heaven
Amelia: (English & Latin America): industrious, striving
America: (English): ruler of the home
Amethyst: (Greek): wine, a purple gemstone
Amira: (Arabic): princess
Amrita: (Hindu): nectar of eternal immortality
Amy/Aimee: (English, French & Latin America): beloved
Anais: (Hebrew): gracious
Anastasia: (Greek): resurrection
Andrea: (Greek & Latin): courageous, strong
Andrina: (English): courageous, valiant
Angel: (Spanish & Greek): angelic
Angela: (Spanish, French, Italian & Latin America): angel
Angelina: (Italian): little angel
Angelique: (Greek): heavenly messenger
Anita: (Italian, Hebrew & Latin America): gracious
Aniyah: (Polish & Hebrew): God has shown favor
Anja: (Russia): grace of God
Anjelica: (Greek): a diminutive form of Angela, which means angel
Anka: (Japanese): color of the dawn
Anna/Ana: (Hebrew): favor or grace; (Native American): mother; (Israel): gracious
Annabel: (Italian): graceful and beautiful
Annabeth: (English): graced with God's bounty
Annalynn: (English): from the graceful lake
Anne: (Hebrew & Israel): favor or grace
Annette: (French & Hebrew): gracious
Annika: (Dutch): gracious
Annmarie: (English): filled with bitter grace
Anona: (English): pineapple
Antonella: (Latin America): praiseworthy
Antonia: (Greek): flourishing or flowering
Antoinette: (French): flowering; (Latin): praiseworthy
Anya: (Russian): graced with God's favor
Anyssa/Anissa: (English): a form of Agnes, which means pure
Aphrodite: (Greek): beauty, love goddess
Apollonia: (Greek): strength
Apple: (America): sweet fruit
April: (English): opening buds of spring; (Latin America): opening, fourth month
Arabella: (Latin): answered prayer, beautiful altar
Arden: (English): passionate, enthusiastic, valley of the eagle
Aretha: (Greek): virtuous
Aria: (Italian): melody
Arianna/Ariana: (Greek & Italian): holy
Ariel/Arial: (Hebrew): lioness of God
Arista: (Latin): harvest
Arizona: (Native American): from the little spring, from the state of Arizona
Arlene/Arleen: (Irish): pledge
Ashanti: (African): great African woman
Ashley: (English & Biblical): lives in the ash tree
Ashlyn: (American): combination of Ashley and Lynn
Asia: (Greek & English): resurrection, rising sun
Aspen: (English): from the aspen tree
Astra: (Latin): of the stars
Astrid: (Scandinavian & German): divine strength
Athena: (Greek): wise, goddess of wisdom and war

Aubrey: (English): one who rules with elf-wisdom
Audrey: (English): noble strength
Audrina: (English): nobility, strength
Augusta: (Latin): venerable, majestic
Aura: (Greek): soft breeze: Latin: golden
Aurora: (Latin): dawn
Autumn: (English & Latin America): the fall season
Ava: (Latin America): like a bird
Avalon: (Latin): island
Avery: (English): counselor, sage, wise
Avril: (English); born in April
Ayanna: (Hindi & African): innocent, resembling a beautiful flower
Azura/Azure: (Persian): a blue, semi-precious stone

Babette: (French & German): a diminutive form of Barbara, which means stranger
Bailey: (English): bailiff, steward, public official
Bambi: (Italian): child
Barbara: (Latin America): stranger
Bathsheba: (Hebrew): oath, voluptuous, famous bearer; (Biblical): seventh daughter
Bea: (American): blessed
Beatrice: (Italian): blessed; (French): bringer of joy
Bebe: (Spanish): a diminutive form of Barbara, which means stranger
Becca: (Hebrew): a diminutive form of Rebecca, which means tied or bound
Bela: (Slovakian): she of fair skin; (Indian): sea shore; (Hebrew): destruction
Belinda: (English): beautiful and tender woman
Belisama: (Celtic): goddess of rivers and lakes
Bella: (Hebrew): devoted to God; (Spanish & Latin America): beautiful
Belle: (French): beautiful
Bernadette: (French): brave as a bear
Bernadine: (English & German): brave as a bear
Bernice: (French & Greek): one who brings victory
Bertha: (Germany): bright
Beryl: (Greek & English): green jewel
Bess: (English): my God is bountiful
Beth: (Scottish): lively
Bethany: (Hebrew & Israel): a life-town near Jerusalem
Bettina: (English): consecrated to God
Beulah: (Hebrew & Israel): married
Beverly: (English): beaver field
Beyonce: (American): one who surpasses others
Bianca: (Italian): white, fair
Bibi: (Latin): lively
Bijou: (French): as precious as a jewel
Billie: (English): desire to protect
Blaine: (Gaelic, Irish & Celtic): thin
Blair: (Irish & Celtic): from the plain, (Gaelic): child of the fields; (Scottish): peat moss
Blake: (English): pale blond or dark; (Scottish): dark-haired
Bliss: (English): joy, happiness
Blossom: (English): fresh, flowerlike
Blue: (English): the color blue
Blythe: (English): happy
Bo: (Chinese): precious
Bonnie: (English): good; (French): sweet; (Scottish): pretty, charming
Brady: (Irish): a large-breasted woman
Brande/Brandy/Brandie: (English): a woman wielding a sword, an alcoholic drink
Brea: (French): champion

Bree: (Celtic): broth; (Irish): hill, strong one
Brenda: (Gaelic): little raven; (Scandinavian): sword
Brenna: (Welsh): like a raven
Brianna/Breanna: (Irish): strong; (Celtic & English): she ascends
Brice/Bryce: (Welsh): alert, ambitious
Bridget/Brigid: (Irish): strong and protective
Brie: (French): from the northern region of France
Bristol: (English): bridge
Britt/Britta: (Swedish): high goddess
Brittany: (English & Celtic): from Britain
Bronte: (Greek): thunder
Bronwyn: (Welsh): dark and pure; (English): white-skinned
Brooke: (English): lives by the stream
Brooklyn: (English): water, stream
Brynn: (Welsh): hill
Buffy: (American): buffalo, from the plains
Bunny: (Greek): a diminutive form of Beatrice, which means blessed, happy
Burgundy: (French): a region of France that is famous for its wine

Caden: (English): battle maiden
Cadence: (Latin): rhythmic and melodious
Cady: (American): happiness
Cairo: (African): the Egyptian city
Caitlyn/Kaitlyn: (Irish): pure
Caledonia: (Latin): woman of Scotland
Callie/Cally: (Greek): beautiful; (English); lark
Calliope: (Greek): beautiful voice
Calista: (Greek): most beautiful
Calla: (Greek): resembling a lily, beautiful
Cambria: (Latin): woman of Wales
Camdyn: (English): of the enclosed valley
Cameo: (Italian): sculptured jewel; (English & Latin America): a shadow or carved gem portrait
Cameron/Camryn: (Irish & Gaelic): crooked nose
Camila/Camilla/Camille: (Italian): a noble virgin, a ceremonial attendant
Campbell: (Scottish): crooked mouth
Candace: (English): pure, glittering white
Candida: (Latin): white-skinned
Candy/Candi: (American): bright, sweet; (Hebrew): famous bearer
Canisa: (Greek): much-loved
Cantrelle: (French): song
Caprice: (Italian): fanciful
Caprina: (Italian): from the island Capri
Cara: (Celtic): friend; (Italian & Dominican Republic): dear, beloved
Carey: (Irish): pure; (Celtic): from the fortress
Cari: (Latin America): beloved
Carina: (Latin): little darling
Carissa/Caressa: (Greek): woman of grace
Carla: (Portuguese & Latin America): strong one
Carleen/Carlene: (English): derivative of Caroline, which means song of happiness
Carlessa: (American): restless
Carlie/Carly: (American): strong one; (Latin America): little, womanly
Carlotta: (Italian): a derivative of Charlotte, which means feminine
Carmel: (Hebrew): garden; (Israel): woodland; (Celtic): from the vineyard
Carmela/Carmella: (Hebrew & Israel): golden; (Spanish): garden
Carmen: (English): garden; (Spanish & Latin America): song
Carnie: (Latin): vocal

Carol: (French): melody, song
Carolina/Caroline: (Mexican): beautiful woman; (French & English): song of happiness
Carolyn: (English): joy, song of happiness
Carrie: (American): melody, song
Carrington: (English): beautiful
Carys: (Welsh): one who loves and is loved
Casey/Cacie/Kasey: (Celtic & Gaelic): brave; (Irish): observant, brave; (Spanish): honorable
Casia: (English): alert, vigorous
Cassandra: (Greek): prophet of doom
Cassidy: (Irish): curly-haired
Catalina: (Spanish): pure
Cate: (English): blessed, pure, holy
Catherine: (English): pure, virginal
Cathleen/Kathleen: (Irish): a form of Catherine/Katherine, which means pure, virginal
Cayenne: (French): hot and spicy
Cayla: (American): crowned with laurel
Caylee: (American): crowned with laurel
Ceara: (Irish): a derivation of Ciara, which means dark-skinned
Cecilia: (Latin): blind
Cecily/Cicely: (Latin): a form of Cecilia, which means blind
Celeste: (Latin): heavenly daughter
Celia: (Italian): heavenly
Celina/Celine: (Latin): of the heavens
Cera: (French): colorful woman
Cerise: (French): cherry
Chai: (Israel & Hebrew): life
Chakra: (Arabic): center of spiritual energy
Chalice: (French): goblet
Chambray: (French): a lightweight fabric
Chanda: (Sanskrit): enemy of evil
Chandelle: (French): candle
Chandra: (Hindi): of the moon
Chanel: (French): from the canal, a channel
Chantal/Chantel: (French): song
Chantrise: (French): a singer
Charisma: (Greek): grace
Charity: (English): kindness, generous, goodwill
Charlaine: (English): feminine form of Charles, which mean manly
Charlize: (French): manly
Charlotte: (French): feminine
Charmaine: (English): song; (French): beautiful orchard
Chastity: (Latin): pure
Chelsea: (English): seaport
Chen: (China): great, dawn
Cher: (English): beloved
Cherise/Cherice/Cherisse: (French): cherry, dear one
Cherish: (English): to be held dear, values
Cherry: (French): dear one; America: cherry
Cheryl/Sheryl: (English): beloved
Chesney: (English): one who promotes peace
Cheyenne: (French): dog; (Native American): an Algonquin tribe
Chiara: (Italian): daughter of the light
China: (Chinese): fine porcelain
Chiquita: (Spanish): little one

Chloe: (Greek): verdant, blooming
Christina/Christine/Christal/Christa/Chrissy: (English): follower of Christ
Chun: (Chinese): springtime
Ciara: (Irish): dark beauty
Cierra: (Spanish): dark-skinned
Cilla: (Latin): sturdy, vision
Cinnamon: (American): reddish-brown spice
Clancy/Clancey: (American): light-hearted
Clara: (French & Catalonia): clear, bright
Clare/Clair/Claire: (English): clear; (French): bright
Clarice: (French): famously bright
Clarissa: (Spanish & Italian): clear; (Latin America): brilliant
Claudia/Claudine: (Spanish & Latin America): lame
Claudette: (Spanish): a form of Clara, which means clear, bright
Clementine: (French): merciful
Cleo/Clio: (English); father's glory
Cleopatra: (Greek): glory to the father; (African American): queen
Cloris: (Greek): goddess of flowers
Clove: (German): spice
Clover: (English): meadow flower
Coby: (Hebrew): supplanter
Cody: (English): cushion
Colleen: (Irish & Gaelic): girl
Collette: (English): victorious people
Concordia: (Latin): peace
Constanza/Constance/Connie: (American): strong-willed
Consuela: (Spanish): provides consolation
Contessa: (Italian): a countess
Cora: (Greek & English): maiden; (Scottish): seething pool
Coral: (English): a reef formation
Corazon: (Spanish): of the heart
Cordelia: (English, Welsh & Celtic): of the sea
Coretta: (Greek): a form of Cora, which means maiden
Corey/Cory: (Irish): from the hollow, of the churning waters
Corina: (Latin): spear-wielding woman
Corinthia: (Greek): woman of Clorinth
Cornelia: (Latin): horn
Cota: (Spanish): lively
Cote: (French): from the riverbank
Courtney: (English): courteous
Cree: (Native American): name of tribe
Cressida: (Greek): golden girl
Crimson: (English): deep red color
Crystal/Krystal: (English): jewel; (Latin America): a clear brilliant glass
Cyan: (American): light blue or green
Cylee: (American): darling daughter
Cynthia: (Greek): moon
Cyrene: (Greek): maiden huntress

Dagmar: (Scandinavian): born on a glorious gay
Dahlia: (Swedish): from the valley, resembling the flower
Daisy: (English); day's eve; (American): daisy flower
Dakota: (Native American): friend, ally, tribal name
Dale: (English): valley
Dalia/Dahlia: (Hebrew): tree branch
Dana: (English, Danish, Irish & Hebrew): a person from Denmark

Dania: (English, Hebrew & Denmark): God is my judge
Danica: (Slavic): the morning star
Daniela: (Hebrew & Spanish): God is my judge
Danielle: (Hebrew): God is my judge
Danna: (Indian): gift
Daphne: (Greek): of the laurel tree
Dara: (Hebrew): compassionate
Darby: (Irish & Gaelic): free man; (English): deer park
Darcy: (Irish & Celtic): dark one
Daria: (Greek): wealthy
Darlene: (English & French): little darling
Davena/Davina: (Scottish): feminine form of David, which means beloved one
Davon: (English): river
Dawn: (English): aurora; (Greek): sunrise
Dea: (Greek): resembling a goddess
Deana/Deanna: (English & Latin America): from the valley
Deborah: (Hebrew & Israel): honey bee
Deidre: (Gaelic): a raging or broken-hearted woman
Dekla: (Latvian): a trinity goddess
Dela/Della: (German, Greek & English): noble
Delaney: (Irish): dark challenger; (French): from the elder-grove tree
Delia: (Greek): visible
Delilah: (Hebrew): a seductive woman
Delora/Delores/Deloris: (Latin America): of the seashore; (English): sorrow
Delta: (Greek): from the mouth of the river, the fourth letter of the Greek alphabet
Demi: (Greek): a petite woman; (French): half
Dena: (Hebrew & Israel): vindicated; (Native American): valley
Denali: (Indian): a superior woman
Dendara: (Egyptian): from the town on the river
Denise: (French): a follower of Dionysus
Deondra/Deandra: (American): a combination of Dee and Andrea
Derry: (English, Irish, German & Gaelic): red-haired, from the oak grove
Desiree: (French): desired
Destiny: (English): fate
Deva: (Hindi): divine
Devin/Devon: (Irish): poet
Dextra: (Latin): skillful
Dharma: (Indian): ultimate law of all things
Diamond: (English): bridge protector; (Greek): unbreakable
Diana: (Greek): divine, goddess of the moon and the hunt
Diane: (Latin America): hunter
Dina: (Hebrew & Israel): avenged, judged; (English): from the valley
Dinah: (Hebrew & Israel): judgment
Dionne: (Greek): divine queen
Dita: (Spanish): a form of Edith, which means gift
Dixie: (American): woman of the south
Dolly: (American): cute child
Dolores: (Spanish): woman of sorrow
Dominique: (French): belonging to God
Donna: (Italian): lady
Dora/Dori/Dory: (Greek): gift
Doreen: (French): golden one; (Gaelic): brooding
Doris: (Greek): sea
Dorothea: (Dutch): gift of God
Dorothy (Greek): gift of God
Dove: (American): bird of peace

Drucilla/Drusilla: (Biblical): fruitful, dewy-eyed; (Latin America): mighty
Drew: (Greek): courageous, strong
Drury: (French): greatly loved
Dulce: (Latin): very sweet

Earlene: (Irish): pledge; (English): noble
Eartha: (English): earthy
Easter: (American): from the holiday or Christian festival
Easton: (American): wholesome
Ebony: (American): dark strength
Echo: (Greek): sound returned
Edana: (Irish): fiery
Eden: (Hebrew): delight; (Israel): paradise
Edie: (English): blessed
Edith: (English): joyous, a treasure
Edna: (Celtic): fire; (Hebrew): rejuvenation; (Israel): spirit renewed
Edwina: (English): prosperous friend
Effie: (Greek): melodious talk
Eileen: (Irish & French): light
Elaine: (French): light
Elana: (Hebrew): from the oak tree
Elata: (Latin): high spirited
Eldora: (Spanish): golden, blond, gift of the sun
Eleanor/Elinor: (English): torch
Electra: (Greek): bright, the shining one
Elena: (Spanish): the shining light
Eleni: (Greek): light
Eliana: (Hebrew): the Lord answers our prayers
Elisa/Elise: (Hebrew): my God is bountiful
Elisha: (Hebrew): God is salvation; (Israel): God is gracious
Eliza: (French): consecrated to God
Elizabeth: (English): my God is bountiful; (Hebrew & Biblical): consecrated to God
Ella: (English); beautiful fairy; (Spanish): she
Elle: (English): torch
Ellen/Ellyn: (Greek): light
Ellery: (English): cheerful
Elliott: (Israel): close to God; (English): the Lord is my God
Elma: (German): having God's protection
Elmira: (English): noble
Eloisa/Eloise: (Latin): famous warrior
Elrica: (German): great ruler
Elsa: (German): noble
Elsie: (English): my God is bountiful
Elvira: (Latin): truthful, trusted
Emerald: (English, Spanish & French): a bright green gem
Emerson: (English): brave, powerful
Emery: (German): industrious
Emilia: (Spanish): flattering
Emily: (Latin America): admiring
Emma: (English, Danish & German): whole, complete, universal
Emmanuelle: (Hebrew): God is with us
Emme: (Latin America): industrious, striving
Emmylou: (American): universal ruler
Enid: (Welsh): life, spirit
Enya: (Scottish): jewel, blazing
Epiphany: (Greek): manifestation

Erica: (Denmark): honorable ruler
Erin: (Irish): peace
Ernestina/Ernestine: (German): determined, serious
Esme: (French): esteemed
Esmeralda: (Spanish): resembling a prized emerald
Essence: (English): scent
Estelle: (French & Latin America): star
Esther: (Hebrew & Africa): star
Estrella: (Spanish): star
Ethyl: (English): noble
Etta: (German): little
Eudora: (Greek): honored gift
Eugenia: (Greek): well-born
Eunice: (Greek): happy, victorious
Eva: (Hebrew, Israel, Indian & Spanish): one who gives life
Evangeline: (Greek): like an angel
Eve: (Hebrew): to breathe
Evelyn: (Celtic): light; (English & Hebrew): life, hazelnut
Ever: (English): strong as a boar
Evita: (Spanish): a derivative of Eve, which means to breathe

Fabiana: (Latin): bean grower
Faith: (English): faithful; (Latin America): to trust
Faline: (Irish): in charge
Fallon: (Irish): a commanding woman
Fang: (Chinese): fragrant
Far: (Chinese): flower
Fantasia: (Latin): from a fantasy land
Farren: (English): wanderer
Fatima: (Arabic): the perfect woman
Fawn: (French & English): young deer
Fay/Faye: (French): fairy; (Irish): raven; (English): faith, confidence
Felicia/Felice/Phylicia: (French & Latin America): happiness
Felicity: (French, English & Latin America): happiness
Fern: (English): the fern plant
Fernanda: (Spanish): adventurous
Fia: (Portuguese): weaver; (Italian): from the flickering fire; (Scottish): from the dark of peace
Fiana: (Irish): warrior huntress
Fidelity/Fidealia: (Latin): faithful, true
Filipa: (Spanish): friend of horses
Fina: (English): God will add
Finley: (Gaelic): fair-haired, heroine
Fiona: (Gaelic): fair, a white-shouldered woman
Fiorella: (Italian): little flower
Flair: (English): natural talent
Flame: (American): passionate, fiery
Fleta: (English): swift
Fleur: (French): flower
Flora: (English): flower: (Latin): flowering
Florence: (English): flowering; (Latin America): prosperous
Florencia: (Spanish): flowering, blooming
Flynn: (Irish): heir to the red-head; ruddy complexion
Fortuna: (Latin): fortunate
Fran/Francine: (Latin America): free
Francesca: (Italian): one who is free
Freda/Freida: (German): wise judge

Frederica: (German): peaceful ruler
Freira: (Spanish): sister
Freya: (Norse): lady
Frida: (German): peaceful
Fujita: (Japanese): field
Fuschia: (Latin): resembling the color
Fury: (Greek): an enraged woman
Fuyu: (Japanese): born in winter

Gabriella: (Israel & Hebrew): God gives strength; (Italian): woman of God
Gabrielle: (French): strength of God
Gail/Gale/Gayle: (English): merry, lively
Galiana: (Arabic): a Moorish princess
Galilee: (Hebrew): from the sacred sea
Gardenia: (English): a sweet-smelling flower
Garnet: (English): gem, armed with a spear; (French): keeper of grain
Gay: (English): merry, happy
Gemma: (French & Italian): jewel
Genesis: (Hebrew): origin, birth; (Israel): beginning
Geneva: (French): juniper berry: (German): of the race of woman
Genevieve: (French): white-skinned
Gentry: (English): gentleman
Georgette/Georgeann/Georgeanna/Georgina: (French): farmer
Georgia: (Greek & German): farmer
Geraldine: (English): mighty with a spear
Germaine: (French): from Germany
Gertrude: (German): adored warrior
Gia: (Italian): God is gracious
Giada: (Italian): jade
Gianna: (Italian): diminutive form of Giovanna, which means God is gracious
Gillian/Jillian: (English): child of the gods; (Irish): young at heart
Gina/Geena: (Italian): garden; (African American): powerful mother of black people
Ginger: (English): the spice
Giovanna: (Italian): God is gracious
Giselle: (French): pledge
Gita: (Hindi): beautiful song; (Hebrew): good woman
Gitana: (Spanish): gypsy
Gladys: (Welsh): lame
Glenna: (Gaelic): from the valley between the hills
Gloria: (Latin): renowned, highly praised
Glynnis: (Welsh): from the valley between the hills
Golda/Goldie: (English): resembling the precious metal
Grace/Gracie: (Latin America): grace of God; (American): land of grace
Greer: (Scottish): alert, watchful
Greta: (German): pearl
Gretchen: (German): a form of Margaret, which means pearl
Gretel: (German & Scandinavian): pearl
Guadalupe: (Spanish): from the valley of wolves
Guinevere: (Celtic): white lady; (English): white wave
Gwen: (Celtic): mythical son of Gwastad
Gwendolyn: (Welsh): fair
Gwyneth: (Welsh): blessed with happiness
Gypsy: (English): wanderer

Hachi: (Japanese): eight, good luck
Hadley: (English): from the field of heather

Hae: (Korean): ocean
Hagan: (Irish): youthful
Hagar: (Hebrew): forsaken, flight, famous bearer; (Israel): flight
Hailey/Hailee/Haley/Haylee: (English): hero, field of hay
Haimi: (Hawaiian): one who searches for the truth
Hallie/Halle: (English): hay meadow
Halsey: (American): playful
Hana: (Japanese): flower; (Arabic): blissful
Hannah: (English & Hebrew): favor, grace; (Biblical): grace of God
Hara: (Hebrew): from the mountainous land
Harley: (English): from the meadow of the hares
Harlow: (American): impetuous
Harmony: (Latin America): a beautiful blending
Harper: (English): musician, harp player
Harriet: (English & German): rules the home
Hattie: (English): a form of Harriet, which means rules the home
Haven: (English): safe place
Haya: (Japanese): quick, light
Hayden: (English): from the hedged valley
Haylee: (English): from the hay meadow, hero
Hazel: (English & Irish): the hazel tree
Heather: (English): a flowering plant
Heaven: (American): from the heavens
Hedda/Hedy: (German): battler
Heidi: (German): noble, serene
Helen: (Greek): light
Helena: (Greek): light
Helene: (French): in the light of the sun
Helga: (German): wealthy, blessed
Heloise: (French): famous in battle
Henrietta: (German): ruler of the house
Hera: (Greek): Goddess of marriage
Hermione: (Greek): earthly
Hermona: (Hebrew): from the mountain peak
Herra: (Greek): daughter of the earth
Hester: (Greek): star
Hilary/Hillary: (English & Greek): joyous, cheerful
Hilda: (German): battle maiden
Hoda: (Indian): child of God
Holly: (French, English & Germany): shrub
Honey: (English): sweet
Honor: (Spanish & Irish): honor; (Latin America): integrity
Hope: (English): trust, faith
Hua: (Chinese): flower
Huan: (Chinese): happiness
Hunter: (English): hunter
Hye: (Korean): graceful

Ida: (English): hardworking
Idona: (Scandinavian): fresh-faced
Ilaina/Ilana: (Hebrew): tree
Ileana: (Roman): torch; (Greek): from the city of lion
Ilene: (Irish): a form of Helen, which means light
Ilia: (Greek): from the ancient city
Ilsa: (German): abbreviation of Elizabeth, which means God is bountiful
Imala: (Native American): one who disciplines others

Iman: (Arabic): having great faith
Imani: (Kenya): faith
Imari: (Japanese): daughter of today
Imelda: (Italian): warrior
Imogene: (Latin): image, likeness
Ina: (Polynesian): moon goddess
Inara: (Arabic): heaven-sent daughter
Inari: (Finnish): successful, woman from the lake
Inca: (Indian): adventurer
India: (English): from India
Indigo: (Latin America): dark blue
Indira: (Hindi): splendid
Ineesha: (American): sparkling
Inez/Ines: (Spanish): a form of Agnes, which means pure
Inga: (Danish & Swedish): beautiful daughter
Ingrid: (Scandinavian): having the beauty of God
Inis: (Irish): woman from Ennis
Iona: (Greek): woman from the island
Ionanna: (Hebrew): filled with grace
Ionia: (Greek): of the sea and islands
Ipsa: (Indian): desired
Ireland: (Irish): country of the Irish
Irena: (Greek): peace
Irene: (Greek & Spanish): peaceful
Iris: (Greek): colorful, rainbow; (Hebrew & English): the flower
Irma: (German): whole, universal
Isabel: (Hebrew): devoted to God; (Spanish & Biblical): consecrated to God
Isabella: (Hebrew): devoted to God; (Spanish): God is bountiful; (Biblical): consecrated to God
Isadore/Isadora: (Greek): gift from the goddess Isis
Isana: (German): strong willed
Ishtar: (Arabic): mythical goddess of love and fertility
Isis: (Egyptian): most powerful goddess
Isla: (Greek & Irish): from the island
Isra: (Arabic): one who travels in the evening
Ivana: (Slavic): God is gracious
Ivanka: (Slavic): God is gracious
Ivette/Yvette: (French): a form of Yvette, which means young archer
Ivory: (English & Latin America): white, pure
Ivy/Ivey: (English): vine

Ja: (Korean): attractive, fiery
Jacey/Jacy/Jacie: (American): resembling the hyacinth
Jacinda: (Greek): beautiful
Jacinta: (Spanish): resembling the hyacinth
Jacqueline: (French): to protect
Jada/Jayda: (Israel): wise
Jade: (Spanish): jewel, green gemstone
Jae: (English): resembling a jaybird
Jael: (Hebrew): mountain goat, climber
Jaffa: (Hebrew): beautiful
Jai: (Tai): heart
Jaiden: (Spanish): a form of Jade, which means jewel
Jailyn: (American): a combination of Jae and Lynn
Jalila: (Arabic): important
Jalisa: (American): a combination of Jae and Lisa
Jamaica: (American): from the island of springs

216

Jamie/Jayme: (Hebrew): supplanter
Jamielee: (American): a combination of Jamie and Lee
Jamielynn: (American): a combination of Jamie and Lynn
Jana: (Slovakian): God is gracious
Janae: (American): a form of Jane, which means gracious
Jane: (Hebrew): gift from God; (English): gracious, merciful
Janelle/Jeanelle: (French): a form of Jane, which means gracious
Janesha/Janessa: (American): a form of Jane, which means gracious
Janet: (Hebrew & English): gift from God
Janice/Janis: (Hebrew): gift from God; (Israel): God is gracious
Janine: (Hebrew): gift from God
Jasmine: (Persian): a climbing plant; (English): a fragrant flower
Javiera/Xaviera: (Spanish): owner of a new house
Jayla: (Arabia): charity; (African American): one who is special
Jayne: (Indian): victorious; (Hebrew): gift from God; (English): Jehovah has been gracious
Jazmin: (Japanese): the flower
Jean: (Hebrew): God is gracious
Jeanette: (French): a derivative of Jean, which means God is gracious
Jeanne: (Scottish): a form of Jean, which means God is gracious
Jemima: (Hebrew): our little dove
Jemma: (English): as precious as a jewel
Jena/Jenna: (Arabic): our little bird
Jennifer: (English & Welsh): fair one; (English & Celtic): white wave
Jensen: (Scandinavian): God is gracious
Jeri/Jerri/Jerrie: (American): diminutive forms of Geraldine, which means mighty with a spear
Jerica: (American): a combination of Jeri and Erica
Jermaine: (French): woman from Germany
Jessica: (Israel): God is watching; (Hebrew): rich, God beholds
Jetta: (Danish): resembling the gemstone
Jewel/Jewelle: (English & French): precious gem
Jezebel: (Hebrew): one who is not exalted
Jia: (Chinese): beautiful
Jiao: (Chinese): dainty
Jiera: (Lithuanian): lively
Jill: (English): girl, sweetheart
Jillian/Gillian: (English): child of the gods; (Irish): young at heart
Jinelle: (Welsh): fair skin
Jing: (Chinese): stillness, luxurious
Jiselle: (American): one who offers her pledge
Jo: (English): God will add
Joan: (Hebrew): gift from God; (English): God is gracious
Joann: (English & Hebrew): God is gracious
Joanna: (Hebrew & French): gift from God
Joba/Joby: (Hebrew): afflicted
Jobeth: (American): a combination of Jo and Beth
Jocelyn/Josslyn/Josselin: (Latin): cheerful, happy
Joda: (Hebrew): an ancestor of Christ
Jody: (Hebrew): praised
Joelle: (Hebrew): God is willing
Jolene/Joleen/Joline: (English): God will add
Jolie: (French): pretty young woman
Jonna/Johnna: (Danish): God is gracious
Jordan/Jordana: (Hebrew): to flow down; (Israel): descendant
Jorja: (English): farmer
Josephina/Josefina: (Hebrew): God will add
Josephine: (French): God will add

Josette: (French): a form of Josephine, which means God will add
Journey: (American): one who likes to travel
Jovana/Jovanna: (Spanish): daughter of the sky
Jovi/Jovita: (Spanish): joyful
Joy: (French, English & Latin America): rejoicing
Joyce: (English & Latin America): cheerful, merry
Juana/Juanita: (Spanish): a form of Jane, which means gift from God
Jubilee: (Latin): joyous celebration
Judith/Judy/Judi: (Hebrew): praised; (Israel): from Judah
Julia/Julie: (French): youthful; (Latin America): soft-haired, youthful
Juliana: (Spanish): soft-haired
Juliet/Juliette: (French): youthful, soft-haired
Julietta/Julieta: (French): youthful, young at heart
June: (Dominican Republic): born in June
Juno: (Roman): mythical queen of the heavens
Justina: (Greek): just
Justine: (English): just, upright; (Latin America): fairness

Kacey/Casey: (Irish): brave
Kacia: (Greek): the adoptive mother of Romulus and Remus
Kady/Katy: (American): a diminutive form of Katherine, which means pure or virginal
Kaelin/Kaylin/Kaelyn: (American): a combination of Kay and Lynn; (Irish): beautiful girl from the meadow
Kaia: (Greek): earth
Kailani: (Hawaiian): sky
Kaitlyn/Caitlyn/Katelyn/Catelyn: (Irish): pure
Kala: (Hawaiian): princess
Kalina/Kaleena/Kalena: (Indian): of the sun
Kallan: (Slavic): stream, river
Kama: (Indian & Japanese): one who loves and is loved
Kamala: (Hawaiian, Hindu & Indian): lotus; (Arabic): perfection
Kami: (Hindu): loving; (Japanese): divine aura
Kamila: (Czechoslovakian): young ceremonial attendant
Kana: (Japanese): dexterity and skill
Kanda: (Native American): a magical woman
Kara: (Greek): pure; (Italian): dearly loved; (Gaelic): a good friend
Karen: (Greek): pure
Kari: (Norwegian): blessed, pure, holy
Karina/Kareena/Karena/Carina/Carena/Careena: (Scandinavian & Russian): dear one, pure
Karisma/Charisma: (English): blessed with charm
Karissa: (Greek): grace, kindness
Karla: (German): a small and strong woman
Karmel: (Latin): of the fruitful orchard
Kasia: (English): alert, vigorous
Kate: (Irish, English & French): diminutive of Katherine, which means pure, virginal
Katherine/Kathryn: (Irish): clear; (English): pure; (Greek): pure, virginal
Kathleen/Kathy: (English, Irish & French): diminutive of Katherine, which means pure
Katniss: (American): female warrior
Katrina: (German): a form of Katherine, which means pure
Kay: (Greek): rejoice; (Scottish & Welsh): fiery
Kayden: (French, English & Arabic): round, gentle; companion
Kayla: (Irish & Greek): pure and beloved
Kaylee/Kayleen/Kaylene: (American): pure
Kayo: (Japanese): beautiful
Keagan/Keegan: (Irish): little, fiery
Keara: (Irish): dark, black
Kearney: (Irish): the winner

Keaton: (English): from a shed town
Keely/Keeley: (Irish): beautiful
Keilani: (Hawaiian): glorious chef
Keira: (Celtic): black-haired
Keisha/Keesha: (African): favorite
Kelly/Kelli/Kelleigh/Kellee: (Gaelic & Irish): warrior; (Scottish): wood
Kelsey: (English): from the island of ships
Kendall: (English & Celtic): from the bright valley
Kendra: (English): having royal power
Kenja: (Japanese): a sage
Kennedy: (Gaelic): a helmeted chief
Kent: (English & Welsh): white; (Celtic): chief
Kenya: (Israel): animal horn
Kenzie: (Scottish): light-skinned; (American): diminutive of McKenzie
Keri/Kerry: (Irish): dusky, dark
Ki: (Korean): arisen
Kiara: (Irish): small and dark
Kiera: (Irish): dusky
Kiley: (Irish): narrow land
Kim: (Vietnamese): as precious as gold; (Welsh): leader
Kimball: (English): chief of warriors
Kimberlin/Kimberlyn: (English): a form of Kimberly, which means ruler
Kimberly: (English): ruler
Kimora: (American): royal
Kin: (Japanese): golden
Kina: (Hawaiian): woman of China
Kinley: (American): diminutive of McKinley
Kinsey: (English): the king's victory
Kira: (Russian): sun
Kirby: (Scandinavian): church village
Kirsten: (Greek): Christian, annointed
Kismet: (English): fate
Kita: (Japanese): north
Kitty: (Greek): a diminutive form of Katherine, which means pure, virginal
Ko: (Japanese): filial piety
Kobe/Kobi/Koby: (African): supplanter; (American): from California
Komala: (Indian): tender and delicate
Kona: (Hawaiian): girly
Kono: (Japanese): dexterity and skill
Kosame: (Japanese): fine rain
Kris/Kristen/Kristi/Krista: (Irish): Christ-bearer
Kristina/Kristine: (English): follower of Christ
Krystal: (American): clear, brilliant glass
Kuma: (Japanese): bear, mouse
Kyla: (English): from the narrow channel
Kyle: (Irish): attractive
Kylee: (Celtic): a straight and narrow channel
Kylie: (Australian): a boomerang
Kyra: (Greek): noble

Lacrecia/Lacresha/Lucretia: (Latin): bringer of light
Lacy/Lacey: (Irish): surname; (English): derived from lace
Laila/Leila/Leyla: (Arabic): beauty of the night
Laine/Lane/Lainey/Laney/Lanie: (English): narrow road, from the long meadow
Lake/Laken/Lakin/Lakyn: (American): body of water, from the lake
Lakeisha: (American): joyful, happy

Lalita: (Indian): playful and charming
Lan: (Chinese): orchid
Lana: (Latin): wooly; (Irish): attractive, peaceful
Lanassa: (Russian): cheerful, lighthearted
Landon: (English): from the long hill
Lani: (Hawaiian): from the sky, heavenly
Laquita: (American): fifth-born child
Lara: (Greek): cheerful; (Latin): shining, famous
Laramie: (French): shedding tears of love
Larissa/Laryssa/Laurissa: (Greek): cheerful
Lark: (English): a lark; (American): songbird
Larue: (American): a medicinal herb
Lashawna: (American): filled with happiness
Lata: (Indian): of the lovely wine
Latanya: (American): daughter of the fairy queen
Latisha/Leticia/Letitia: (Latin): a form of Lucretia, which means bringer of light
Latoya: (American): a combination of La and Toya
Laura: (English, Spanish & Latin America): crowned with laurel, from the laurel tree
Laurel: (English & French): crowned with laurel, from the laurel tree
Lauren/Laryn/Lauryn: (French): crowned with laurel
Laurie/Lori: (English): crowned with laurels
Lavender: (English): a purple flowering plant
Lavina/Lavinia: (Latin): purified
Layla/Leila(h): (Indian): born at night; (Arabian): dark beauty
Layne: (English): path, roadway
Leah/Leia: (Hebrew): weary
Leann: (English): gracious meadow
Lecia: (English): noble, truthful
Leeza: (Hebrew & English): a form of Lisa, which means devoted to God
Leigh: (English): from the meadow
Leighton: (English): herb garden, town by the meadow
Leila/Leyla: (Persian): night, dark beauty
Leilani: (Hawaiian): heavenly flower, heavenly child
Lena: (Israel): illustrious
Lenora/Lenore/Leora: (Greek & Russian): a form of Eleanor, which means torch
Leona: (Latin): strength of a lion
Leslie/Lesley: (Gaelic): from the holly garden
Leta: (Latin): glad
Levin: (Hebrew): heart; (English): dear friend
Levona: (Hebrew): spice, incense
Lexa/Lexia: (Czech): defender of mankind
Li: (Chinese): upright
Lia: (Greek): bearer of good news
Liane/Liana: (English): daughter of the sun
Libby: (English): my God is bountiful
Liberty: (English): free, independent
Libra: (Latin): balanced, the seventh sign of the zodiac
Lien: (Chinese): lotus
Lila: (Arabia): night
Lilac: (Latin America): bluish purple; (American): a flowering bluish purple shrub
Lilith: (Babylonian): woman of the night
Lillian: (Latin): resembling the lily
Lily/Lilly: (Hebrew, English & Latin America): lily, blossoming flower
Lin: (Chinese): resembling jade
Lina: (Arabic): tender
Linda: (Spanish): pretty; (English): lime tree; (German): snake, lime tree

Linden: (English): from linden hill
Lindley: (English): from the pasture land
Lindsay/Lindsey/Lyndsay/Lyndsey: (English): from the land of linden trees
Linette/Lynette: (Welsh): idol; (French): bird
Ling: (Chinese): dainty
Lisa: (German): devoted to God; (Israel): consecrated to God
Lisette/Lissettte/Lizette: (French): derivation of Elizabeth, which means my God is bountiful
Liv: (Norwegian): protector
Livia: (English): life
Liza: (Hebrew): consecrated to God
Lois: (Israel): good; (German): famous warrior
Loki: (Norse): a trickster god in mythology
Lola: (Spanish): woman of sorrow
Lolita: (Spanish): sorrowful
Lona/Loni: (English): ready for battle
London/Londyn: (English): capital of England; fortress of the moon
Lora: (Latin): crowned with laurel
Lorelei: (German): from the rocky cliff
Loretta: (Italian): crowned with laurel
Lori: (English) the laurel tree; (Latin America): crowned with laurel
Lorita: (Latin America): laurel
Lorraine: (French): from the kingdom of Lothair
Lotus: (Greek): the flower
Louise/Louisa: (German): famous warrior
Love: (English): full of affection
Luana/Luann: (Hawaiian): contented
Lucile: (English): a form of Lucy, which means bringer of light
Lucinda: (Latin): a form of Lucy, which means bringer of light
Lucy/Lucia/Luciana: (Latin America): bringer of light
Lulu: (Arabic): pearl; (English): soothing
Luna: (Latin & Latin America): the moon
Lupe/Lupa/Lupita: (Latin): wolf
Lurleen/Lurlene: (Scandinavian): war horn
Lydia: (Greek): beautiful maiden
Lyla/Lila: (Arabic): born at night
Lynn(e): (English): waterfall
Lyric: (Greek): melodic word; (French): of the lyre
Lysandra: (Greek): liberator
Mabel: (English): lovable, beautiful
Mackenna: (Gaelic): daughter of the handsome man
Mackenzie/Mackinsey: (Irish & Scottish): fair, favored one
Macy: (English): enduring; (American): stone worker
Maddox: (English): born into prosperity
Madeline/Madalyn: (Greek): high tower
Madge: (English): pearl
Madison: (English): son of Matthew
Madonna: (Italian): my lady
Maeve: (Irish): intoxicating, joyous
Magdalena: (Hebrew): from the tower; (Spanish): bitter
Maggie: (English): resembling a pearl
Magnolia: (French): resembling the flower
Mahogany/Mahogony: (Spanish): rich, strong
Maia: (French): May; (Greek): mother
Maisie: (Scottish): resembling a pearl
Maite: (Spanish): loved
Makala: (English): princess; (Hawaiian): resembling myrtle

Makayla: (English & Irish): like God
Makena: (African): filled with happiness
Mako: (Japanese): truth, grateful
Mali: (Thai): resembling a flower; (Welsh): from the sea of bitterness
Malia: (American): calm, peaceful
Malika: (African): queen, princess
Mallory/Malerie: (French): unfortunate; ill-fated; (German): war counselor
Mamie: (American): a diminutive form of Margaret, which means pearl
Mana: (Japanese): truth
Mandy: (Latin America): worthy of love
Mara: (English, Italian, Hebrew & Israel): bitter
Marcela/Marcella: (Spanish): warring
Marcia/Marsha: (Latin): dedicated to Mars
Marcy: (Latin America): marital
Maren/Marin: (Latin): sea
Margaret: (Greek & Latin America): a pearl
Mari: (Finnish): bitter
Maria/Marie: (Latin): bitter
Mariah: (English): bitter; (Latin): star of the seas
Mariana: (Spanish): star of the sea; (French): bitter
Marianne/Marian: (French): bitter; (Spanish): star of the sea
Maribel: (French): beautiful
Mariel: (Hebrew): bitter
Marietta: (French): star of the sea
Marika: (Danish): star of the sea
Marjorie/Margery: (English): resembling a pearl
Marlie/Marley/Marleigh/Marly: (American): bitter
Marlo: (English): one who resembles driftwood
Marilyn/Marlyn: (Israel): descendants of Mary
Marina: (Greek, Italian & Slovakian): from the sea
Maris: (Latin): sea
Marissa: (Latin America): of the sea; (Hebrew): rebellion, bitter
Marita: (Dutch): bitter
Marla: (Greek): high tower
Marlene: (German): bitter; (Hebrew): from the tower
Marlowe: (English): from the hill by the lake
Marnie/Marny: (Hebrew): rejoice
Marquesa: (Spanish): she who works with a hammer
Marquise: (French): noble woman
Marsala: (Italian): from the place of sweet wine
Martha: (Israel): lady
Martina: (Latin America): warlike
Mary: (Biblical, English & Slovakian): bitter
Matilda: (German): powerful battler
Maude: (French): strong in war; (Irish): strong battle maiden
Maura: (Italian, Irish & French): dark
Maureen: (Irish): star of the sea, from the sea of bitterness
Mauve: (American): purplish color
Maven: (English): having great knowledge
Mavis: (French): resembling a songbird
Maximiliana: (Latin): eldest
Maxine/Maxie: (Latin): greatest
May/Mae: (English): name of month; (Hebrew & Latin America): from Mary
Maya/Mya: (Indian): an illusion or dream; (Hebrew): woman of the water
Maybelline: (Latin): a form of Mabel, which means lovable, beautiful
McKayla: (Gaelic): fiery

McKenzie: (Irish): fair, favored one
McKinley: (English): offspring of the fair hero
Meadow: (American): beautiful field
Meagan/Megan: (Irish): soft and gentle; (Greek): strong and mighty
Medea: (Greek): cunning ruler
Medina: (Arabic): the site of Muhammad's tomb
Medora: (Greek): wise ruler
Medusa: (Greek): a Gorgon with snakes for hair
Megara: (Greek): wife of Hercules
Meili: (Chinese): beautiful
Melanie: (Greek): dark-skinned beauty
Melba: (Greek): slender, thin-skinned
Meli: (Native American): bitter
Melia: (German): industrious
Melika: (Greek): as sweet as honey
Melina: (German): industrious, striving
Melinda: (Latin): sweet and gentle
Melissa: (Greek): honey bee
Melita: (Greek), a form of Melissa, which means honey bee
Melody: (Greek): beautiful song
Melora: (Greek): golden apple
Mena: (German & Dutch): strong
Mercedes: (Latin): reward, payment; (Spanish): merciful
Mercy: (English): compassion; (French): merciful
Meredith: (Welsh): great ruler, protector of the sea
Merrilee: (American): a combination of Merry and Lee
Merry: (English): joyful, mirthful
Meryl: (German): famous; (Irish): shining sea
Mia: (Italian): my; (Biblical): mine
Michaela: (Celtic, Hebrew, English, Gaelic & Irish): who is like God
Michelle: (French & Hebrew): like God, close to God
Midori: (Japanese): green
Mika/Micah: (Finnish): like God; (Japanese): new moon
Mikala/Mikaela: (Hawaiian): who is like God
Mila: (Russian): dear one; (Serbian): favor, glory
Mildred: (English): gentle counselor
Miley: (American): virtuous
Millicent: (English): industrious
Mimi: (French): a diminutive form of Miriam, which means rebellious
Mindy: (English): sweet and gentle
Minerva: (Latin): wise
Ming: (Chinese): brilliant light
Mingzhu: (Chinese): bright pearl
Minka: (Teutonic): great strength
Minnie: (Irish): bitter; (Hebrew): wished for a child
Mira: (Hindu): prosperous
Mirabel: (Spanish): of uncommon beauty
Miranda: (Latin): worthy of admiration
Miriam: (Hebrew): rebellious; (Israel): strong-willed
Mischa: (Russian): like God
Misty: (English): shrouded by mist
Mitzy/Mitzi: (German): diminutive form of Mary, which means bitter
Miya: (Japanese): from the sacred temple
Miyo: (Japanese): beautiful daughter
Mizuki: (Japanese): beautiful moon
Moesha: (American): drawn from the water

Moira: (Irish): bitter
Molly: (Israel & English): bitter
Mona: (Gaelic): born into nobility
Monica: (Greek & Spanish): advisor
Monique: (French): one who provides wise counsel
Monroe: (Gaelic): from the red swamp; (Scottish): from the river; (Irish): near the river roe
Monserrat: (Latin): jagged mountain
Montana: (Latin America): mountainous
Morgan: (Celtic): lives by the sea; (Welsh): bright sea
Mulan: (Chinese): magnolia blossom
Muriel: (Arabian): myth; (Celtic): shining sea
Murphy: (Irish): sea warrior
Mya: (American): emerald
Myka: (Hebrew): who is like God
Myra: (Greek): fragrant
Myrina: (Latin): an amazon in mythology
Myrtle: (Greek): the tree, victory; (English): the flowering shrub

Nadia: (Slovakian): hopeful
Nadine: (French): hopeful; (German): the courage of a bear
Nadira: (Arabic): rare, precious
Nailah/Naila: (Arabic): successful
Nala: (African): successful; (Tanzanian): queen
Nami: (Japanese): wave
Nan: (English): gracious
Nana: (Hawaiian): born in the spring
Nancy: (Hebrew & English): grace
Nandita: (Indian): delightful daughter
Nanette: (English): favor; (French & Hebrew): gracious
Naoki: (Japanese): honest tree
Naomi: (Hebrew & Israel): pleasant
Nara: (Greek): happy; (English): north; (Japanese): oak
Narella: (Greek): intelligent
Narelle: (Australian): woman from the sea
Nari: (Japanese): thunder
Narissa/Narcissa: (Greek): dafodil
Natalia/Natalie: (French): to be born at Christmas; (Slovakian): to be born
Natasha: (Greek): rebirth
Naveen: (Hindu): new; (Irish): beautiful, pleasant
Navida: (Iranian): brings good news
Nazareth: (Hebrew): religion
Neda: (Slovakian): Sunday's child; (English): wealthy guardian
Neena: (Hindi): beautiful eyes
Nefertiti: (Egyptian): queenly
Neila/Neela/Neely: (Irish): champion
Nelle/Nelly: (English): torch
Nena: (English): girl
Neriah: (Israel): light lamp of the Lord
Nerissa: (Italian): black-haired beauty; (Greek): sea nymph
Nessa: (Hebrew): miracle child; (Greek): pure, chaste
Neta: (Hebrew): plant, shrub
Neva: (Spanish): covered with snow
Nevada: (English): covered in snow
Nevaeh: (American): gift from God, heaven spelled backwards
Neve: (Irish): radiant; (Hebrew): life
Nevena: (Irish): worshipper of the saint

Neylan: (Turkish): fulfilled wish
Nia: (Irish): champion; (African): purpose
Nicole: (French): victory of the people
Nicolette: (French): a form of Nicole, which means victory of the people
Nikita: (Russian): victorious people
Nila: (Indian): blue
Nina: (Hebrew); grace; (Spanish): girl; (Native American): strong
Nirel: (Hebrew): light of God
Nishi: (Japanese): west
Nissa: (Hebrew): sign, emblem
Nita: (Hebrew): planter; (Choctaw): bear
Noa: (Israel): movement
Noelle: (French): born at Christmastime
Nola: (Irish): champion
Nona: (English): ninth
Noor: (Aramaic): light
Nora/Norah: (Hebrew): light
Noriko: (Japanese): child of principles
Norleen: (Irish): honest
Norma: (Latin America): from the north
Nuala: (Irish): white, fair-shouldered
Nula: (Irish): white: shouldered
Nuna: (Native American): land
Nuo: (Chinese): graceful
Nyala: (African): resembling an antelope
Nyssa: (Greek): the beginning

O'Shea: (Irish): child of Shea
Oba: (Yoruba): chief, ruler
Ocean/Oceana: (Greek): ocean
Octavia: (Latin America): eighth; (Italian): born eighth
Odelia: (Greek): melodic
Odessa: (Latin America): the odyssey
Odette: (German & French): a form of Odelia, which means melodic
Odina: (Latin): from the mountain
Okalani: (Hawaiian): from the heavens
Oksana: (Russian): hospitality
Ola: (Nigerian): precious; Scandinavian: ancestor
Oleda: (English): resembling a winged creature
Olena: (Russian): a form of Helen, which means light
Olethea: (Latin): truthful
Olga: (Slovakian): holy
Oliana: (Polynesian): oleander
Olina: (Hawaiian): joyous
Oliva: (Latin): olive tree
Olive: (Irish): olive; (Latin America), olive branch, peace
Olivia: (Spanish & Italian): olive; (Biblical): peace of the olive tree
Olympia: (Greek): from Mount Olympus
Oma: (Hebrew): reverent
Omri: (Arabic): red-haired
Ona: (Hebrew): grace
Ondrea: (Slavic): courageous and strong
Onida/Oneida: (Native American): the one expected
Onyx: (Greek): the onyx stone
Oona: (Gaelic): pure, chaste
Opal: (English & Indian): precious gem

Ophelia: (Greek): useful, wise
Ophrah/Oprah: (Hebrew): resembling a fawn
Orabella: (Latin): a form of Arabella, which means answered prayer
Oriana: (Latin): born at sunrise
Orin: (Latin): dark-haired beauty
Orion: (Greek): huntress
Orla: (Irish): golden woman
Orli: (Hebrew): light
Orna/Ornice: (Irish): pale skinned
Ornat: (Irish): green
Ornella: (Italian): of the flowering ash tree
Orpah: (Israel): fawn
Osaka: (Japanese): from the city of industry
Osita: (Spanish) divinely strong
Overton: (English): from the upper side of town
Ozora: (Hebrew): wealthy

Padma: (Hindi): lotus
Paige: (French): assistant, attendant
Paloma: (Spanish): dove-like
Pamela: (Greek, English & Indian): honey
Pandora: (Greek): gifted and talented woman
Paola: (Italian): little
Parker: (English): keeper of the park
Paris: (Persian): angelic face; (Greek): downfall; (French): the capital city of France
Parthenia: (Greek): virginal
Pasha: (Greek): sea
Patience: (English): patient, enduring
Patricia: (Spanish & Latin America): noble
Patrina/Patrice: (American): born into nobility
Paula/Paulette: (Latin America): small
Pauline/Paulina: (Latin America): small
Peace: (English): peaceful
Peaches: (English): fruit
Pearl: (English): gemstone
Pembroke: (English): from the broken hill
Penelope: (Greek): weaver
Penny: (Greek): diminutive form of Penelope, which means weaver
Peony: (Greek): resembling the flower
Pepita: (Spanish): God will add
Perdita: (Latin): lost
Peri: (Persian): fairy; (English); from the pear tree
Perlita: (Italian): pearl
Peta: (Blackfoot): golden eagle
Petra/Petrina/Petrisse: (Greek & Latin): small rock
Petunia: (English): resembling the flower
Peyton: (English): village
Pheodora: (Greek): supreme gift
Phernita: (American): well-spoken
Phia: (Italian): saintly
Philana: (Greek): lover of mankind
Philippa/Pippa: (English): friend of horses
Philomena: (Greek): friend of strength
Phoebe: (Greek): bright, shining one
Phoenix: (Greek): dark-red color, an immortal bird
Phylicia/Felicia: (Latin): fortunate, happy

Phyllis: (Greek): green leaf
Pia: (Italian): devout
Pilar: (Spanish): pillar of strength
Ping: (Chinese): peaceful
Piper: (English): plays the flute
Pippi: (French): friend of horses; (English): blushing
Pita: (African): fourth daughter
Pixie: (English): mischievous fairy
Plato: (Greek): strong shoulders
Plena: (Latin): abundant, complete
Polina: (Russian): small
Polly: (Latin America): bitter
Pollyanna: (American): overly optimistic
Poloma: (Choctaw): bow
Pomona: (Latin): goddess of fruit trees
Poppy: (English & Latin America): the poppy flower
Portia/Porsha/Porscha/Porsche: (Latin): offering
Posy: (English): God will increase
Precious: (American): treasured
Presley: (English): priest's land
Prima: (Latin): first, beginning
Primrose: (English): the first rose, primrose flower
Princess: (English): born to royalty
Priscilla: (Latin): from an ancient family
Prudence: (English): prudent or cautious
Pua: (Hawaiian): flower
Pyria: (American): cherished
Pythia: (Greek): prophet

Qi: (Chinese): fine jade
Qiana/Quiana: (American): living with grace, heavenly
Qiang: (Chinese): beautiful rose
Qing: (Chinese): dark blue
Quana: (Native American): sweet
Quarralia: (Australian): star
Quartilla: (Latin): fourth
Queen/Queenie/Quenna: (English): queen
Querida: (Spanish): dearly loved
Queta: (Spanish): head of the household
Quilla: (Incan): goddess of the moon
Quincy: (English): fifth-born child; (French): estate belonging to Quintus
Quinn: (Celtic): queenly; (Gaelic): one who provides counsel
Quintana/Quinella: (Latin): the fifth girl; (English): the queen's lawn
Quintessa: (Latin): of the essence

Rachel: (Hebrew): ewe; (Israel): innocent lamb
Racine: (French): root
Rae: (Scottish): grace; (German): wise protection
Raeden: (Japanese): thunder and lightning
Raelene/Rayleen: (American): a combination of Rae and Lee
Raelynn: (American): a form of Raylene
Rafaela/Raphaela: (Hebrew): healed by God
Rafiki: (African): friend
Rain/Raine/Raina: (American): blessings from above; (French & Latin): ruler; (English): lord, wise
Rainbow: (English): rainbow
Raisa: (Russian): a form of Rose

Raja: (Arabic): filled with hope
Ramona: (Spanish): wise protector
Randi: (English): shielded by wolves
Rani: (Sanskrit): queen
Ranita: (Hebrew): song, joyful
Raquel: (Spanish): innocent lamb
Rasha: (Arabic): resembling a young gazelle
Rashida: (Swahili & Turkish): righteous
Raven: (English): to be black, blackbird
Rayna: (Hebrew): pure; (Scandinavian): wise counsel
Razi: (Aramaic): secretive
Reagan: (Celtic): regal; (Irish): son of the small ruler
Reba: (Hebrew): fourth
Rebecca: (Biblical): servant of God
Reese/Reece: (English &Welsh): ardent, fiery, enthusiastic
Regina: (Italian, Spanish & Latin America): queen
Rein: (German); advisor, counselor
Reina: (French & Spanish): queen; (English): wise ruler
Remi/Remy: (French): oarsman or rower from Rheims
Rena: (Hebrew): song
Renata: (French): a form of Renee, which means reborn
Renee: (French): reborn
Reta: (African): shaken
Reva: (Hebrew): rain
Reya: (Spanish): queenly
Reza: (Hungarian): harvester
Rhea: (Greek): rivers
Rhianna: (English): goddess; (Welsh): nymph
Rhiannon: (Welsh): pure maiden
Rhoda: (Greek): roses
Rhonda: (Welsh): carrying a good spear
Rhonwyn: (Irish): a form of Bronwyn, which means light-skinned
Ria: (Spanish): from the river's mouth
Richelle: (French): feminine form of Richard, which means strong ruler
Ricki/Rickelle: (American): a form of Erica, which means honorable ruler
Rielle: (Hebrew): a feminine form of Gabriel, which means God is my strength
Riley: (English): from the rye clearing; (Irish): a small stream
Rio: (Spanish & Portuguese): river
Rippina: (Japanese): brilliant light
Risa: (Latin): one who laughs often
Rita: (Greek): precious pearl
Riva: (French): river bank
River: (Latin & French): stream, water
Roberta: (English): bright with fame
Robin/Robyn: (English): a small bird
Rochelle: (French): from the little rock
Roja: (Spanish): red-haired woman
Rolanda: (German): well-known
Romina: (Arabian): from the Christian land
Romy: (French): a form of Rosemary, which means bitter rose
Rona: (Hebrew): my joy
Rong: (Chinese): martial
Rory: (Irish): famous brilliance, famous ruler; (Gaelic): red-haired
Rosa: (Spanish): rose
Rosalind/Rosalee: (Spanish): beautiful one
Rosario: (Filipino & Spanish): rosary

Rose: (English, French & Scottish): flower, a rose; (German): horse, fame
Roseanne/Rosanna: (Greek): graceful rose
Rosemary: (English): bitter rose
Rosetta: (Italian): rose
Roshonda/Roshawna: (American): a combination of Rose & Shawna
Rosina/Rosita: (Celtic): little rose
Roslyn/Rossalyn: (Scottish): cape, promontory
Rowan: (Irish): red-haired; (English & Gaelic): from the rowan tree
Rowena: (Welsh): fair and slender: (German): happy and famous
Roxanne: (Persian): sunrise
Roz/Roza: (Polish): rose
Ruby: (English & French): a precious jewel, a ruby
Rue: (Greek): herb of grace
Rula: (Latin & English): ruler
Rumer: (English); gypsy
Ruth: (Hebrew & Israel): companion, friend
Rylan: (English): the place where rye is grown
Rylee/Rylie: (Irish): a form of Riley, which means a small stream

Sabine/Sabina: (Latin): a tribe in ancient Italy
Sable: (English): sleek
Sabrina: (English): legendary princess
Sada: (Japanese): pure
Sadie: (English): a lady
Saffron: (English): resembling the yellow flower
Sahara: (Arabian): wilderness
Saige/Sage: (English & French): wise one; (English): from the spice
Sailor: (American): sailor
Sakari: (Native American & Hindi): sweet girl
Salina: (French): solemn, dignified
Sally/Sallie: (English): princess
Saloma/Salome: (Hebrew): peace and tranquility
Samantha: (Hebrew & Biblical): listener of God
Samina: (Hindi): happiness
Samira: (Arabic): entertaining
Sandra: (Greek): helper of humanity; (English): unheeded prophetess
Sandrine: (Greek): defender of mankind
Saniya: (Indian): a moment in time preserved
Santana: (Spanish): saintly
Santina: (Spanish): little saint
Sapphira/Sapphire: (Hebrew): sapphire; (Israel): beautiful
Sara(h): (Hebrew, Spanish & Biblical): princess
Sarafina/Saraphina: (Greek): gentle wind
Sardinia: (Italian): from the mountainous island
Sasha: (English): defender of mankind
Sato: (Japanese): sugar
Savannah: (Spanish): open plain, field
Sayo: (Japanese): born at night
Scarlett: (English): red
Scout: (French): scout
Season: (Latin): a fertile woman
Sedona: (American): the American city
Sela(h): (Israel): pause and reflect
Selene/Selena/Seline/Selina: (Greek): of the moon
Selma: (Scandinavian): divinely protected
Sena: (Persian): blessed

Sequoia: (Cherokee): giant redwood tree
Seraphina: (Israel): burning fire; (Hebrew): fiery-ringed
Serefina: (Latin): a winged angel
Serena/Syrena/Sirena: (Latin): peaceful disposition; (African American): calm, tranquil
Serenity: (Latin & English): peaceful
Shaba: (Spanish): rose
Shada: (Native American): pelican
Shae/Shea/Shay/Shayla: (Celtic & Irish): gift
Shahina: (Arabic): falcon
Shaina: (Yiddish): beautiful
Shakila: (Arabic): beautiful one
Shakira: (Arabic): grateful
Shamara: (Arabic): ready for battle
Shana/Shanea/Shanae: (Hebrew): God is gracious
Shandy/Shandie/Shandi: (English): rambunctious
Shane: (Hebrew): gift from God; (Irish): God is gracious
Shanel/Shanell/Shanelle/Shannel: (American): a form of Chanel, which means from the canal
Shani: (African): marvelous
Shania: (Native American): on my way
Shanika: (American): a combination of Sha and Nika
Shannon/Shannen: (Gaelic): having ancient wisdom
Sharlene: (English & French): manly, from the name Charles
Sharon: (Hebrew & Israel): a flat clearing
Shasta: (Native American): from the triple-peaked mountain
Shawn: (Irish): a form of Sean, which means God is gracious
Shawnee: (Native American): name of tribe
Shawnda: (English): God is gracious
Shaylee: (Gaelic): fairy princess
Sheba: (Hebrew): an ancient country in Arabia
Sheena: (Gaelic): God's gracious gift
Sheila/Sheela: (English & Irish): blind; (Italian): music
Shelby: (English): from the willow farm
Shelley/Shelly/Shellie: (English): meadow on the ledge
Sheridan: (Irish, English & Celtic): untamed; (Gaelic): bright, a seeker
Sherry/Sheree/Sheri/Sherri: (Israel): beloved; (French): dear one
Sheryl/Cheryl: (English): beloved
Shiloh: (Hebrew): he who was sent, God's gift, the one to whom it belongs; (Israel): peaceful
Shilpa: (Indian): well proportioned
Shima: (Japanese): true intention
Shirley: (English): bright meadow
Shona/Shonda: (Irish): a form of Jane, which means gift from God
Shoshana: (Arabic): white lily
Shu: (Chinese): kind, gentle
Shula: (Arabic): flaming, bright
Shura: (Russian): defender of mankind
Sibley: (English): sibling, friendly
Sibyl/Sybil/Cybil: (English): a seer or prophetess
Sidney/Sydney: (French): from Saint Denis
Sienna: (Italian): reddish brown in color
Sierra: (Spanish): mountain; (Irish): dark
Signe/Signy: (Latin): sign
Signourney: (English): victorious conquerer
Silvia/Sylvia: (Latin): forest
Silver: (English): precious metal
Simone: (French): one who listens well
Sinead: (Irish): gift from God

Siobhan: (Irish): gift from God
Siri: (Scandinavian): beautiful victory
Skye: (English): sky
Skylar/Skyler: (English): a scholar
Sloan: (English): raid; (Irish, Celtic, Scottish & Gaelic): fighter, warrior
Snow: (American): frozen rain
Solana: (Latin): from the east; (Spanish): sunshine
Solange: (French): religious and dignified
Soledad: (Spanish): solitary
Solita: (Latin): solitary
Sondra: (Greek): defender of mankind
Song: (Chinese): pine tree
Sonja/Sonia/Sonya: (Scandinavian): wisdom
Sonora: (Spanish): pleasant sounding
Sophia/Sofia/Sophie: (Greek & Biblical): wisdom
Sophie: (Greek): wisdom
Sora: (Native American): chirping songbird
Sorina: (Romanian): sun
Spencer/Spenser: (English): dispenser of provisions
Spica: (Latin): ear of wheat, a star in the constellation Virgo
Spring: (English): the spring season
Stacy/Stacey: (English): productive, resurrection
Starr: (English & American): star
Stella: (French, Italian & Greek): star
Stephanie: (Greek): crowned in victory
Stevie: (English & American): from the name Steven, which means crowned one
Stormy: (English): tempest; (American): impetuous nature
Suki: (Japanese): loved one
Sula: (Icelandic): large sea bird
Summer: (English): the summer season
Suni: (Zuni): native, a member of our tribe
Sunshine: (English): brilliant rays from the sun
Suri: (Todas): pointy nose
Surya: (Sanskrit): a sun god
Susan/Suzanne/Susannah/Suzie: (Hebrew): graceful lily; (Israel): lily
Sybil: (Greek): prophet
Sydney: (English): wide island
Sylvia/Silvia: (Latin): forest

Tabitha/Tabatha/Tabbitha: (Hebrew): beauty, grace; (Israel): a gazelle
Tacita/Taci/Tacey: (Latin): silent
Taffline/Taffy: (Welsh): beloved
Tahira: (Arabic): virginal, pure
Tai: (Chinese): large; (Vietnamese): prosperous, talented
Taima: (Native American): clash of thunder
Taja/Tajah: (Hindi): crowned
Taka: (Japanese): borrowed
Takenya: (Hebrew): animal horn
Taki: (Japanese): waterfall
Takia: (Arabic): worshipper
Tala: (Native American): a stalking wolf
Talia/Tahlia: (Hebrew): morning dew from heaven; (Greek): blooming
Talisa/Talissa: (American): consecrated to God
Talisha: (American): damsel, innocent
Tallis: (French & English): forest
Tallulah: (Choctaw): leaping water

Tama: (Japanese): precious stone
Tamaka: (Japanese): bracelet
Tamara/Tamra/Tamyra: (Hebrew): palm tree; (Israel): spice
Tameka: (Aramaic): twin
Tamika/Tamiko: (Japanese): child of the people
Tamira: (Hebrew): palm tree, spice
Tandy: (English): team
Tangia: (American): angel
Tani: (Japanese): valley
Tania/Tonya/Tanya: (Slovakian): a fairy queen
Tanisha: (English): worthy of praise
Tao: (Chinese & Vietnamese): peach
Tara/Tari/Tarin/Tarryn: (Irish & Scottish): a hill where the kings meet
Tasha: (Greek): born on Christmas day
Tatiana: (Slavic): fairy queen
Tatum: (English): joyful, spirited
Taura: (Latin): bull
Tavi: (Aramaic): well-behaved
Tawny/Tawnee: (Gypsy): little one: (English): brownish yellow, tan
Tayanita: (Cherokee): beaver
Taylor: (English & French): a tailor
Teagan: (Gaelic): handsome, attractive
Temperance: (English): temperate, moderate
Tempest/Tempestt: (French): stormy
Terelle: (German): thunder ruler
Teresa/Theresa: (Finnish): summer, harvester; (Greek): reaper
Terrene: (Latin): smooth
Terrwyn: (Welsh): valiant
Tertia: (Latin): third
Tess/Tessa: (English): harvester
Thalia: (Greek): plentiful, blooming
Thea: (Greek): gift of God
Thelma: (English): ambitious, nurturing
Thema: (African): queen
Theodora: (English): gift of God
Theora: (Greek): a watcher
Theta: (Greek): eighth letter of the alphabet
Thomasina: (Hebrew): a twin
Thora: (Scandinavian): thunder
Tia: (Greek); princess; (Spanish): princess, aunt; (African American): aunt
Tiana: (Greek): princess
Tiara: (Latin): crowned
Tiegen: (Aztec) : princess
Tierney: (Gaelic): regal, lordly
Tiffany: (Greek): lasting love
Tijuana: (Spanish): border town in Mexico
Tilda: (English): strength in battle
Timothea: (English): honoring God
Tina: (English): river
Ting: (Chinese): graceful and slim
Tipper: (Irish): water pourer
Tira: (Hindi): arrow
Tirranna: (Australian): stream of water
Tirza: (Hebrew): pleasant
Tisa: (Swahili): ninth-born
Tisha/Tish: (Latin): joy

Tobi/Toby: (Hebrew): God is good
Toki: (Japanese & Korean): one who grabs opportunity
Tola: (Polish): praiseworthy
Tomiko: (Japanese): wealthy
Tomo: (Japanese): intelligent
Tomoko: (Japanese): two friends
Toni: (Greek): flourishing; (Latin): praise-worthy
Tonia/Tonya: (Slavic): fairy queen
Topagna: (Native American): from above
Topaz/Topaza: (Mexican): golden gem
Tory/Tori: (American): victorious
Toshi: (Japanese): mirror image
Tova/Tovah: (Hebrew): well-behaved
Tracy/Tracey: (English): brave
Trang: (Vietnamese): intelligent
Treasa: (Irish): great strength
Trevina: (Irish): prudent; (Welsh): homestead
Trina: (Greek): pure
Trinity: (Latin): the holy three
Trish/Trisha: (English & Latin): noble
Trixie: (American): a form of Beatrice, which means blessed
Trudy: (German): adored warrior
Tryna: (Greek): third-born child
Tula: (Hindi): balance
Tully: (Irish): at peace with God
Twila/Twyla: (English): woven of double thread
Tyne: (English): of the river Tyne
Tyra: (Scandinavian): God of battle; (Scottish): land

Ualani: (Hawaiian): rain from heaven
Udele: (English): prosperous
Ugolina: (German): bright mind and spirit
Ula: (Irish): sea jewel
Ulima: (Arabic): wise, astute
Ulrica: (German): wolf ruler
Ultima: (Latin): last
Ulva: (German): wolf
Uma: (Hindi): mother
Umiko: (Japanese): child of the sea
Una: (Welsh & Celtic): white wave; (Irish): unity: (Native American): remember; (English): one
Unique/Unika/Uniqua: (Latin): only one; (American): unlike others
Unity: (American): unity, togetherness
Urbana: (Latin): from the city
Uriana: (Greek): heaven, the unknown
Uriel: (Hebrew): light of God
Urika: (Omaha): useful
Ursula: (Danish & Scandinavian): female bear
Uta: (German): rich; (Japanese): poem
Utina: (Native American): woman of my country
Uzzia: (Hebrew): God is my strength

Vail: (English): valley
Vala: (German): chosen one
Valencia/Valentina/Valene: (Spanish & Italian): brave; (Latin America): health or love
Valeria/Valerie/Valery: (French): brave, fierce one; (English): strong, valiant
Vanessa: (Greek): resembling a butterfly

Vanity: (English): excessive pride
Vanna: (Cambodian): golden
Vanora: (Welsh): white wave:
Vara: (Scandinavian): careful
Veda: (Sanskrit): sacred lore
Vega: (Arabic): falling star
Venecia/Venetia: (Italian): from Venice
Venus: (Greek): love goddess, little bird
Vera: (Russian): verity, truth
Verda: (Latin): young and fresh
Verna: (English): alder tree
Verena/Verity: (Latin): truthful
Veronica: (Latin): displaying a true image
Vespera: (Latin): evening star
Vesta: (Latin): keeper of the house
Victoria/Vicki/Vicky/Vickie: (Latin America): winner
Victory: (Latin): victory
Vienna: (Latin America): from wine country
Vignette: (French): from the little vine
Villette: (French): small town
Vina: (Hindi): musical instrument; (Spanish): vineyard
Viola: (Italian): violet flower
Violet: (French): resembling the flower
Violeta: (Bulgarian): violet
Virgilia: (Latin): staff bearer
Virginia: (English, Spanish, Italian & Latin America): pure
Vita: (Latin): life
Viv: (Latin America): alive
Viveka/Viveca: (German): little woman of the strong fortress
Vivian: (Latin): lively
Vivianne/Vivienne/Vivian/Vivien: (English): the lady of the lake
Vixen: (American): flirtatious
Vonna: (French): young archer; (Latin): true image

Wallis: (English): from Wales
Wanda: (German): wanderer
Waneta: (Native American): charger
Wanetta: (English): pale face
Waynette: (English): wagon maker
Wednesday: (American): born on a Wednesday
Wen: (Chinese): refinement
Wendy: (English): white-skinned, literary
Wesley: (English): western meadow
Whisper: (English): soft-spoken
Whitley: (English): from the white meadow
Whitney: (English & African American): white island
Wilhelmina/Wilma: (German): resolute protector
Willa: (English): protector
Willow: (English): willow tree
Winetta: (American): peaceful
Wing: (Chinese): glory
Winifred: (Irish): friend of peace; (Welsh): reconciled, blessed
Winnie: (Irish & Celtic): white, fair
Winola: (German): gracious and charming
Wren: (Welsh): ruler; (English): small bird
Wynonna/Winona: (American): oldest daughter

Xanadu: (African): from the exotic paradise
Xantara: (American): protector of the earth
Xanthe: (Greek): yellow, blond
Xavier: (Arabic): bright
Xema: (Latin): precious
Xena/Xenia: (Greek): hospitable
Xenosa: (Greek): stranger
Xerena: (Latin): peaceful disposition
Xiang: (Chinese): pleasant fragrance
Ximena: (Greek): heroine
Xiu: (Chinese): grace
Xoana: (Hebrew): God is compassionate and merciful
Xuan: (Vietnamese): spring
Xyleena: (Greek): forest dweller

Yadira: (Hebrew): friend
Yadra: (Spanish): mother
Yael: (Hebrew): strength of God
Yaffa: (Hebrew): beautiful
Yalena: (Greek): shining light
Yama: (Japanese): from the mountain
Yaminta: (Native American): minty
Yamka: (Hopi): blossom
Yamuna: (Hindi): sacred river
Yana: (Hebrew): he answers
Yanaba: (Navajo): brave
Yang: (Chinese): sun
Yanessa: (American): resembling a butterfly
Yara: (Brazilian): goddess of the river; (Iranian): courage
Yashira: (Japanese): blessed with God's grace; (Afghan): humble
Yasmine/Yasmeen: (Persian): resembling the jasmine flower
Yei: (Japanese): flourishing
Yeira: (Hebrew): light
Yelena: (Russian): a form of Helen, which means light
Yen: (Chinese): yearning
Yenay: (Chinese): she who loves
Yeo: (Korean): mild
Yepa: (Native American): snow girl
Yesenia: (Arabic): flower
Yessica: (Hebrew): the Lord sees all
Yetta: (English): ruler of the house
Yin: (Chinese): silver
Yitta: (Hebrew): one who emanates light
Yoki: (Native American): of the rain, bluebird
Yoko: (Japanese): good girl
Yolanda: (Greek): resembling the violet flower
Yon: (Korean): lotus blossom
Yori: (Japanese): reliable
Yoshi: (Japanese): respectful and good
Yu: (Chinese): universe
Yuki: (Japanese): snow
Yukiko: (Japanese): happy child
Yumiko: (Japanese): beautiful and helpful child
Yuna: (African): gorgeous
Yuri: (Japanese): lily
Yvette/Ivette: (French): a form of Yvonne, which means young archer

Yvonne: (French): young archer

Zaba: (Hebrew): she who offers a sacrifice to God
Zada: (Arabic): prosperous
Zahara: (Arabic): shining, luminous, the bright dawn
Zaidee: (Arabic): rich
Zakia: (Swahili): smart; (Arabic): chaste
Zakila: (Swahili): born to royalty
Zakiyyah: (Muslim): sharp, intellectual, pious, pure
Zaltana: (Native American): high mountain
Zana: (Romanian): the three graces
Zara: (Hebrew & Israel): princess
Zaynah: (Arabic): beautiful
Zelda: (Yiddish): gray-haired
Zelene: (Greek): sunshine
Zelia: (Greek): having zeal; (Spanish): of the sunshine
Zelmira: (Arabic): brilliant
Zemira: (Hebrew & Israel): praised
Zena: (African): famous; (Greek): hospitable; (Persian): woman; (Ethiopian): news
Zenda: (Persian): sacred, feminine
Zenia: (Greek): hospitable
Zenobia: (Greek): child of Zeus
Zephrine: (English): breeze
Zephyr: (Greek): of the west wind
Zera: (Hebrew): seeds
Zerlina: (Latin & Spanish): beautiful dawn
Zesta: (American): with zest or gusto
Zeta: (English): rose
Zetta: (Portuguese): rose
Zi: (Chinese): flourishing, beautiful, with grace
Zia: (Arabic): one who emanates light
Zila: (Hebrew): shadow, shade
Zilla/Zillah: (Hebrew): shadows, shade
Zina: (African): secret spirit; (English): hospitable, welcoming
Zinnia: (English): the flower: (Latin America): beautiful
Zipporah: (Hebrew & Israel): bird
Zita: (Spanish): little rose
Ziva: (Hebrew): bright, radiant
Zoe/Zoey/Zooey: (Greek): life, alive
Zora: (Slavic): sunrise
Zoya: (Greek): life
Zudora: (Sanskrit): laborer
Zula: (African): brilliant
Zuri: (French): lovely and white